Unique Games
and Sports
Around the World

Unique Games and Sports Around the World

A Reference Guide

Edited by Doris Corbett,
John Cheffers,
and Eileen Crowley Sullivan

Greenwood Press
Westport, Connecticut • London

Library of Congress Cataloging-in-Publication Data

Unique games and sports around the world : a reference guide / edited by Doris Corbett, John Cheffers, and Eileen Crowley Sullivan.
    p. cm.
  Includes bibliographical references and index.
  ISBN 0-313-29778-9 (alk. paper)
    1. Games—Cross-cultural studies. 2. Sports—Cross-cultural studies. I. Corbett, Doris. II. Cheffers, John, 1936– III. Sullivan, Eileen Crowley.
  GV1201.38.U55 2001
  790.1—dc21   00–033125

British Library Cataloguing in Publication Data is available.

Library of Congress Catalog Card Number: 00-033125
ISBN: 0-313-29778-9

First published in 2001

Greenwood Press, 88 Post Road West, Westport, CT 06881
An imprint of Greenwood Publishing Group, Inc.
www.greenwood.com

Printed in the United States of America
The paper used in this book complies with the
Permanent Paper Standard issued by the National
Information Standards Organization (Z39.48-1984)

10 9 8 7 6 5 4 3 2 1

Every reasonable effort has been made to trace the owners of copyright materials in this book, but in some instances this has proven impossible. The author and publisher will be glad to receive information leading to more complete acknowledgments in subsequent printings of the book, and in the meantime extend their apologies for any omissions.

Contents

Acknowledgments

Mary C. Lydon has through her internet and typing expertise contributed strongly to the recruiting phase of this text. We thank her for very human reasons.

The many contributors to this text are listed along with their games and deserve special praise for the quality of the unique games they have submitted. The editors thank them profusely.

Four people have helped in the preparation of this manuscript, their efforts lying well beyond the call of duty: *Elizabeth Hoeffner* has worked on this text for over three years; *Rachel O'Brien* volunteered much of her time and has helped in the assembly of games from the sparser areas, as did *Melissa Doyle; Margaret Beames* worked tirelessly for three months on the typing and classification of the games submitted. These four people are especially praised because they were asked to transcribe, as well as type the games. The end result is a compliment to their transcription abilities.

Further thanks is given to *Janet Stankiewicz, Jessica Hochbaum, Tube Blower, Abishag, Little Jules, Michelle, Margaret, Donna, Diana, Katie,* and *Steve Ellenwood* for their support in the final assembling of these pages.

The editors would also like to thank *Emily M. Birch* of Greenwood Press who liaisoned with the editors throughout the conceptual and gathering processes.

Introduction

The purpose of this volume is to introduce students to the importance of games and sports to different cultures, examining games from both a sociological perspective as well as an anthropological one. Play is almost universally an important part of becoming an adult as well as an important part of leisure time activity among adults. Many of the games children and teenagers play in different cultures help them to develop the skills they will need to assimilate into the adult worlds of their cultures, whether these are decision-making skills, diplomatic skills, hunting skills, skills that teach coordination, or any number of other skills children might need once they reach adulthood. Many of the games adults play represent the challenges they may face in their day-to-day living, whether they be warfare, decision making, or the need to act quickly, among others.

Since game playing is such a basic component of living and learning, studying the games of other cultures can help us understand these cultures. Examining games and sports while studying other aspects of different cultures as well provides us with broader pictures of what is important to cultural members, and what they feel is necessary to survive. By comparing these games, we can note the differences and similarities among the maturing processes and leisure activities of cultures from all over the world.

This volume profiles a variety of games and sports played around the world. Some of the games in this book represent real dangers and tests of bravery that members of certain societies have to face as adults. Others focus on other skills, such as coordination. Many different types of games have been presented in this volume to help us understand the many different cultures from which they have come. Some of the games are suitable for replication in the classroom or on the playground. Others are not due to the use of dangerous or impractical equipment, diagrams, or play areas, or due to the fact that purposely hurting other players is a necessary part of the game. Each entry indicates whether or not the game is suitable for replication in schools.

This book is relatively unique in that it focuses on less familiar, rarer games and promotes many that represent the more far-flung cultures of the world. The book informs students, teachers, educators, coaches, program leaders, recreators, and parents of particular cultural games and activities for studying the various peoples these games emanate from. It is hoped that this book will lead to further investigations of the world's rare and unique games. Educators introducing students to another culture can do no better than to begin playing the games of that culture. The editors have enjoyed collecting games from many parts of the world. Included in this volume is a lengthy and impressive contributors list. We have assembled the games by country within continents. Due to the fact that the focus in choosing these games and sports was on finding those that are rare and unique to their particular cultures, some countries are overrepresented, while others seem to be underrepresented. This reflects the fact that some cultures seem to have more unique games than others. However, all world regions are well represented here.

An attempt has also been made to preserve the language styles of the contributors as these different protocols contribute to the uniqueness of the respective games. Yet for the purposes of this book, an essential universal routine has been established for the study of these games. The *players* are described first and in this text they are mostly secondary school students, college students, and adults. The *object of the game* gives meaning to the behaviors and helps all players understand what the goals are for winning, losing, and participating. *Number of players* is the next heading, followed by *costume, apparel, and equipment required*. The *area, arena, field, or space* where the game is played is important as roughhouse games must be confined to safe areas. The *time length* of the game is important as is a description of the rules of play and the plays themselves. The category *symbolism* attracted a variety of comments and interpretations from the contributors, which we have not tried to make uniform. This heading covers game symbolism of various ways of life and folklore within particular communities yet sometimes gives meaning and historical perspective to the submitted games as well. Sometimes the symbolism is vague and sometimes it is very specific, but the editors felt this entry should be included in order to enhance the enjoyment and understanding of each game. The *rules of play,* which include *scoring,* rounds out the protocol for each game.

Some games submitted have not been used and others arrived too late. An emphasis, especially with the American games, has been placed on integrative games involving both physical and classroom fare.

Very few of the games played around the world can be attributed exclusively to one person or one tribe. Similar games are played in countries far away from one another under different names, but where we have been able to find a game not played elsewhere, we have displayed the contributor in the first part of this book. Where games are not attributed to one contributor, their practice is widespread. Many games are played in many countries, especially popular games, and it behooves us to give universal recognition. Further, rule changes and adaptations, while providing great variety, also make the national designation of that game at times difficult. The editors are confident, however, that games attributed to particular nations and people are accurate.

Even the simplest of games requires interpretation and figuring things out, which combines cognitive and physical activity. Teachers who succeed in perfecting this combination are performing a great service for their students. It is this linkage between the games and important classroom subjects such as literacy, science, and math, which not only facilitates specific learning, but usually engages the student with positive emotion. This volume introduces us to rare and popular games of the world from which more formidable and sophisticated texts will evolve.

PART I

Africa

Ghana

ALOKOTO
Reginald Ocansey
Not appropriate for replication.

Players:

Male pre-teens and teens from the Kasena-Nankana, Dagombas, and Akans tribes.

Object of game for players:

Given a small funnel-shaped shell, a player spins the shell on a sandy surface attempting to manipulate the shell so that it rests with its spinning edge facing up.

Number of players:

Four to ten.

Costume, apparel/equipment required:

One shell per player, and a small knife.

Area/arena/field where played—space required:

Dirt or sand.

Time length of game. How is end of game determined?:

Until a predetermined score is reached by one player.

Symbolism of game:

- Object manipulation with control.
- Bravery, initiation into teenage/adulthood.
- Acceptance by peers as worthy to be a man.

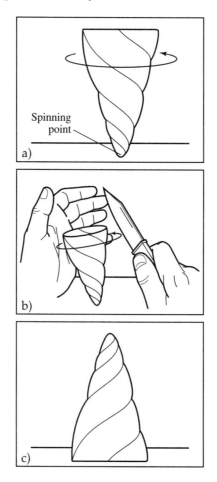

a) Shell spinning on point; b) Player manipulating shell; c) Target position of shell.

Rules of play, including scoring:

Players sit in a circle or in any convenient formation. Each player prepares loose dirt or sand for spinning in. Select a player to start the game by spinning the shell into the loose dirt or sand. As the shell "dances" the spinner applies force to it with the fingers of right or left hand. The player slightly cups the shell with his left hand as his right hand "cuts" it with a knife, upending the shell and bringing it to rest on its wide base with the tip pointing upwards. This is one score or point. The spinner continues to spin and cut the shell in the same manner until the shell falls on its side, then the next player takes over. The winner is the one who is first to reach an arbitrarily set target score. The one with the lowest score of the game places the thumb of one hand on the floor palm down, with the other fingers close together and off the floor. The winner then attempts to spin the shell to hit the knuckles of the loser (to cause pain).

The player to reach the specified number first is the winner. Points are earned when the shell faces up (i.e., the spinning edge is up). If the shell closes half way while spinning, the spinner is given a handful of dirt to throw at the shell to bring it to the desired position. The player may then continue spinning. The player forfeits a turn after any failed spinning attempt.

AMPE

Reginald Ocansey
Appropriate for replication.

Players:

Females, three to sixteen years of age, from the Ashanti tribe.

Object of game for players:

Players form small groups of four or more with a leader. On command, a leader vies with each player in turn. To begin each contest, both the leader and the player make two forward quick hops on the spot. The leader attempts to disguise the leg that she will put out in front (criterion leg) so as to score points and maintain leadership as long as possible.

Number of players:

Twenty.

Costume, apparel/equipment required:

Everyday wear.

Area/arena/field where played—space required:

Field or gymnasium.

Time length of game. How is end of game determined?:

The game is over when one player reaches the previously determined score.

Symbolism of game:

- Development of lower body strength, endurance, and coordination.
- Development of rhythm and coordination.
- Development of skills in counting and addition.
- Analysis of the odds and decision making in predicting leg selection of opponents.

Rules of play—including scoring:

First, players elect a starter or leader who establishes the standard or criteria for movement of the legs. The leader chooses either crossed legs, in which one leg is crossed over the other, or the straight leg position, in which one leg is placed in front of the other, and then declares this choice to the other players. At her command, and in unison, the leader and the first player prepare with two small hops on both feet while clapping. On the third hop, they quickly put out one foot. If the leader's choice was straight and they both put out the same leg (for example, left and left), then the leader wins a point and she continues with the next player. If they put out opposite legs (for example, leader puts out left and player puts out right), then the other player becomes the new leader. If the leader has chosen the crossed-position, leader and player on the third hop cross one foot in front of the other. If they both cross the same foot in front (e.g., both cross right foot over left), the leader wins a point and moves to the next player. If, however, they cross opposite feet in front (e.g., leader crosses right foot over left and player crosses left foot over right), then the player becomes the new leader. Each player keeps her own score. Each play must be completed in two trials. While players wait their turn they may clap to a steady beat or sing a song.

ANOTOBA

Reginald Ocansey
Appropriate for replication.

Players:

Pre-teens from the Ashanti tribe.

Object of game for players:

Players sit in a circle with one player acting as performer, standing outside the circle holding a beanbag. On command, the performer runs around the circle and quietly drops the beanbag behind another player sitting in the circle. The performer, after dropping the beanbag, runs around the circle to touch the player behind whom the beanbag was placed. If the player does not discover the beanbag before being touched by the performer, they switch roles.

Number of players:

Ten to 20 (or more).

Costume, apparel/equipment required:

Stone, beanbag, rag, and handkerchief.

Area/arena/field where played—space required:

Field or gymnasium.

Time length of game. How is end of game determined?:

Any preset amount of time.

Symbolism of game:

- Spatial awareness and/or alertness.
- Sprint runs and jogs for fitness.
- Played in moonlight in the village after completing household chores.

Rules of play—including scoring:

Players sit in a circle in an area about 20 x 20 meters and begin the game with a song—the whole group sings. The first player runs around the outside of the circle with a stone, beanbag, piece of rag, or handkerchief in one hand. During the run, the player quietly drops the beanbag (or rag, etc.) behind one of the other players seated in the circle. Following the drop, the player runs around the circle to return to the beanbag. If a complete circle run is made, the player gently taps (with open palm) the back of the player behind whom the beanbag was dropped. Both runners then compete by sprinting around the circle to determine who gets to join the circle. Whoever arrives at the vacant spot first sits in the circle while the other player becomes, or continues to be, the player holding the beanbag. If the player behind whom the beanbag was dropped discovers the beanbag sooner, he or she picks it up and sprints all the way around the circle to occupy the vacant spot he or she has just left.

The player holding the beanbag continues until the beanbag changes hands. All players must sit in the circle on the ground and start all runs from a sitting position. Players cannot turn to look at the one with the beanbag as he or she runs around the circle. While in the initial process of running in order to drop the beanbag, the player runs slowly or jogs, but when competing to occupy the vacant spot in circle, the players sprint.

BASERIGO

Reginald Ocansey
Appropriate for replication.

Players:

Teens.

Object of game for players:

Players assume a spot on a circle designated by a line drawn on the floor or ground. At the command of the leader, all players attempt to rush out of the circle to avoid being designated the ghost.

Number of players:

Unlimited.

Costume, apparel/equipment required:

Garments permitting climbing.

Area/arena/field where played—space required:

Treed area with clearings or gym with rings and wall bars.

Time length of game. How is end of game determined?:

Typically, the game lasts for 30 minutes.

Symbolism of game:

Involves a lot of climbing, jumping, and running. Attempt to escape death through running for fitness.

Rules of play, including scoring:

Draw a circle on the ground large enough to accommodate the number of players in the game. The circle represents the "grave." Typically played in areas where there are trees and obstacles within the natural habitat (for dodging and climbing), it could also be played in an open gymnasium that has wall bars and climbing ropes. Players enter the grave (represented by the circle) and then select a leader. At the command of the leader, all participants run out of the circle. The last to leave the circle becomes the *kogo* (ghost). The kogo chases and attempts to touch other participants. Players run, jump, and climb to escape from being touched. When a kogo touches another player, the player becomes the new kogo. The new kogo runs back into the grave, then runs out and chases the other players. The cycle is repeated.

No slapping, pushing, or pulling other players. To avoid being touched, players may run back into the circle (this is a time-out period for about 60 seconds). Players can only be touched when they are outside the circle. Players may be disqualified for staying more than 60 seconds in the grave.

CHASIKELEN
Reginald Ocansey
Appropriate for replication.

Players:

Male pre-teens and teens from the Kasena-Nankana, Dagombas, and Gonjas tribes.

Object of game for players:

A guard stands with a stick in his hand behind or in front of a target circle. The rest of the players stand five to six meters away from the target circle with a tin can in hand. The players attempt to throw the tin cans into the circle while the guard hits them to keep them from entering the circle.

Number of players:

Two to ten.

Costume, apparel/equipment required:

One stick and tin can per player.

Area/arena/field where played—space required:

Field or gymnasium.

Time length of game. How is end of game determined?:

Game ends when all players get their tin cans into the target.

Symbolism of game:

- Throwing and hitting accuracy.
- Development of stick-hand-object coordination.
- Development of reaction speed.
- The game takes place after the crops have germinated and flowered.

Rules of play, including scoring:

Players select a guard (by self-nomination, coin tossing, or any other means) to determine the starter. After selecting the guard, the rest of the players become the throwers. Throwers attempt to throw empty tin cans or objects about the size of a tennis ball into the circle (if outdoors, the circle can surround a target hole within the circle). Throwers stand behind a line five to six meters from the target circle, which is under the vigilant eye of the guard. On command by the guard, players take turns throwing their tin cans into the circle. With a stick in his hand, the guard vigilantly watches over the target and redirects all incoming tin cans by hitting them away from the circle. Once a tin can is hit by the guard the thrower runs to pick it up and then attempts the throw again from the spot where it landed. When the guard swings and misses a tin can thrown toward the target circle, the thrower is given a second chance if the tin can did not enter the target hole. (The spot from where the tin cans are thrown should be marked to facilitate second chances.) Throwing and hitting continues until all players get their tin cans into the circle. Once a tin can lands in the circle, the player removes it and then waits for the others to do likewise.

Use light empty cans, a tennis or soft, slow-moving ball about the size of a tennis ball, and straight sticks of a manageable size. If possible, dig a hole in the ground about six inches wide and three inches deep. May substitute with a large drawn circle on the floor and a hoola hoop to demarcate the hole. The guard must stand in front of or behind the hole and hit all tin cans or balls away. Players must throw their hit tin cans from wherever they landed.

KURA YA KURA
Jepkorir Rose Chepyator-Thomson
Appropriate for replication.

Players:

Male and female teens.

Object of game for players:

To develop physical speed, eye-hand coordination, and to produce rhythmic movement.

Number of players:

Any number.

Costume, apparel/equipment required:

A small stone for each player; traditional colorful costumes.

Area/arena/field where played—space required:

Any clear grassy area outdoors or an open area inside.

Time length of game. How is end of game determined?:

The game continues until the players are too few to make the game interesting; then the eliminated players join in and the leader starts the game all over again.

Symbolism of game:

The game is used to initiate males and females separately into adulthood. Boys and girls sing separate songs.

Rules of play (include scoring):

Each player finds a small stone that could fit in one hand and easily be passed to the next player. Players first squat, sit, or kneel in a circle to start the game. Next, all players pass the stones to the leader. The leader then starts to sing local or regional songs, and the other players follow suit with appropriate responses. When the leader is satisfied that all players are in tune and singing together—it does not take long—then she or he starts to pass out the stones one by one counterclockwise, in time with the rhythm of the song. When a player misses the pitch or beat of the song, his or her stone is placed on the ground. When a player makes a predetermined number of mistakes, indicated by the stones piled in front of her or him, that player is eliminated from the game. Then the leader restarts the game.

OWARE (A MARBLE GAME)*
Reginald Ocansey
Appropriate for replication.

Players:

Teens and up.

---

*A similar game known as Ajua is played by males of all ages in Kenya.

Object of game for players:

Given a carved wooden board with two rows of six to eight holes each containing four marbles, players attempt to move the marble sets by placing them in each hole strategically in order to win houses or cows, which represent the two important possessions in the village.

Number of players:

Two or more.

Costume, apparel/equipment required:

Carved wooden board with 12 or 16 holes, four marbles for each hole (48 or 64 marbles in all).

Area/arena/field where played—space required:

Two rows of holes in a wooden board or in the ground—either two rows of six or two rows of eight.

Time length of game. How is end of game determined?:

When all the marbles are won.

Symbolism of game:

- This game was very popular among women during the tribal wars. A story is told of an Ashanti king, Ntim Gyakari, who after committing his soldiers to war stayed home just to play the game with his wife.
- Computation—including addition and subtraction.
- Critical thinking.
- Judgment and decision making.

Rules of play, including scoring:

Players sit on either side of a set of two rows of holes (carved in wood or dug into the ground). A row may contain six to eight holes, each hole containing four marbles. At the beginning of the game, a player strategically picks four marbles from a hole on his or her side of the carved wooden game board. The marbles are about the size of the last digit of a finger. Small stones can also be used. One player starts the game by picking four marbles from any of the six holes in front of him or herself and drops them one at a time in the next four holes to the right. In the fourth hole, the player picks five marbles and drops them one at a time in the next five holes to the right. The picking up and dropping of the marbles in the holes continues until the last marble is dropped into a vacant, or empty, hole. There is a time-out at this time. The process is repeated by the opponent. Marbles are regrouped, and holes become empty as the marbles keep piling in certain holes. Houses or cows are won when a hole is regrouped to the starting four marbles. The player in whose half of the game board more marbles in fours are regrouped wins the most houses or cows. In the event a player drops the last marble in a hole of three marbles on the opponent's half of the game board, the player "steals" all four marbles and adds them to his or her pile of houses and cows. The game continues until the last marbles are in the player's pile. The player with the greatest count out of the 48 or 64 marbles wins the game. At the end of the game, players reset their holes by placing four marbles in each hole. Any player with extra marbles occupies the holes in the opponent's half of the game board starting at the right and filling up in a counter-clockwise manner. The holes that are occupied by the extra marbles become the property or territory of that player. Lost houses are redeemable by winning more marbles in subsequent play.

At any time during the game while the process of regrouping is going on, if a hole contains four marbles the player on whose side the marbles are picks them up and keeps them. Each player should attempt to prevent any rearrangement of the marbles in twos or threes in the territory of the opponent.

STRAW ROLLING
Reginald Ocansey
Not appropriate for replication.

Players:

Teens and up from the Kasema-Nankans and Builasas tribes.

Object of game for players:

Standing side by side in a line in a forward-bending position, one player rolls the target straw ring forward. The other players roll their straw rings in attempts to knock down the rolling target ring or any other ring aimed at the target ring. To win, a player must knock down another ring so that his or her ring lies on top of that ring.

Number of players:

Two to 12.

Costume, apparel/equipment required:

Rings of straw.

Area/arena/field where played—space required:

An open area.

Time length of game. How is end of game determined?:

When all the rings are won.

Symbolism of game:

- Develop accuracy in rolling and knocking or hitting targets.
- Negotiation and decision-making skills.
- Object manipulation and control.

Rules of play, including scoring:

Players stand side by side in a straight line facing the same direction. The leader bends and rolls the straw ring forward on the ground while the others momentarily wait. Immediately following the leader's roll, the other players tactically roll their straw rings attempting to knock down the leader's or any other straw ring. To win, a player's straw ring must lie completely or partially on another straw ring.

One player rolls his or her straw ring first; others roll their straw rings to hit down the first one. When two or more straw rings lie on one, the topmost one wins and takes them all. In the event two straw rings lie side by side on top of another, the winner is the player whose straw ring occupies the most space. The one with the most rings wins. The game is played on a flat, smooth area, such as a road or floor. The area can be of any size. The game ends when others have very few or no more straw rings left.

TU- MA-TU (GHANA)
CHEMETYER (KENYA)
Reginald Ocansey
Not appropriate for replication.

Players:

Teens. Most tribes in Ghana and the Kalenjins tribe in Kenya play this game.

Object of game for players:

Given a floor diagram similar to the one used to play hopscotch, players toss a small piece of clay or play-dough into squares. They use various jumping and landing techniques to go through the squares and acquire home blocks upon successful completion.

Number of players:

Four to nine.

Costume, apparel/equipment required:

A small piece of clay or play-dough.

Area/arena/field where played—space required:

Open area with twin squares marked on the ground. These are the starting squares.

Time length of game. How is end of game determined?:

When all the houses are owned.

Symbolism of game:

- Fitness.
- Develops throwing accuracy through aiming play-dough at particular squares.
- Body control—jumping, landing, balancing.

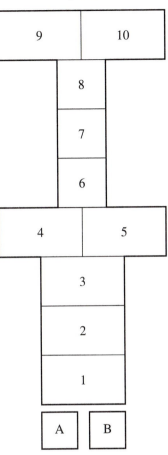

Starting squares

Rules of play, including scoring:

Similar to the American version of hopscotch.

- At least four but less than ten players are allowed in each game.
- The rectangular space to be used is designed by all players before the game.
- The rectangle has ten spaces and each represents a house.
- A piece of dry (circular) clay is used as a button for aiming at the houses.
- One button is used by all the players.
- All the players choose a method of balloting that is used to determine who will start the game, who will go second, and so on.

- The first player starts by standing on the starting squares (A and B) in astride position.

- A player tosses the clay or play-dough to land in square #1.

- He or she then hops or jumps from both feet and attempts to land in square #2 on one leg.

- The player jumps off with the same leg from square #2 and lands on the same leg in square #3.

- The player jumps on the same leg from square #3 and lands astride in blocks #4 and #5 simultaneously.

- From the astride position in blocks #4 and #5, the player jumps into block #6 and lands on either foot. (The player may change jumping and landing feet but must land on one foot.)

- From block #6, the player jumps and lands in block #7 on the same foot as in block #6.

- From block #7, he or she jumps or hops and lands in block #8 on the same foot.

- From block #8, he or she jumps on the same leg and lands astride in blocks #9 and #10.

- The player turns by hopping to face the starting square and repeats the process in a reverse manner until he or she lands in square #2.

- While in square #2 and on one leg, the player bends to pick up the piece of clay or play-dough and then jumps over square #1 to land in astride position in the starting squares.

- Repeat the game from the beginning, but this time toss the play-dough into square #2 and go through the entire process.

- From squares #9 and #10, standing astride, hop or jump and land in square #8 on the same foot.

- Hop or jump on the same foot into square #7; hop on the same foot into square #6; then hop and land in astride position in squares #4 and #5; and then hop on one foot into square #3.

- In square #3 bend over to pick up the piece of clay or play-dough in square #2, hop over square #2, and then land in square #1 on the same foot.

- Hop from square #1 on the same foot and land in the starting squares astride.

- A player is eligible to "own" a house or square after successfully hop-scotching through all the houses or squares, #1 through #10, without error.

- Upon completing square #10, the player returns to the starting squares (A and B) to assume astride position with his or her back to the game.
- The player then throws the play-dough or clay behind and over the shoulder. Where the clay or play-dough lands becomes the participant's "own" house.
- Repeat the entire process to own as many blocks or houses as possible.

A player loses a turn when a line of the floor diagram is fouled by stepping on or touching a line. Once a square or house is owned, no other participant can step or land on it. Only the owner can make occasional but strategic rest stops at his or her convenience to facilitate performance. When a player who faulted previously returns to the game, he or she resumes where he or she left off. The game comes to an end when all the houses are owned. The winner of the game is the player who owns the most houses.

WOR-HU! GUMIA! (COBRA! RUN!)

Reginald Ocansey
Appropriate for replication.

Players:

Young teens.

Object of game for players:

Players in small groups work cooperatively and uniformly to describe a curled snake by wrapping themselves around one player in the group; they then carefully unwrap themselves from the "curled snake wrap" and move forward on each occasion.

Number of players:

Eight to ten.

Costume, apparel/equipment required:

Nothing special.

Area/arena/field where played—space required:

Open area.

Time Length of game. How is end of game determined?:

Any preset amount of time.

Symbolism of game:

- Coordination.
- Team work.
- Cooperation.

Rules of play, including scoring:

Eight to ten players hold hands firmly to form a long chain that will not break. The player at the end of the chain stands still while the rest of the players run in a circle, trying to wrap themselves around the stationary player until all the players are wound together like a curled-up snake. Once successful, children run in the opposite direction until a single long chain is formed again. The process is repeated and they move forward on each occasion.

Kenya

CATTLE RAIDING GAME
March Krotee
Not appropriate for replication.

Players:

Male pre-teens and teens of the Maasai Tribe.

Object of game for players:

To throw the *rungu* (club) for distance and accuracy.

Number of players:

Five to 20.

Costume, apparel/equipment required:

Maasai warrior outfit: brilliant red cloth, long hair, braided ochred spear, shield, and rungus.

Area/arena/field where played—space required:

Open pasture or clearing similar in size to one large enough to throw a javelin in.

Time length of game. How is end of game determined?:

Usually until exhaustion or when one dominant warrior emerges.

Symbolism of game:

Represents one of the young warrior training methods often associated with battle or cattle raiding missions. It is also used as a measure of fitness and physical prowess.

Rules of play, including scoring:

Actual rungus (18-inch clubs) are used. Rungus are usually thrown alternately at a specified target for distance. This requires balance, strength, and throwing accuracy. Only male warrior groups participate and the contest is usually watched by male tribal elders. The young male warriors (*morans*) test their manhood by throwing their rungus the farthest distance within a prescribed target-throwing area, at a specific target, or for distance.

FENCING GAMES (FORKED STICK "FIGHTING")
Jepkorir Rose Chepyator-Thomson
Not suitable for replication.

Players:

Pre-teens and teens.

Object of game for players:

To "fight" by putting marks on an opponent's forked stick.

Number of players:

Two.

Costume, apparel/equipment required:

Forked stick for each player.

Area/arena/field where played—space required:

Any clear area that is free of dangerous objects.

Time length of game. How is end of game determined?:

Players usually play until exhaustion.

Symbolism of game:

Represents the times when Keiyo ethnic groups used to go to war to defend Keiyo territory from being invaded by neighboring ethnic groups.

Rules of play, including scoring:

Each player cuts a forked stick from a tree called Leketwo. This is a local tree that marks easily when struck. Current players may coat their sticks with chalk or flower so that hits can be registered and counted. No hits on an opponent's body are permitted. The game requires the following skills: speed, endurance, and strategy.

To start the game, a player says "Let us start," and the game finishes when a player says "I am tired," or after both players have been hit ten times. Whoever has the most marks on the stick loses the game. Sometimes players agree on a given time to play. For instance, before the start of the game players may agree on ten hits, and whoever has the most marks on the stick loses the game.

KIROROKTET

Reginald Ocansey
Not appropriate for replication.

Players:

Typically male teens, from the Kalenjins Tribe.

Object of game for players:

Given a cobweb-like net between two trees or sticks, players in teams attempt to send their members through at least ten of the "web" spaces in the net within the shortest possible time without touching any part of the net.

Number of players:

Twenty.

Costume, apparel/equipment required:

Web of sisal strings.

Area/arena/field where played—space required:

The forest.

Time length of game. How is end of game determined?:

Typically, 30 minutes.

Symbolism of game:

- Develops cooperative spirit.
- Develops ability to problem solve in a group.

Rules of play, including scoring:

In the woods, teams of players use sisal strings to create a cobweb-like net between two trees or sticks. The different-sized spaces in the web range from large and easy to go through to small and difficult to go through. Each team of six to ten players attempts to move its members through the spaces in the cobweb without any part of their bodies touching the strings within the shortest time possible.

Each player on the team should go through at least one space. Each team should come up with their best solutions on how to go through the given spaces.

KORA (KENYA)
BIA (ALSO IN GHANA)
Reginald Ocansey
Appropriate for replication.

Players:

Young female teens.

Object of game for players:

Given six small stones, one designated as a queen, the player throws up the queen stone gently and attempts to pick the other stones in different combinations without dropping any of them.

Number of players:

Six to 24.

Costume, apparel/equipment required:

Six small stones, one designated as a queen stone.

Area/arena/field where played—space required:

Open area.

Time length of game. How is end of game determined?:

Game stops when each player has completed the tasks.

Symbolism of game:

- Long life, decision making, and problem solving.
- Throwing accuracy, catching, and coordination.
- Estimations for throwing at relative heights and corresponding judgments, selections, and picking target combinations of stones.

Rules of play, including scoring:

1. Players work in small groups determined by the number of players available.
2. The game starts with the rolling of six small-size stones (about the size of dice). The player picks one of the six stones to be designated as "queen" (or "king") and does the following:
   - Toss the queen stone up just high enough to give time to pick up the other stones.
   - Start first by picking up one stone at a time, until all five stones have been picked up.

- Repeat #2 above, and then pick up two, two, and then one, or one, two, and then two stones.
- Repeat #2 above, and then pick up three, and then two, or two, and then three stones.
- Repeat #2 above, and then pick up one, and then four, or four, and then one stones. Repeat 2 above, and then pick up all five stones.

3. Pick up all six stones in one hand, toss them up slightly, then catch them with the backs of both hands put together, the sides of the two index fingers touching each other and palms facing down.
4. Flip the six stones up slightly and catch them in the palms.
5. Successful completion of tasks #2 through #4 earns the player a year of life.
6. Repeat the entire process to accumulate more years.

Always toss the queen stone before picking up a stone or a set of stones. Caught stone(s) should be kept in the non-tossing hand. Under special circumstances the caught stone(s) may be placed on the floor. A player continues to accrue more years of life until the queen or any of the other stones are dropped. Players are not allowed to touch any additional stones except according to the combinations. For example, in the two-two-one or one-two-two pick-up sequences, the player may not touch any of the other stones while attempting to pick up two at a time. The player loses a turn when she fails to pick up any stone in the correct combination.

MAROBA (KENYA)
KRUJE KRUJE E-KPE, E-KPE (GHANA)
Reginald Ocansey
Appropriate for replication.

Players:

Pre-teens and young teens in Ghana. Pre-teen and young teen females in Kenya.

Object of game for players:

Sitting in a circle with a small stone (or pair of shoes) placed in front of each player, players move the stone or pair of shoes (and all subsequent stones or shoes placed in front of them) to the next player on their right, all the while maintaining the coordinated movement of the stones or shoes to the accompanying rhythm and tempo of the song.

Number of players:

Unspecified.

Costume, apparel/equipment required:

Stones (or shoes, or beanbag).

Area/arena/field where played—space required:

Open area.

Time length of game. How is end of game determined?:

Any preset amount of time.

Symbolism of game:

- Development of hand-eye-object coordination.
- Development of cooperation and team work.
- Development of concentration and rhythmic movement.
- Development of coordination and a sense of rhythm.
- Initiation into adulthood for Kenyan female teens—teaching responsibility through lyrics of songs, teaching girls to become women.

Rules of play, including scoring:

Eight to ten players sit, squat, or kneel in a circle, each with a small stone (the size of a lemon) or beanbag in front of him or her. Girls in Kenya use pairs of shoes instead and sit in a circle with legs crossed (leg crossing is indicative of good discipline). On command, each player taps the floor three times with the stone or beanbag. After the third tap, each player places the stone or beanbag in front of the next participant to the right. (The speed and/or swiftness of the execution is dictated by the tempo of an accompanying song.) On command, in the Kenyan marabo, for example, the leader introduces a song with lyrics outlining the common responsibilities that women undertake in their daily lives, for example, what to do when a visitor comes to the house. Players continue to move the stones/shoes/beanbags in a circular rotation to the rhythm of the song. As the tempo of the accompanying song gets faster, the rhythmic rotation increases in speed. The object of the game is to keep the shoes or beanbags moving around the circle in time to the beat of the music. Players continue to pick up the shoes/stones from the left and pass them on to the player on their right in a rhythmic manner. In the event an object is not placed in front of a player on time, he or she goes through the motion(s) of picking up the object and putting it in front of the next player anyway, in order to keep the rhythm. At the end of a song, if a player has two or more stones/shoes/beanbags, he or she is out of the game. In the Kenyan version, the leader may stop the song and/or change the direction of shoe rotation at any time. When the leader stops the song, the person who has more than one pair of shoes or less than one pair is out of the game. In Kenya, the winner is the one who stays in the game longest without fumbling. In Ghana, as the elimination continues, the last two players use three stones to determine the winner. The winner is the one who is best able to maintain sustained coordination in moving the stones in a timely fashion.

Players who fumble leave the circle, taking their stones with them; or the stone is placed in the center of the circle and they may rejoin the game after running around the circle a given number of times. Start with a slow tempo and then increase to fast tempo. A girl who sits incorrectly in the Kenyan shoes game is disqualified. Players take turns leading songs.

SENGENYA DANCE
March Krotee
Not appropriate for replication.

Players:

Teens of the Digo tribe.

Object of game for players:

Entertainment. The dance depicts a beautiful young woman showing off her movements in order to attract a suitor.

Number of players:

Equal numbers of young male and female tribal members.

Costume, apparel/equipment required:

Players wear colorful skirts, knee and ankle rattles, and large feathered headdresses. Women wear jewelry and other ornaments. Kayamba rattles, drums, and whistles are also requisite.

Area/arena/field where played—space required:

Any flat surface will suffice.

Time length of game. How is end of game determined?:

Ten to fifteen minutes, though often extended and repeated.

Symbolism of game:

The Sengenya is a popular coastal dance where the women gracefully move and entice the men to follow their movements. Its origin may be traced to the once matrilineal society of the Digo, who traditionally traced their descent through the female line.

Rules of play, including scoring:

Dancers enter in two separate lines, one of men, one of women. Music accompanies the dance, and dancers keep in step with the music. The two lines move in a clockwise dance pattern by employing a shuffling foot pattern. The dance is done in a crescent line formation with the male partners in back of each respective female partner. Mostly upright and crouching positions are alternated in time to the music while the lines pass through each other. This dance is often performed in competitions or exhibitions.

SIMBII
Reginald Ocansey
Appropriate for replication.

Players:

Young male teens from the Kalenjins tribe.

Object of game for players:

Given ten buttons, each player throws them consecutively into a hole five to six yards away. Players attempt to throw all ten buttons into the hole. First finished is the winner.

Number of players:

Ten.

Costume, apparel/equipment required:

A hole for a target and a button for each player.

Area/arena/field where played—space required:

Open area.

Time length of game. How is end of game determined?:

After the ten players have thrown, a judge rates their efforts. In other words, at the end of the first round of ten throws, a judge determines who has been the best thrower.

Symbolism of game:

- Developing throwing accuracy through aiming at a target.
- Portrays a unique part of the cultural heritage regarding the old male dating practices.

Rules of play, including scoring:

Players dig a hole about two inches across and two inches deep. They then draw a line five to six yards away from the hole (this is the starting line). In turn, each player is given all the buttons and stands with both feet behind the starting line. He throws each button into the hole one at a time (players determine their own throwing techniques). After all ten buttons have been thrown, a designated judge counts and declares the score. If the player gets a perfect score, then he wins a "wife," and continues with a second turn. The turn ends when a perfect score is not obtained.

- Each player is supposed to get a button from an old shirt or pair of pants.
- No player can step on or beyond the starting line.
- Each player should aim all the buttons into the hole.
- Each player continues to play and wins "wives" as perfect scores are obtained. A player loses a turn when a perfect score is not obtained.
- Any player who behaves inappropriately is completely disqualified.

SPEAR GAME
Dell Smith
Not appropriate for replication.

Players:

Teens of the Samburu tribe.

Object of game for players:

To toss "spears" and stop a rolling hoop; also to see how many spears can be thrown into the hoop. Samburu do not use their actual spears because they do not want to risk breaking a valuable spear.

Number of players:

Typically six to ten, divided into two teams.

Costume, apparel/equipment required:

Six- to eight-foot straight willows that are smooth (similar to an international javelin). A thin willow that has been curved into a hoop and tressed to withstand vigorous tossing and rolling.

Area/arena/field where played—space required:

An open space at least 50 x 50 yards on ground capable of allowing a spear to stick upright. (Obviously if the ground is too hard or too soft then some adjustment in the rules is necessary.)

Time length of game. How is end of game determined?:

The game ends when one team wins a predetermined number of cattle (points).

Symbolism of game:

This game develops basic physical skills necessary to live in the Samburu environment. It is not unusual for a lion or leopard to attack the domestic herds of the Samburu who must then protect their food source (i.e., milk producing animals), and their investment. This game provides the practice necessary to develop the strength, fitness, and accuracy skills used for survival among the Samburu people. Cattle represent the main feature of the economy of the Samburu people. Cattle are part of the "bride price" and are essential in the basic economic structure of this society. Also, milk is the basic food source for the Samburu.

Rules of play, including scoring:

The participants are divided into two teams. The team that is up first will form a line approximately 20–30 yards away from the point where one of the opponents will throw the hoop in a line parallel to the spear tossers. The objective is to see how many spears can be thrown into the center of the hoop. If the first spear stops the hoop then the other team members have a chance to throw at a stationary target that is laying on the ground. The hoop must be stopped by a spear in order for points to be gained. If the hoop is not stopped and rolls dead on its own then no points are awarded. Points are awarded in the form of cattle. Therefore, the winner is determined at the end of the game by the number of cattle a team has earned. The teams rotate after each toss of the hoop. The length of the game is arbitrary and is usually set at a specific number of cattle won.

1. Spear tossers cannot step across the throwing line that is marked on the ground.
2. A thrown spear must stop the hoop before the hoop stops rolling on its own or else no points are awarded.
3. Spears must stick in the ground to be counted.
4. The hoop tosser must throw the hoop hard enough so that it travels at least past the last person on the spear tossing line.
5. The hoop must be thrown so that it is touching the ground when it passes the first person on the spear tossing line. Hoops in the air at that stage will have to be rolled again.
6. Spear tossers can run along their line but cannot cross to the hoop side of the line.

Nigeria

BIG SNAKE*

Tom Sharpe

Appropriate for replication.

Players:

Pre-teens and teens.

Object of game for players:

The snake tries to capture other players. When a player is caught he or she joins hands with the snake, causing it to gradually grow longer. Only players on either end of the snake may tag others.

Number of players:

Unlimited. Can be played with individual snakes or snake teams.

Costume, apparel/equipment required:

Jump ropes or cones to delineate home for the snake.

*This game has many different names. It is also called Blob, Amoeba, Chain-tag, and Add-on, and is very popular in many countries. The basic rules are designed to optimize active participation and be fun for all players. It is not an elimination game.

Area/arena/field where played—space required:

Open area or large indoor gymnasium.

Time length of game. How is end of game determined?:

The game is over when all players are caught by the snake.

Symbolism of game:

Hunting, chasing, running, and evading. Players have to problem solve to avoid capture and to capture others.

Rules of play, including scoring:

Only players on either end of the snake may catch others. If the snake breaks because players let go their hands, runners may tag the snake and send it home. If the snake becomes long enough, the runners can be encircled. Encircled players may break through the snake and send it home, giving other runners a chance to avoid capture. There is no scoring.

COLLEGE
Aminu Momodu
Not appropriate for replication.

Players:

Female teens.

Object of game for players:

To "build" as many houses as possible.

Number of players:

Two to four.

Costume, apparel/equipment required:

No particular costume is worn. Players wear dresses that will not disturb them during the game. A marble is needed for each player.

Area/arena/field where played—space required:

A rectangular diagram is enclosed showing the set-up area. Usually the diagram is 8 x 15 feet divided into "houses" and "apartments."

Time length of game. How is end of game determined?:

No specific length. The game is played until all the available houses have been acquired.

Symbolism of game:

Represents the benefits of Western education, or college. That is, how Western education can facilitate better living conditions and economic prosperity, which the built houses represent.

Rules of play, including scoring:

Features and Rules: A marble is used by each player. No player should touch the endline with her foot. A player should not step on the opponents' built houses while playing the game. A player's marble should not touch any line or drop out of the playing area. A player's foot must not touch the house where the marble is dropped. The player steps into a house with a single apartment on one foot, and into a house with two apartments on both feet, with one in each apartment. An opponent takes over in the event of any violation. A player who has forfeited her turn continues from the point at which she left off when it becomes her turn again. That is, when her opponent commits an offense and loses her turn.

The Game: By mutual agreement, the first girl stands behind the endline and starts the game by throwing a marble into house no. 1. She jumps over the house where the marble is. She starts jumping from house no. 2, landing on the houses on one or both feet, depending on the number of apartments in the house. When she gets to house no. 6, she then returns in the same manner to house no. 2, picks up the marble in house no. 1, and then jumps out of the playing area. The next step is to drop the marble in house no. 2 and continue the process until she completes all six houses.

College Stage: After completing the exercise in the six houses, the player throws the marble into the college area. If she succeeds by the same process in reaching the "college" area and makes it back again, she can then build a house.

Building a House: The player stands at the starting area, turns her back to the playing area and throws the marble into any house. If the marble lands in a house, the player writes her name on the house, indicating ownership. A player can acquire as many houses as she is able by repeating the entire process described. The no. 1 house and college are the last to be acquired.

Winning: The player with the highest number of houses is declared the winner. More than one player, however, can acquire a college.

DAOLIKHABO

Aminu Momodu
Appropriate for replication.

Players:

Pre-teens and young teens of the Owan tribe.

Object of game for players:

To be able to say the name of the player who touches you when blind-folded.

Number of players:

Typically 10 to 15.

Costume, apparel/equipment required:

A blindfold.

Area/arena/field where played—space required:

Any open space approximately 40 x 60 feet, such as the village square, school compound, or family compound.

Time length of game. How is end of game determined?:

Varies.

Symbolism of game:

Played by the Owan tribe 340 miles from Lagos. Suggests recognition can occur other than through sight and sound.

Rules of play, including scoring:

Rules: There must be two groups of equal number. A player's eyes must be closed by another player from the opposite team. When a group wins a player, its size increases by one as the opposing player joins them.

The Game: The players are divided into two groups. They sit in rows facing each other, with group A on one side and group B on the other. The leader of group A will go to group B and blindfold the first person. A player from group A will come to group B to touch the blindfolded player and go back to his or her position. The blindfolded player's eyes are then uncovered and he or she is asked to guess who touched him or her. If the guess is right, the player who touched him or her joins that group, in other words, group B. But if the guess is wrong, he or she joins the opposite group, in other words, group A. The leader of group B will then go to group A and blindfold one of their players. Correct and incorrect guesses determine who moves to which group.

Winning: At the end, the group with the highest number of players wins the game.

ENU GAME
Aminu Momodu
Not appropriate for replication.

Players:

Male teens and young men of the Etsako tribe.

Object of game for players:

To hold the ankle of an opponent.

Number of players:

Two groups, typically two to ten in each.

Costume, apparel/equipment required:

Locally made shorts and vests. The two groups use headbands of different colors made from a piece of cloth.

Area/arena/field where played—space required:

Can be of any shape, usually 30 x 40 yards.

Time length of game. How is end of game determined?:

Until an opponent's ankle is held or both groups capitulate.

Symbolism of game:

Fitness, courage, strength. Represents war experience.

Rules of play, including scoring:

The two groups confront each other. The objective is to hold the ankle of any member of the opposing group. Any member of the group that succeeds in holding the ankle of his opponent scores a point and the game is restarted. The group with the higher number of points are declared the winners.

- Village center is arena.
- Very energetic. Uses wrestling skills.
- Often watched by the entire village.
- Accompanied by war songs.

IFI-UVIN

Aminu Momodu
Appropriate for replication.

Players:

Teens.

Object of game for players:

To catch a coconut when it is thrown.

Number of players:

Seven to ten in each of two groups.

Costume, apparel/equipment required:

No specific costume but participants wear any dress that will not inhibit their movements. They wear locally made headbands of two different colors for easy identification of teammates. A small coconut—underdeveloped—or a ball is also needed.

Area/arena/field where played—space required:

Any open field about 100 x 100 feet is adequate. The village square, school playground, or any other spacious play area could be used as an arena.

Time length of game. How is end of game determined?:

Thirty to 40 minutes, or as agreed to before commencement of the game.

Symbolism of game:

Fitness, courage, and survival measures (to fight for food).

Rules of play, including scoring:

Features and Rules: No pushing or holding during the game. Duration of play is 30–40 minutes. Often watched by the entire village during festivals or by interested persons at other times.

The Game: A center line is drawn and both teams move to the endline, 50 feet away. The referee stands at the center line and shouts "Are you ready?" The players answer "yes" if they are ready. The referee then throws the coconut and tries to avoid giving any of the teams undue advantage. The players on both sides run to catch or retrieve the coconut. A player who gets the coconut wins a point for his or her team.

Winning: The group with the highest number of points are the winners. Where there is a tie, a final throw is taken to break the tie.

LANGA (ONE LEGGED GAME)
Jimoh Shehu
Not appropriate for replication.

Players:

Male teens and young men of the Hausas tribe.

Object of game for players:

To outrun, outwit, outmaneuver, and unbalance the opponent.

Number of players:

Two to 11.

Costume, apparel/equipment required:

Nothing is worn beside shorts or a skirt (*bante*) made from cow or goat hide.

Area/arena/field where played—space required:

Standard oval track, an open field, or the village arena, depending on the type of game chosen.

Time length of game. How is end of game determined?:

When the race or combat is over.

Symbolism of game:

Virility, courage, physical fitness, teamwork, and resourcefulness.

Rules of play, including scoring:

Version 1: Dual combat involving two contestants trying to wrestle and destabilize one another. The one who loses his grip or balance loses the match.

Version 2: Team combat involving equal numbers of opposing players. The mode of play is similar to Version 1. The team that has more players with intact holds wins.

Version 3: King scoring. Another team game in which a player of the defending team is designated king. The king's teammates try to protect him as he hops from their endline to that of the opponents. The defending team is defeated either when the king is touched by an opponent or when he is brought down or forced to lose his grip, depending on the covenant and sanction agreed to by the teams. In the king version different agreements are developed before the game begins.

Version 4: Adapted sprints (80 meter, 150 meter, 5 x 80 meter relay) by athletes hopping on the same foot from start to finish. Standing start is adopted. Competitors must keep to their lanes. May involve two to eight sprinters.

- Entails hopping about to ward off an opponent or get to a destination.
- Played in the morning or evening during dry season.
- Between two and 11 men divided into junior, intermediate, and senior categories.
- Watched by a large crowd that forms a ring round the players.
- No rule restricting the use of any foot; the player holds the toes of any foot he finds most convenient.
- Player or team with intact toegrip wins.
- Blows and kicks not permitted.

LION AND THE GOAT
Aminu Momodu
Appropriate for replication.

Players:

Male or female pre-teens and teens of the Bini tribe.

Object of game for players:

The lion tries to catch the goat; the goat avoids being caught by the lion.

Number of players:

Twenty to 30 males or females.

Costume, apparel/equipment required:

Any dress such as shorts and sleeveless shirts that allow players to run easily.

Area/arena/field where played—space required:

Any open space.

Time length of game. How is end of game determined?:

Typically, a game lasts 15 minutes before exhaustion sets in.

Symbolism of game:

Represents war and hunting experiences, fitness, and courage.

Rules of play—including scoring:

The game is between two teams: the lions and the goats. The remaining children act as "villagers" while the eldest serves as referee. The villagers form a circle by joining their hands together. The lions and the goats each send a participant to compete for them. The lion stays outside the circle while the goat stays inside the circle. The game is begun with the following song:

Ekpen la mum ebhe bhu utodin,
eee jole mun, jole mun non mum gbele,
eee jole mun, jole mun no mun yowa
eee jole mun.

All players sing this song. The lion makes desperate efforts to go into the village (i.e., break into the circle) to catch the goat, but the villagers will not allow it. When the lion gains entry into the circle, the villagers then allow the goat to get out, and vice versa. The goat becomes a lion when it is caught by the lion and the lion becomes a goat if it cannot catch the goat after a specified amount of time. Substitutions are made at the end of each round until every member has taken part. The team with the greatest number of players (i.e., more captured opposing team members) are declared the winners.

• Requires a lot of running.
• Accompanied by songs.

OGHILI (TARGET HITTING)
Aminu Momodu
Not appropriate for replication.

Players:

Pre-teens and teens of the Etsako tribe.

Object of game for players:

To aim and hit the opponents' four marble seeds.

Number of players:

Two players.

Costume-Apparel/Equipment required:

Four marble seeds and small coconut-shaped objects about half as large as a regular-sized coconut, one for each player.

Area/arena/field where played—space required:

Open area.

Time length of game. How is end of game determined?:

Usually three rounds are played.

Symbolism of game:

Represents hunting experiences, shooting for accuracy and coordination.

Rules of play—including scoring:

The two players stand opposing each other, about ten to twelve feet apart. The two players arrange four marble seeds in such a way that three are placed on the ground with the fourth on top of them. One of the participants starts the game by using a marble seed to aim at the marble seeds arranged by the opponent. If a player hits and scatters the seeds arranged by an opponent, he then aims at individual seeds on his subsequent attempts. Any seed hit is removed and used to aim at and possibly hit other marble seeds in subsequent attempts. The first to hit all four marble seeds of his or her opponent wins the round. The two players can go through several rounds. The player who wins more rounds becomes the overall winner.

- Played mainly by males.
- Any seed that is hit is kept aside by the owner and given to the opponent. These are added to the number of throwing seeds used by both participants.
- The player that hits all four marble seeds of his or her opponent becomes the winner.
- Played during the daytime.
- Turns are alternated between the two players.

- Any marble seed thrown toward the opponents' marble seeds should not be obstructed. A rethrow is ordered if this happens.

OGHILI (TRIBAL HUNTING)
Aminu Momodu
Not appropriate for replication.

Players:

Male teens of the Etsako tribe.

Object of game for players:

To capture opposing team members.

Number of players:

Sixteen to 20 males on two teams.

Costume, apparel/equipment required:

Participants wear only pants. Teams wear their own colors, which usually consists of a color band, to avoid confusion between teammates and opponents.

Area/arena/field where played—space required:

Executed on a grass field, sandy surface, or in the village square.

Time length of game. How is end of game determined?:

The game is finished when both teams' members are tired.

Symbolism of game:

Represents preparation for war, fitness, courage, team spirit, and self defense.

Rules of play, including scoring:

The two oldest boys choose up sides, forming two teams. Three men or older boys form a panel of judges. At a signal from one of the judges, a member from one of the teams begins a song thus:

Akpanuhomhon Oghehe Omihilan - O!

The two teammates respond in chorus:

Yo go you—Omhilan O!

The prompter (i.e., one of the judges) begins another song:

Aba iyole Khaiyo Omhilan O!

The players respond:

Yo yo yo—Omhilan—O!

After the second response, all the players run about the field trying to capture opposing team members while defending themselves. The captor must grip the captive between the knee and the ankle. As soon as a player is captured, the game is stopped, the captive is given to the team that caught him, and then the game is restarted. The game continues until one team completely eliminates the other by capturing all of its players. If, however, the game is disrupted for any reason (e.g., inclement weather), the team with the higher number of captives is declared winner.

- A team game for males, 8–10 on each team.
- One player or two teammates joining forces may capture one member of the opposing team.
- High-energy game.
- Accomplished with tribal war songs.
- Watched by the entire village.
- Physical contact is allowed.
- A player is captured only if his opponent succeeds in gripping him firmly between the knee and the ankle.
- Any player must signal his capture of another player immediately by raising the victory alarm, *Oailo*, as many times as possible.
- No player may strike his opponent. If a player violates this instruction, he is sent off the field and cannot play.
- No player may run out of the field of play, which should be demarcated.
- Played at night when there is moonlight and sometimes between the hours of nine and ten in the morning.

OKHO KHO VARE (CHICKEN COME HOME)

Aminu Momodu
Appropriate for replication.

Players:

Pre-teens and teens.

Object of game for players:

For the hawk to touch all of the chickens.

Number of players:

Ten to 20. One player is designated the hawk and one is designated the hen; all the rest are chickens.

Costume, apparel/equipment required:

None.

Area/arena/field where played—space required:

Any open area about 60 x 100 ft in the village square, school, or family compounds.

Time length of game. How is end of game determined?:

The game ends when all the chickens are caught by the hawks or the hawks are too exhausted to continue.

Symbolism of game:

Represents the struggle for survival in the midst of enemies. Speed, fitness, and agility are emphasized.

Rules of play—including scoring:

The Game: The players representing the chickens line up behind the endline. One player, the hen, stands on the opposite endline. The hawk stands in the middle of the arena, between the hens and the chickens. Then the hen calls the chickens to come home. They respond by saying "No, the hawk will catch us." The hen insists they come home.

The chickens try to run to the hen but the hawk pursues and tries to touch them. Anyone touched by the hawk automatically becomes a hawk and then hunts and tries to touch the other chickens. The game is repeated until all the chickens are touched by hawks.

Winning: The hawks win if they touch all the chickens and the chickens win if the hawks are exhausted and want to stop playing.

South Africa

CROWS AND CRANES

Eileen Crowley Sullivan

Appropriate for replication.

Players:

Pre-teens.

Object of game for players:

To avoid being tagged and giving points to the other group.

Number of players:

Eight to 20, divided into two groups.

Costume, apparel/equipment required:

None.

Area/arena/field where played—space required:

Gymnasium, play area, or field.

Time length of game. How is end of game determined?:

As directed by the teacher.

Symbolism of game:

Represents tribal/community rivalry, survival, and fitness.

Rules of play, including scoring:

Children are divided into two groups, crows and cranes. Groups face each other, toeing the center line. The teacher calls "crows" or "cranes." If he calls crows, they run to the goal line behind them while the cranes chase them. All players tagged by the cranes count as points for the cranes or are put out of the game. Both groups return to the center line and the game continues. The teacher calls again. The group with the most points or the most players at the end of the playing time wins.

FLAGS GALORE
Eileen Crowley Sullivan
Appropriate for replication.

Players:

Teens.

Object of game for players:

To gather the most flags.

Number of players:

Variable.

Costume, apparel/equipment required:

Small flags or pieces of plastic hose. Rope and markers, and a tape recorder and music tapes.

Area/arena/field where played—space required:

Open area.

Time length of game. How is end of game determined?:

Race time, typically 90 seconds.

Symbolism of game:

Team goal orientation.

Rules of play, including scoring:

This event may be started by a whistle blast. There are two methods of conducting this event.

Walking Away: All players breast a tape of rope (players stand with chests against a rope held by two nonparticipants). If a player does not maintain position of breasting the rope, looks back toward the flags, hangs back, or retards the forward movement of the judges with the rope before the starting signal (or while the music is still playing), he or she shall be disqualified.

On the go signal, players run to capture as many flags as they can. Flags are scattered in the race area. Typically, each race is over within 90 seconds, depending on the size of the play field, the number of flags, and the number of players. All subsequent variations have the same objectives but different conditions.

On the Sand: The competitors are on their backs with their heels, shoulders, and heads on the sand and their heels on the starting line. Should any competitor lift his or her head, heel, or body while the music is still playing, he or she will be disqualified.

- Jostling or obstructing another competitor so as to impede his progress shall result in disqualification.
- Any competitor picking up two flags will be disqualified. Should two competitors be holding a flag, the judges will decide the winner.

Scoring: In the event of five or fewer competitors being left in a heat or final, and they all break, then all of them will be recalled and the heat or final must be recontested. Judges should arrange the flags so that first, second, and third places can be obtained.

Variations: Sack Musical Flags: Players start on their backs in sacks, and continue to wear the sacks to race and reach the flags. This event was actually contested at carnivals.

PART II

The Americas

Argentina

CONTINENT BALL

Eileen Crowley Sullivan
Appropriate for replication.

Players:

Pre-teens and teens.

Object of game for players:

To bump two or three balls up and down on a blanket and pass the ball without touching the ground. Working cooperatively in a group is stressed and this game can be used to reinforce curriculum through games.

Number of players:

Scattered groups of three or four.

Costume, apparel/equipment required:

Blankets, sheets, cloth, or several parachutes, and beach balls.

Area/arena/field where played—space required:

Gymnasium, play area, or field.

Time length of game. How is end of game determined?:

As directed by the teacher.

Symbolism of game:

Represents the hazards and determination involved in early world exploration and travel.

Rules of play, including scoring:

Several students hold onto a small blanket or sheet. Each sheet could be decorated to represent a continent. The players holding each continent blanket try to work together and bump two or three beach balls up and down off the blanket. How many times can North America bump their balls? Can South America skip around in a circle as they bump their balls? Can they bump them to each other?

Brazil

BIRIBOL

Vera Regina Toledo Camargo
Appropriate for replication.

Players:

All ages. This game was started in Birigui, in the state of Saõ Paulo.

Object of game for players:

To be the team that wins the best of three sets of fifteen.

Number of players:

Two teams, with four players each.

Costume, apparel/equipment required:

Bathing suits.

Area/arena/field where played—space required:

A 4 x 8 meter area in a swimming pool at least 1.3 meters deep. A net is set across the middle of the playing area at 2.62 meters in height.

Time length of game. How is end of game determined?:

Best of three sets wins the game.

Symbolism of game:

Teamwork with agility and self discipline

Rules of play, including scoring:

This game is similar to volleyball, but played in a pool. Rules are like those for volleyball, with only three touches for each team each time the ball crosses the net. The advantage rule applies: A team can only win a set when it is up by two points after fifteen is reached. Tie breakers are played. One variation is that the players can use a wide ball and scoop it back into play (once).

FUTEBAL DE ARERIA (BEACH SOCCER)

Vera Regina Toledo Camargo
Appropriate for replication.

Players:

All ages, males and females playing separately.

Object of game for players:

This game is similar to soccer. The team that scores the most goals in the time allowed wins.

Number of players:

Twelve; two teams with six players on each team (five field players and one goalie).

Costume, apparel/equipment required:

Often played among men as skins and shirts, though among women, in more populous areas, uniforms are worn. No shoes. Two goal posts with nets and a ball are needed.

Area/arena/field where played—space required:

A flat sandy area approximately 20 x 25 yards—about the same size as for indoor soccer.

Time length of game. How is end of game determined?:

Two thirty-minute halves.

Symbolism of game:

Teamwork with head, body, and leg dexterity.

Rules of play, including scoring:

Soccer rules apply. Goals are scored from the body (not hands) of the attacking team. (Goals can also be made off the defending team, even their feet).

MARATHON BACKWARDS
Vera Regina Toledo Camargo
Appropriate for replication.

Players:

Older teens and adults race in the city of San Vincente Ferre in Pernambuco state.

Object of game for players:

To get to the finish line first, and for some to finish the event.

Number of players:

Unlimited.

Costume, apparel/equipment required:

Comfortable clothes and sneakers or running shoes.

Area/arena/field where played—space required:

Determined locally—some establish 21 kilometers as a maximum distance.

Time length of game. How is end of game determined?:

Until the finish line is reached.

Symbolism of game:

Courage, endurance, and total body awareness.

Rules of play, including scoring:

Players must run backwards until they reach the finish line. Anyone looking backwards is disqualified.

PUNHOBOL OR FAUSTEBOL

Vera Regina Toledo Camargo
Appropriate for replication.

Players:

Boys and girls of all ages. This game is commonly played in southern Brazil.

Object of game for players:

Each team wants to score the highest number of points in thirty minutes.

Number of players:

Two teams, each with five players.

Costume, apparel/equipment required:

Soccer shoes and comfortable clothing. A net (two posts with a nylon cable two meters high), and a ball weighing 320 to 380 grams, with a circumference of 62 to 68 centimeters. Either a soccer ball or volleyball can be used.

Area/arena/field where played—space required:

A grass court 50 x 20 meters. A variation can be played in sand with the distances halved.

Time length of game. How is end of game determined?:

Thirty minutes.

Symbolism of game:

Teamwork with agility, manual manipulation, and self discipline.

Rules of play, including scoring:

Like volleyball, each player can only touch the ball once, but the ball can touch the ground one time during rallies on either side of the net. The game is a mixture of soccer and volleyball, and players can kick or punch the ball. The forearm must be used when defending (not the hands). A point is scored each time the ball goes into the net, falls outside the court, is not defended, or takes more than three attempts to get back over the net.

TAMBOREU
Vera Regina Toledo Camargo
Appropriate for replication.

Players:

All ages.

Object of game for players:

The team that wins the best of three sets is the winner.

Number of players:

Two teams of two.

Costume, apparel/equipment required:

Comfortable outfits, one ball, a net one meter high, and posts.

Area/arena/field where played—space required:

A court, usually 10 x 6 meters. The net is midfield.

Time length of game. How is end of game determined?:

The game ends after the best of three sets. Each set is divided into three games of ten points each.

Symbolism of game:

Teamwork with agility and manual dexterity.

Rules of play, including scoring:

The ball is thrown into play by the member of the team that wins the toss. The ball is caught and thrown to the other side, over the net. When the ball is not caught, or is batted up (with hands), and/or hits the ground or the net, the point is lost. There are ten points each game, and the best of three sets wins (three games each set).

Canada

INDIAN KICKBALL
Tom Sharpe
Appropriate for replication.

Players:

Pre-teens and teens. Played by the Hopi Indians.

Object of game for players:

Kicking and chasing a kickball over a prescribed course, perhaps a mile long, with plenty of twists, turns, and obstacles.

Number of players:

Two teams of equal number (three to six players).

Costume, apparel/equipment required:

Brightly colored team shirts, shorts, bandanas, and sneakers. Colored kickball, four to six inches in diameter, for each team.

Area/arena/field where played—space required:

Outdoor area such as a football or soccer field. Marked lanes several yards apart for each team. Clearly marked starting and finishing lines.

Time length of game. How is end of game determined?:

Start: At a predetermined signal, one player on each team gives the ball a lifting toss with his off (or kicking) foot and kicks it toward the racecourse. Other team members chase after their own team's ball and advance it the same way. The team stays together during the race and acts as a cooperative group.

Finish: The team that kicks their ball over the finish line first wins.

Symbolism of game:

A spiritual ceremony of the Hopi Indians of the Southwestern United States. Each of the teams represents a sacred shrine (Kiva). The name of the Tarahumara Indians of Mexico is derived from an Indian word meaning foot runners, and kicking is an important part of their culture. Race day is festive, with lots of food, beverages, and games.

Rules of play, including scoring:

Ball must be lifted (tossed) with the non-kicking foot to the kicking foot before kicking to advance the ball. Each team member must kick the ball during each cycle of kicks; no one player should kick the ball twice in succession. The team whose ball is kicked over the finish line first are the winners.

LABRATHON
Greg Wood
Not appropriate for replication.

Players:

A highly regarded event, often featuring skilled hunters and trappers. A popular spectator sport, usually won by "old timers." Always played by men.

Object of game for players:

An endurance and outdoor survival triathlon covering a distance of approximately 2,400 meters. The course is completed by snowshoeing the total distance and completing three survival activities (tilts) that are culturally significant in Northern Canada.

Number of players:

Individuals or three teams competing in regional Olympic-style games. Heats usually are limited to four individuals, or teams, at a time.

Costume, apparel/equipment required:

Outdoor wear, normally a parka or anorak, leggings, seal skin boots, and mitts or cuffs. Snowshoes, tea kettle, matches, and an ax are used. Only authorized equipment is permitted.

Area/arena/field where played—space required:

In a snow covered area, preferably on a sheltered trail near a pond or lake. Spectators need to be able to observe competitors at critical stages of the event (tilts).

Time length of game. How is end of game determined?:

Variable.

Symbolism of game:

Represents the day-to-day survival skills needed to live in Northern Canada. Speed, endurance, and strong traditional outdoor skills are required.

Rules of play, including scoring:

Each player or team starts at the starting line. At the sound of a whistle, all commence snowshoeing to tilt #1. Each player or team one after another starts having their starting times recorded. At tilt #1 the competitors chop wood (must be provided) into splits with an ax (provided as well). Competitors must carry the split wood to tilt #2 (as a variation, some wood may be green, and the competitor must be able to tell apart the green wood from the dry wood). Tilt #2 is located on a pond or lake. Here competitors chop a hole in the ice using an ax. Once the competitors reach water they fill their kettles and proceed to tilt #3 (as a team event, teammates take turns chopping the hole). At tilt #3, the competitors use the wood chopped at the previous station to light a fire and boil the water in the kettle. Once the kettle is judged boiled, the competitor immediately proceeds to the finish line where his final time is recorded. The winner is the individual or team completing the course requirements in the shortest time.

MONKEY DANCE
Greg Wood
Appropriate for replication.

Players:

Male and Female adults of the Inuit tribe.

Object of game for player:

A novelty game using monkey-like movements, where players try to outlast each other.

Number of players:

Unlimited.

Costume, apparel/equipment required:

None.

Area/arena/field where played—space required:

An open area.

Time length of game. How is end of game determined?:

Continues until only one player remains.

Symbolism of game:

Persistence.

Rules of play, including scoring:

The players assume the starting position by squatting down with their arms out to their sides. On the command ("Go"), the players must stay in the squat position and alternate outstretched legs in rapid progression. The player who continues the movement correctly the longest wins. The player cannot stop the movement and continue again. The legs must extend either to the side or in front of the player and extension of the leg is mandatory on each hop.

PULIITUT ILKIKATTAUT (SEAL RACE)

Greg Wood
Appropriate for replication.

Players:

Pre-teens and teens of the Inuit Tribe.

Object of game for players:

Using seal-like movements, competitors race against each other to the finish line.

Number of players:

Unlimited individual players in mass start.

Costume, apparel/equipment required:

Players may wear gloves.

Area/arena/field where played—space required:

Open space, with a usual set racing distance of 100 feet.

Time length of game. How is end of game determined?:

The first player to cross the finish line wins the game.

Symbolism of game:

A novelty game that mimics the movements of a traditional animal (seal) while testing upper body strength.

Rules of play, including scoring:

The player lies belly down on the floor behind the starting line with his or her hands palm down and under the shoulders. The legs are straight and crossed at the ankles. The player then straightens his or her arms so that the upper body is raised off the floor. Knees may touch the floor, but at no time may the toes lose contact with the floor. On the command "Go" the players pull themselves along a set distance using only their hands. The winner is the first player with both hands completely across the finish line.

Chile

CHOIKEPURUN (COMPETITIVE TRIBAL DANCE)

Carlos Lopez von Vriessen
Not appropriate for replication.

Players:

Males and females of all ages from the Mapuche Indians.

Object of game for players:

Each team has to show its nimbleness in the dance that imitates the movements of the *nandu* (*Rhea americana*) or ostrich of South America.

Number of players:

Different families from the same community form teams, each family having six to eight dancers.

Costume, apparel/equipment required:

The *chiripa* wraps around the waist and is covered with a colored woolen *manta*; a knot imitates the bird's tail. The dancers are barefoot, have colored feathers on their heads, and their bodies are painted. On their chests hang bronze chains of bells.

Area/arena/field where played—space required:

The field is about 70 x 50 meters on a hard dusty earth field.

Time length of game. How is end of game determined?:

The dance lasts almost the whole day, each team dancing nearly half an hour, with five or six teams alternating. Sometimes teams dance their series twice a day and repeat them during the two days of their religious feast.

Symbolism of game:

The dance which imitates the *nandu*, or South American ostrich, takes place during the two-day religious feast called *nguillatun*, a prehispanic ceremony still held among the Mapuche Indians of Chile. The nandu, a fast runner, is very useful because it eats poisoned grass that is dangerous to cattle and also eats insects. The meat and eggs of the nandu are edible. Its feathers are beautiful and to the Mapuche symbolize liberty.

The dance takes place in the middle of the nguillatun field, around the *pehuen*, or holy tree. At the beginning and end of the presentations of the groups of dancers a troupe of horse riders (about 40 men and women with their *lonko*, or leader, ahead who holds a large cane called a *colihue* with white and blue pennons in his hand) follows the sound of the wind instruments and the magic drum, called a *kultrung*. With loud screams they make several revolutions in an ellipsoidal area of about 100 meters, galloping in two rows counterclockwise making a big dust. With their *awun*, or horse gallop, they want to scare away the bad spirits that try to interfere with the ceremony. The object of the dance is the demonstration of artistic experience, and of the ability to withstand heat, fatigue, tediousness, foot pain, and dust. The referees determine the end of the feast and announce the winners, who enjoy a banquet of goat and horsemeat. There are no prizes for the winner but simply honor for the family group. There are also no alcoholic drinks during the two-day feast, but traditional drinks, such as the *muday* of maize and the fruit of the pehuen tree. Those who are foreigners or not Pehuenche Indians must have a special invitation to attend and may not take photographs.

Rules of play, including scoring:

Features and Rules: Each family team participates with six to eight dancers. The families of the dancers participate during the two days of the feast and maintain fires for 48 hours in front of their *ramadas*, or branch huts, even though the day might be very hot. The family members have to imitate bird movements—walking, springing, tracing their feet on the earth, and running—while at the same time wearing a woolen manta on the shoulders as if they had wings. They must follow the rhythm of the magic drum of the *machi*. During the dances family members make sounds with the little bronze bells on their breast. All assistants to the ceremony are painted with a dark blue line on their cheeks twice a day. The dancers must dance without rest and without drinking water. Foreigners are not allowed to come near the dancers.

The Game: The dance imitates the ostrich. In other regions it imitates the *guanaco*, the puma, or other animals. The dance includes little jumps and dancers walk moving their feet just like birds, their heads moving left to right. The mantas tied to their waists are untied and put on their shoulders, and they make dancing movements just like the wings of an ostrich.

PALIN (TRIBAL BALL GAMES)

Carlos Lopez von Vriessen
Not appropriate for replication.

Players:

Males.

Object of game for players:

To make a goal by beating a ball with a wooden stick.

Number of players:

Seven to 15 players on each team.

Costume, apparel/equipment required:

Players wear woolen head bands (each team with a different color) and are barefooted with their trousers tucked up. Fifteen curved sticks (*weng*), wooden ball (*pali*), two goals (*raya*), and prizes (typically mutton or wine).

Area/arena/field where played—space required:

The field is approximately 200 meters long and 12 meters wide on grooved grass or earth.

Time length of game. How is end of game determined?:

The match consists of two sets, 20 to 30 minutes in length. The team with the most points wins.

Symbolism of game:

It is possible that palin has its origins in funerals and religious ceremonies, however, with the Spanish invasion, it changed to a warrior game, then to a competitive game, and finally to a social recreative game, which has contributed to the unity of the Mapuche people.

In some regions the game is still closely related to religious and magical ceremonies and communal festivities. Players, field, ball, and sticks are submitted to magic proceedings by shamans called *Machis* and leaders called *Lonkos*. Sometimes the night before the match the whole community performs a religious rite called *Nguillatun*, with leaders and shaman women. The shaman of each reservation and many fans stand behind the goal line. Throughout the game they help their team with music, dances, songs, and the sound of the magic drum. The game is rough, but there is always a joyous atmosphere and a spirit of good fun. This local game from Chile was originally played by Mapuche men, women, and children. Since the eighteenth century it has been the national game. Once the size of the field and the number of players was bigger than it is now. Previously, a team had to win four points to zero, and some games lasted several days. The players did not have sexual relations, nor did they eat salt or meat during the eight days before the match. Players slept in the open air in the field and had a daily bath with cold water. They injected themselves with a powder of rocks and bones of the puma or mountain lion. In order to have good luck players brought along the skull of a famous dead player to the match, which they hid between the branches of the *canelo* tree. In former times, big bets were made as well. In the nineteenth century there were professional players who won a lot of money.

Between the seventeenth and nineteenth centuries both the Chilean church and state prohibited the game and punished organizers and players severely. But players continued playing in secret. Traditionally, facial painting, feathers, and masks were used. The ideal of the Mapuche youth was to become bold warriors and qualified palin players. Nowadays, the Mapuche organizations and the government are interested in saving the game. There are palin *chueca* (matches) in the country, in villages, in towns, in the south of Chile, and even in Santiago.

Rules of play, including scoring:

Features and Rules: Each reservation has its own team and one reservation invites another to come compete in the Palingames. A tribal match between two reservations is called *Fuchapalin*. In playing the game, each player takes the curved stick, called a *weno*, in both hands in order to strike a wooden ball, called a *pali*. The players, normally ages 15 to 65, play barefooted. At the beginning of the match the two teams face each other, standing in two rows along the pitch (the active area). The teams then shake hands and promise each other a fair game. The play begins with the ball placed in the middle of the field. Each team tries to play the ball to its left down to the end of the field, or the goal, called *raya*. The team that wins invites the losers to a revenge play the next year. Today there are games held among several teams, which is due to foreign influence, called *winkapalin*.

The Game: A coin is tossed in order to decide in which direction each team has to play. After a cattle horn signal from the referee the play begins; each team leader stands in front of the ball, which is placed in a hole in the middle of the field. A point is scored when the ball passes the narrow side of the field or goal line (12 meters wide). When the ball passes the lateral line (200 meters long) the play begins again in the middle of the field. The game is played roughly and seriously, but always with good feeling and a sense of fair play. There is no run-off game, but ties are resolved with free strikes. The winners receive small prizes, such as mutton, wine, and so on. Normally the games are held in summer (January to March) during the harvest. There is no betting allowed. When the match is finished the guests are welcomed officially by their hosts, and a banquet begins. After dinner, dancers perform and the leaders make speeches.

TAPATI RAPA-NUI OR RAPA-NUI WEEK

Carlos Lopez von Vriessen
Not appropriate for replication.

Players:

Male and female adults of Easter Island.

Object of game for players:

To pass on through games the knowledge of former methods of survival; to pass on the knowledge of folklore of the past and present.

Number of players:

The entire tribe.

Costume, apparel/equipment required:

It depends on the different activities. During the games the participants are dressed with a cover, or *taparrabo*, and have painted bodies.

Area/arena/field where played—space required:

Almost the whole of Easter Island, including the surrounding sea.

Time length of game. How is end of game determined?:

The game is played from the end of January until the beginning of February (and has been every year since 1968).

Symbolism of game:

Originally, life on the island was idyllic in one half and very hard in the other, because of lack of food. The hunt, navigation, fishing, and the war were existential activities. Fighting for survival was dramatic and cruel. In the eighteenth century almost the entire population of the island was taken prisoner to Peru, where most of them died. Years later, the Chilean government rescued the remaining Easter Islanders and brought them back to their island, but by then their culture had disappeared almost entirely. During the Rapa-Nui week there are numerous events that recall this era. The program includes activities of sport, recreation, culture, society, arts, and production. The culmination of the festivities is the election of a king and queen for one year, true representatives of Rapa-Nui beauty. For Easter Islanders it is important to maintain their ancestors' roots, and to resist a repeat of the banishment of the people of the island, an ethnic group, and any renewed submission to a dominant culture.

Rules of play, including scoring:

Features and Rules: The week of Rapa-Nui is divided into periods of several activities:
A. Social activities related to local games, sport, and foreign games.
B. Social cultural activities of an artistic character.
C. Social productive activities introducing fun and happiness.
D. Social festive activities.

The participants in the different activities proceed according to set rules when they prepare and perform. A committee is in charge of each activity. Participants are generally artisans, the typical profession of the people of Easter Island, and are very much esteemed by tourists. The winners' prizes are the social acknowledgment and a portion of the proceeds of the events, which are shared by the community and municipality, which organizes the activities.

The Game:

A. The Social activities characterized by game and sport are:
1. *Te-Kau*: swimming as a group.
2. *Pora*: swimming with floats of reed or *totora*.
3. *Haka-Ngaru*: sliding on the waves with a board.
4. *Haka-Honu*: sliding by imitating the turtle.
5. *A'ati Vaka Ama*: race with boats of reed, or *piragua*.
6. *Haka-Pei*: sliding on a banana trunk, like a sledge, from Pu'i hill.
7. *Tau-Tanga*: free-throwing with a spear.
8. *Tute-Moa*: race following a wild chicken.
9. *Akavenga*: using feet.
10. *Hi-Kua*: fishing while swimming.
11. *Hi-Rua*: fishing with a rod from the shore.
12. *Haka-Ranga*: fishing from shore using a stick with a hook on the distal end.
13. *Puhi*: fishing for lobster, eel, and *morena* (type of eel) at night from the shore with a hook and torch.
14. *Tu'Utong*: eel fishing with string and hook from a high place on the shore.
15. *Here-Ruku*: eel-fishing, plunging into the water.
16. *Hehere*: fishing with meat bait between the rocks.
17. *Hi-Kau Kupenga*: fishing with a net.
18. *Mata e Horu*: fishing with a spear.
19. *A'Ati Vaka*: race of wooden boats.
20. *Pere Popo Hai Tuamini*: football with a sheep or cow bladder.
21. *A'Ati Hoi*: horse race.

B. The artistic cultural activities are:
1. Exposition of art and handicraft of the people of the island.
2. Ornamental, wood-carved work.
3. Sculpture and painting.
4. Weaving of carpets.
5. Stiffening of shirts.
6. Carving of *Moai* figures.
7. Linking of chains.
8. Exhibition of old boats.
9. *Kai-Kai* exhibition and recitation with string figures.

     10. *Takona*: competition of body painting.
     11. Representations of ancient and modern folklore.

C. Social productive activities are:
     1. *Ruku*: submarine hunting.
     2. *Hi Vaka*: fishing on the high seas.
     3. *Here Koreha*: traditional eel fishing.
     4. *Haki Takatore*: extraction of mollusks.
     5. *Runi Pipi*: extraction of shells.
     6. Exposition of agricultural products.
     7. Culinary and gastronomic activities.

D. Social/festive activities are:
     1. Election of the king and queen of the island.
     2. Feast and costume parade.

Mexico

BULL FIGHTING COMPETITION

Greg Narleski
Not appropriate for replication.

Players:

Adolescents and adults from all parts of Mexico. Typically boys play, but girls can play, too.

Object of game for players:

To determine which owner or village maintains the strongest bull. Ceremonial and as entertainment for the community on special occasions such as the end of the harvest season.

Number of players:

Unlimited, but each player must own a bull.

Costume, apparel/equipment required:

Occasionally the owner of a bull and the representative of the village dress in traditional regalia.

Area/arena/field where played—space required:

A closed-in area, usually by a fence or brush, allowing spectators to gather safely.

Time length of game. How is end of game determined?:

Sometimes contests can last all day before a winner is determined.

Symbolism of game:

Bull fighting is a social occasion usually marking the end of the harvest. It functions in community building and entertainment. For the victorious bull owner, the competition brings strength, stature, and wealth.

Rules of play, including scoring:

Special fighting bulls are selected from among the players with mock horns. The bulls fight to the sounds of a drumbeat. The spectators are usually male tribal members. Wagering is permitted. The bull fights until defeated through fatigue. The last bull standing wins recognition for the owner and the village.

COCONUTS
Kevin McAllister
Appropriate for replication.

Players:

Young teens.

Object of game for players:

To manipulate a ball by carrying it while working under pressure.

Number of players:

Classroom group.

Costume, apparel/equipment required:

Hoop, spider ball, cone, beanbag. (A spider ball is a small soft ball with long hairs attached.)

Area/arena/field where played—space required:

Gymnasium, play area, or field.

Time length of game. How is end of game determined?:

As directed by the teacher.

Symbolism of game:

This game represents food gathering experience and fitness.

Rules of play, including scoring:

Each player has a hoop, representing a coconut tree, and two "coconuts," which could be any of various objects that will not roll, such as a spider ball, cone, beanbag, or others. Hoops are spread out around the playing area with the two coconuts in the center of each. On a signal, players try to gather as many coconuts as possible and bring them back to their hoop before time expires. Only *one* coconut can be taken at a time and players cannot guard their hoops nor can they "steal" coconuts from the same hoop twice. Vary the game by having players travel between hoops performing various motor skills. You could call the game "Scavenger Hunt," where the object is to collect just one of each item to store in your own coconut tree (hoop).

Native American

BOWL GAME

Betty Sue Benison
Appropriate for replication.

Players:

All ages from the Crow tribe.

Object of game for players:

To get as many fruit pits into the bowl as possible.

Number of players:

Two teams of equal numbers.

Costume, apparel/equipment required:

Headbands and shorts or jeans for males and colorful skirts and blouses for females. The equipment needed is one small salad bowl of turned wood or a small woven breadbasket. A small wooden or cardboard box may be used. You will also need six peach or plum pits, a small bottle of India ink, a pen point and holder, and marbles, arrowheads, gumdrops, or similar items for rewards.

Area/arena/field where played—space required:

Any designated area.

Time length of game. How is end of game determined?:

No limit.

Symbolism of game:

This game was played by the Crow Indians, as well as the Plains and Woodland Indians and Indians of the Southwest. Originally, a group of Crow Indians played the bowl game in the teepee around a small fire made of buffalo chips. One player held a small wooden bowl in his hand (Indians of the Southwest more often used a fine, woven blanket). As the others looked on, he tossed into the air a number of peach pits that were in the bowl. He then skillfully caught them in the bowl again. The men were divided into two teams and both teams watched closely to see how the stones landed and how the play was scored. Both sides wanted to win, for each man on the winning side would be given a pony by the losers. Today the game is played with the following changes.

Rules of play, including scoring:

Wash the pits or stones and let them dry thoroughly. With the pen and ink draw a broad line across one side of each stone. Any even number of people can play this game, even as few as two. It is more exciting if there are three or four players, or even more, on each team. Drop the six pits into the bowl or basket. Hold the bowl in one hand and with a slight toss flip the pits up into the air and catch them again in the bowl. Score by counting the number of pits that land with the marked side up. Each one that lands with the marked side up counts one point. After scoring your turn, pass the bowl over to your opponent. Your opponent makes a toss, counts his or her score, and passes the bowl back to you. Each player keeps his or her own score with toothpicks or a score pad (a scorekeeper may be used). The winner is the one who has the most toothpicks (or the most marks on the score pad) after twenty tosses. If as many as six are playing the game, divide up into two teams, facing each other, with three players on each team. The first player on your team makes the first toss and counts his or her score. The player then passes the bowl to the opponent directly opposite. The opponent tosses, counts his or her score, and then the bowl goes to the second player on your team. Usually each player keeps his or her own score, but an official scorekeeper may be appointed. At the end of ten tosses by each player, the final team scores are tallied and the team with the largest score wins. The game can be played for marbles, arrowheads, or gumdrops. The losing team hands over one marble, for example, for each point won by the other team. The winnings are then divided among the players whose team has won.

GUESSING GAME
Betty Sue Benison
Appropriate for replication.

Players:

All ages from the Plains Indians.

Object of game for players:

To guess in which of two bundles the odd stick is hidden.

Number of players:

Two teams with four to eight on each side.

Costume, apparel/equipment required:

Headbands of colorful material (usually red) and jeans for males. Females wear white blouses and jeans. Eight sticks, each 12 inches long and one-quarter inch in diameter. One sack is marked as the odd stick. You will also need India ink, a brush, and a blanket or robe.

Area/arena/field where played—space required:

Any designated area.

Time length of game. How is end of game determined?:

No limit.

Symbolism of game:

This was a great time-passer among the Plain Indians. It can be a good rainy day activity, easy to make and fun to play, and the necessary materials cost very little.

Rules of play, including scoring:

Teams of four to eight on each side are seated on the ground so that they face each other, and a folded robe or blanket is placed between them. One team holds the sticks. Hiding them under the blanket, two teammates divide the eight sticks into bundles of four each. The two players then grasp the bundles in such a manner that the painted ends are covered by their hands. They then hold out the bundles of sticks toward their opponents. As all eight of the sticks have a center marking, it is no easy task to guess in which of the two bundles the odd stick is hidden. The odd stick is the same as the other seven sticks but has one small distinguishing mark not readily observable (e.g., a small India ink spot may be used). If the rival team misses its guess, the first team gets one point. The player shuffles the sticks again under the blanket and the next two players grasp the bundles and hold them forward. If, on the other hand, the opponents guess right, then it is their turn to hold the sticks and the first team must guess. The members of each team take turns guessing. Each team can keep its own score or a scorekeeper may be appointed. The scorekeeper sits between the teams at one end of the folded blanket. Colored toothpicks may be used for keeping score. One team is indicated by red and the other by blue toothpicks, for example. The scorekeeper holds 20 of each color. When a member of a team guesses correctly, the scorekeeper places a toothpick belonging to that team in front of him- or herself. The team whose 20 toothpicks are first used up is the winning team.

TRICK THE DANCERS
Christine M. Conboy
Appropriate for replication.

Players:

Children, pre-teens, and teens.

Object of game for players:

To move to the beat of the drum, and to stop immediately, as the drumming often stops at an awkward moment. To learn of the American Indian culture through games.

Number of players:

Classroom group.

Costume, apparel/equipment required:

Drum and drumsticks, or substitutes for these.

Area/arena/field where played—space required:

Indoors or outdoors.

Time length of game. How is end of game determined?:

When one player is left.

Symbolism of game:

Represents the games played by the native children from many of the tribes on the Northwest coast of the United States.

Rules of play, including scoring:

The drummer stands in the middle of the circle beating his or her drum while the dancers move around the circle in time to the beat. When the drum stops the dancers must freeze even if in an awkward position. One may have a foot high in the air; another may be crouched down ready to jump. The dancers still in motion when the music stops must leave the circle and become watchers. The longer the music continues the faster the drummer plays. The drumming can vary from fast to slow but the dancers must keep time to the beat.

ZUNI KICK STICK

Betty Sue Benison
Appropriate for replication.

Players:

Children through teens play this game, males and females separately. It comes from the Zuni Indians.

Object of game for players:

To kick a stick around the circle and back without kicking it out or hitting a spectator.

Number of players:

Two teams of equal number.

Costume, apparel/equipment required:

The only necessary equipment are some branches, each about 12 inches long and one inch thick of approximately equal weight.

Area/arena/field where played—space required:

Any designated circle.

Time length of game. How is end of game determined?:

No limit.

Symbolism of game:

Long ago, a festive day would be held in the Zuni village when the prayers and dances of the people had been answered. Rain had come at last the day before to water the crops and settle the dry, swirling dust on the plaza. In the center of the plaza a stout stick was set into the ground. A Zuni tied a long braided rawhide lariat to the stick. He stretched out the lariat as far as it would go, about 30 feet, and tied another stick to the free end. Then, making sure to keep the lariat taut, he walked backwards, with the end of the stick scratching a deep circular groove in the hard-packed earth. Another Zuni followed him and made the circle visible to everyone by sprinkling white corn meal in the groove. When the circle was finished, two officials stepped into its center. Each held up a stick about 12 inches long. Each stick was carved and decorated with a different pattern. Together the officials called for contestants. The people teased and joked and called out the names of friends and relatives. Then a roar of laughter went up and two old men, each almost ninety years old, stepped into the circle. The two officials greeted them ceremoniously and with much head shaking told them that they were too young. As the two old men walked away, two young Zuni men stepped into the ring. A hush came over the crowd. One official walked to the edge of the circle and drew a line on the ground with his foot. The contestants took their places on the line and in front of each one the officials placed one of the carved sticks. One official gave a quick spoken signal and the young men began kicking their sticks ahead, making sure not to kick them outside of the circle. The spectators shouted encouragement as the players rounded the circle and came back toward the starting line. Then one swift kick sent a stick over the line and the player dashed after it. He was the winner. Kick is still played among the Zuni Indians and it is a very useful game to know.

Rules of play, including scoring:

Instruct all of the players to sit in a circle (the council ring). One of the players is appointed to be chief. Now draw a starting line within the council ring in front of the chief's seat. Two players are selected to kick their stick around the circle and back. If on their way around a player kicks his stick out of the circle, or if it touches a spectator, the player is disqualified. The other player must continue, however, for if he or she should also kick out of the circle, then there is no winner and the players must start over—or at this point two new players may be chosen. The group may be divided into two groups and as one set of two players finishes, a new representative from each group takes a turn. Some tribes make permanent sticks out of two birch dowel rods the same size as the branches. To tell the dowels apart, paint one red and one green or else paint each with a different colored band.

United States

"A" MY NAME IS ALICE

Eileen Crowley Sullivan
Appropriate for replication.

Players:

Teens to college level.

Object of game for players:

To use the beginning letter of your own name in a chanting game where the important nouns all get replaced with words starting with your initial. Listening, waiting your turn, fun.

Number of players:

Small groups.

Costume, apparel/equipment required:

None.

Area/arena/field where played—space required:

Classroom or playground.

Time length of game. How is end of game determined?:

When everyone has had a turn.

Symbolism of game:

Represents identity and belonging to a group within a culture.

Rules of play, including scoring:

In a circle or small group one person says his or her name and then uses the first letter of the name to create a husband's or wife's name with the same beginning letter. Next a place and an object with the same beginning letter are added. For example, "B my name is Brendan, I come from Brookline, my wife's name is Brenda, and we sell baked beans." Continue around the circle until everyone has had a turn. Can anyone remember all the names and facts? Try having the groups call out names and facts as you tap each individual on the head. Do not progress in order around the circle, but mix up the order.

AEROBIC STRIKE

Eileen Crowley Sullivan
Appropriate for replication.

Players:

Late elementary and young pre-teens, males and females.

Object of game for players:

To score a run, which occurs when each member of the hitting team runs around a cone before the fielders run and place the ball at the starting cone.

Number of players:

Two equal teams of any number.

Costume, apparel/equipment required:

Any size ball (playground ball works well), three cones.

Area/arena/field where played—space required:

Gymnasium or large playing area.

Time length of game. How is end of game determined?:

After each team has had a turn to hit, or after several "innings" have been played. Two innings allow each team to be up to hit and in the field twice.

Symbolism of game:

Represents survival of a culture through teamwork, cooperation amongst teams or groups, as well as fitness and courage.

Rules of play, including scoring:

The game is quite active and aerobic for both teams as everyone must run on each play.

There are two versions of the game.

VERSION I: The group is divided into two teams, with one team designated as the *hitters*, and the second, the *fielders*. The hitters line up behind a starting line, or an endline, in a horizontal pattern. The first person in the line is the first hitter, and kicks the stationary ball beside the starting cone into the outfield as far as possible. After kicking the ball, the player runs around the designated cone straight ahead of the hitters and returns to the starting cone/line. The second person in the hitting line then runs around the cone. This pattern repeats until the hitters have run around the outfield cone one at a time. As the hitting team is running, the fielders catch the ball. It is not an "out" if the ball is caught on the fly. Rather, when the ball is caught, the fielders form a line behind the person who caught the ball. Next, the members of the fielding team run one at a time to their respective cone. A run is scored when each hitter has a turn to run before the fielders place the ball beside the hitters' starting cone. Teams switch positions after each hitter has had a turn to kick the ball. The hitting team is the only team that can score a run. If the fielders place the ball at the starting cone, they do not score a run.

Diagram of Version I:

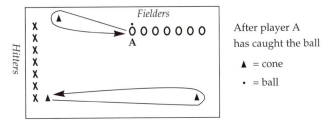

VERSION II: The first player of the hitting team kicks the ball and runs around the designated cone and back to the starting cone. The *entire* hitting team then runs around the cone and back to the start. One of the fielders catches the ball, and the team lines up behind the player who caught it. Instead of running, as in Version I, the fielders pass the ball over their heads and under their legs in this over–under pattern until the last person in line receives the ball. The last person to have possession of the ball then runs the ball to the hitters' starting cone. The last person to have possession of the ball then runs the ball to the hitters' starting cone. A run is scored each time the hitters succeed in reaching their starting cone before the hitter runs to the cone with the ball.

Diagram of Version II:

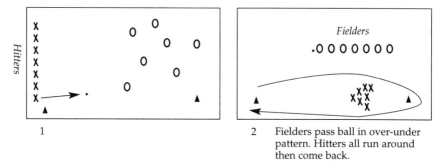

1

2   Fielders pass ball in over-under pattern. Hitters all run around then come back.

Modifications: Instead of kicking the ball, hitters can throw or roll it into the outfield. Hitters can also strike a ball with a bat. Different size balls can be used, and the size of the playing area can be changed to suit the players' aerobic capacities.

ANGLE BALL

Mike Davey
Appropriate for replication.

Players:

Pre-teens and young teens. Commonly played in rural, central Kansas.

Object of game for players:

To score points by dislodging their own "goal ball" with the ball in play while preventing the opposing team from doing the same.

Number of players:

Twenty-four, divided into two teams, A and B.

Costume, apparel/equipment required:

An outseamed ball (slightly heavier than a soccer ball).

Area/arena/field where played—space required:

Playing field 240 x 160 feet, free from obstructions except for the goals set equal distance from the sideline and 60 feet from the endlines. The game is played between the 10-yard lines of a football field with the goals on the 30-yard lines.

Time length of game. How is end of game determined?:

Two halves, 15 minutes each, ten minutes between halves. Each team is permitted four time-outs of two minutes duration each half.

Symbolism of game:

Represents a unique combination of the traditional games of football, basketball, volleyball, and soccer. Angle Ball was conceived and is played exclusively in rural, central Kansas. It has been introduced in Oregon.

Rules of play, including scoring:

The object of each team is to dislodge their own "goal ball" with the ball in play (one point is awarded for each score), and to prevent the opposing team from doing likewise. There is no score if Team A's (offense) goal is interfered with by Team A, or if the Angle Ball should hit the goal below the goal ball and cause it to be dislodged. A score results if Team B (defense) interferes with Team A's goal while A is attempting to score.

RULE I. Method of Penalizing Fouls

1. Fouls shall be penalized by giving the player at fault a prescribed number of laps to make around the playing area, and by giving possession of the ball to the opposing team at the point of the foul.
   Note: By mutual agreement, a penalty box may be substituted for laps. One lap = three minutes.

2 When the ball is awarded to the opposing team at an indicated point, all players must remain at least six feet away from the player putting the ball in play. Said player is permitted three seconds to put ball in

play and must not take more than one step in doing so. Goals made from here are not permissible.

3. In executing the penalty the penalized player shall start at midfield on his or her own team's side of the field and at no time enter onto the field of play until he or she has discharged the assigned penalty.
   Note: A penalized player's team is one player short until he or she has taken the prescribed number of laps. The player may return to the field or tag in a teammate.

RULE II. Playing Regulations, Violations, Fouls, and Penalties

1. The visiting team has choice of goals in the first half; for the second half the teams switch goals.

2. Each half is started at midfield by a jump ball between one member from Team A and one from Team B. Teams A and B remain in their respective halves of the field (the half farthest from their goal) until the ball has been tapped. Players jumping face their own goal.

3. Players can run with the ball, pass it, or strike it with hands open or closed.

4. A ball carrier may carry the ball in any direction. However, if the player is touched or tagged by an opponent he or she cannot at this time throw for a goal or continue with the ball, but must pass the ball *before taking three steps.*
   Penalty: The ball goes to the opposing team at the point of violation.
   Note: A tag cannot be a push or a stiff arm. Unnecessary roughness penalties can be applied.
   If the throwing arm is in forward motion when a player is tagged it is still a legal attempt to score.

5. If it is advantageous for a player, he or she may attempt to tie up the ball carrier rather than tag him. This must be done without jumping off the ground or charging or driving the opponent to the ground, but by grasping the ball carrier between the waist and shoulders.

   a. A legal tie-up results in a jump ball.

   b. A penalty is given for an illegal tie-up; the ball goes to the opposing team at the point of violation and the roughness penalty is applied (laps).

6. A free ball in the air: same rule applies as rule governing pass interference on a forward pass in football.

7. Use of hands on opponents by members of the team in possession of the ball is not permitted. For example, ball carrier may not stiff-arm an opponent, as in football.
   Penalty: One lap. Ball goes to opposing team at point of foul.

8. The offensive team may screen for its ball carrier with an upright screen but must not jump or use a shoulder block.
Penalty for illegal screen: One lap. Ball goes to opposing team at point of foul.

9. a. Defensive team may use hands on the body of an opponent to ward off a screen. Player warding off a screener uses his or her hands to push the screener away but does not use them to strike or stiff-arm an opponent.

   b. There shall be no unnecessary roughness such as tackling, using hands about the head of an opponent, tripping an opponent, holding an opponent who is not in possession of the ball or charging an opponent before or after he or she passes the ball.
   Penalty: Loss of ball to opponent at point of foul. One to three laps depending on the seriousness of the penalty.

10. After a goal is made the team scored upon may advance the ball to the quarter line (the line 30 feet from the scoring team's goal) without interference from the scoring team. Ten seconds are allowed to put the ball in play after the official turns ball over to team that has been scored on.
Penalty for interference with intention of delaying the game: One lap; ball goes to opposing team at quarter line.

RULE III. Out of Bounds

1. When the ball goes or is carried out of bounds, an official shall award it to a nearby opponent of the player who caused it to go out. This player may carry or throw the ball in bounds and must do so within three seconds after being awarded the ball. If the ball is carried in bounds, the player must come in bounds at the point the ball has been awarded to him or her.
Penalty for failure to comply: Ball goes to opponent.

2. A player cannot throw for a goal while taking the ball in from out of bounds. If a goal occurs, no score, and the ball goes to opponent.

3. The 15-foot circle around each goal is out of bounds for players but not for the ball. The ball may roll through the circle and not be considered out of bounds.

RULE IV. Substitutions

1. When time is out (e.g., (1) a called time out, (2) a jump ball, or (3) an out of bounds) any number of substitutes may enter the game.

2. When time is in a player on the field may be substituted for by going to his bench and tagging a teammate who may enter the field of play at this time.

Note: If a team's time outs are exhausted and a player is injured on the field, an official's time out should be called to remove the injured player.

ARACH ATTACK

Eileen Crowley Sullivan
Appropriate for replication.

Players:

Children and pre-teens.

Object of game for players:

To warm up while bowling a spider ball toward a designated target. To work cooperatively with a partner.

Number of players:

Classroom group, in pairs.

Costume, apparel/equipment required:

Equipment or objects suitable for targets, spider ball.

Area/arena/field where played—space required:

Gymnasium, play area, or field.

Time length of game. How is end of game determined?:

As directed by the teacher.

Symbolism of game:

Represents ancient games.

Rules of play, including scoring:

Partners set up their own course using various pieces of equipment or objects in the playing area as targets. Running alongside a partner, while each carries a spider ball players bowl (roll) the spider ball toward a designated target on the course. See how close you can get to the object.

The partner coming closest to the target with his or her spider ball chooses the target object on the course.

AUTHORS
Elenie Tsarhopoulos
Appropriate for replication.

Players:

Pre-teens and young teens.

Object of game for players:

To determine an author's identity, and raise awareness of oral and written communication through games.

Number of players:

Classroom group.

Costume, apparel/equipment required:

Paper or cards with names of different authors for each player.

Area/arena/field where played—space required:

Classroom, gymnasium.

Time length of game. How is end of game determined?:

As directed by the teacher.

Symbolism of game:

Represents experience in understanding the environment and associated culture.

Rules of play, including scoring:

An author's name is taped on each player's back. Players do not know what name they have taped on their backs. Players move around the room asking questions that can be answered with a "yes" or a "no," such as "Am I alive today?" "Do I write fiction?" or "Am I female?" If players think they have determined their identity they stand in a designated area, call out "Author" and make their guess.

BAT BALL
Elenie Tsarhopoulos
Appropriate for replication.

Players:

Pre-teens and young teens.

Object of game for players:

To run around base to home without being hit by the ball.

Number of players:

Eight to 15.

Costume, apparel/equipment required:

One playground ball.

Area/arena/field where played—space required:

Gymnasium, play area, or field.

Time length of game. How is end of game determined?:

Teams change sides after three outs, or one inning. Three innings make up the game.

Symbolism of game:

Represents surviving while threatened by a dangerous force.

Rules of play, including scoring:

One team is at bat, the other spreads out in field. The first batter holds the ball in palm of one hand and bats it with the fist of the other hand into the field. (The ball must go over the restraining line, which is 10 feet from the batting plate.) The batter then runs up and around the base and back home. The team in the field recovers the ball and tries to hit the batter out with the ball by hitting the shoulders or below, before the batter can return home. After three outs the teams change sides.

Fielders may not walk or run with the ball, hold the ball more than three seconds, or play catch with one another while waiting for a runner. If a foul is made, the run is scored even though the runner is hit.

A runner fouls by running out of bounds, by stepping inside the restraining line more than three times, or by failing to circle the base or touch home plate. If a foul is made, the runner is out.

Fielders either hit the runner with the ball or pass the ball to another fielder nearer to the runner, who tries to hit the runner.

Variation: The ball may be kicked by the team at bat instead of being batted out of the hand.

Note: Bat ball is one of the best games for encouraging teamwork and passing and throwing skills. The team that passes the ball to get in a more favorable position to hit the runner out is far more successful than a team on which one player ignores his or her team and makes a long, wild throw at a runner (generally not hitting him or her). The runner, in order to score, must learn to keep his or her eye on the ball, run an irregular course out of the path of the ball, and be able to switch directions quickly with the passing of the ball by the fielders.

BEANBAG BALANCE RELAY
Donna Duffy
Appropriate for replication.

Players:

Pre-teens and young teens.

Object of game for players:

To run around marker and back to team with beanbag balanced on head.

Number of players:

Classroom group divided into teams.

Costume, apparel/equipment required:

One beanbag per team.

Area/arena/field where played—space required:

Gymnasium, play area, or field.

Time length of game. How is end of game determined?:

When the runners on the winning team have completed the relay.

Symbolism of game:

Represents determination and work in a community group under difficult circumstances.

Rules of play, including scoring:

All relay teams start seated. The first player on each team has a beanbag. When the teacher says "Go," the first player places a beanbag on her head, stands up, and runs up and left around a marker and back to her team, balancing the beanbag without using her hands to keep it on her head. If the beanbag falls off, the runner must stop, replace the beanbag, and continue the relay. When back to her team, the runner hands the beanbag to the next player, goes to the end of her line, and sits down.

BEAT BALL
Donna Duffy
Appropriate for replication.

Players:

Pre-teens and young teens.

Object of game for players:

To run around the bases and home before the ball is passed around the bases to home.

Number of players:

Ten to 18, in two teams.

Costume, apparel/equipment required:

Playground ball (softball, football, or soccer ball may be used); batting tee or kicking tee; two sets of bases or one set of bases and four rubber cones.

Area/arena/field where played—space required:

Gymnasium, play area, or field.

Time length of game. How is end of game determined?:

As directed by the teacher.

Symbolism of game:

Represents beating the odds in a hostile environment.

Rules of play, including scoring:

Two sets of bases placed in a baseball diamond arrangement, one set five to ten feet inside the other set. With unskilled players it is advisable to place the fielders in their respective positions in the inside diamond. After the ball is hit, players pass the ball to first base, to second, to third, and then to home. The "batter" runs around all the bases (regardless of whether the ball is caught on the fly) in the outside diamond, thus preventing any contact with the basemen. If the ball arrives at the fielder's homeplate before the batter gets to his homeplate, the runner is out. If not, he is safe and a run is scored. All players on each team should be allowed to bat in each inning. All players will therefore have the same number of turns. The team scoring the greatest number of runs is the winner.

Variations

a. For more skilled players, it may be advisable to have the fielders use the outside bases while the batter runs the inside bases. Adjusting the two sets of bases will equalize the difficulty of the game between the runners and fielders, thus making the game more interesting.

b. In base-football or soccer-baseball, "batting" may be done by punting, place-kicking, or passing.

c. The use of a batting or kicking tee will speed up the game.

BECKON

Donna Duffy
Appropriate for replication.

Players:

Pre-teens and young teens.

Object of game for players:

To stay in hiding as long as possible.

Number of players:

Classroom group.

Costume, apparel/equipment required:

None.

Area/arena/field where played—space required:

Gymnasium, play area, or field.

Time length of game. How is end of game determined?:

As directed by the teacher.

Symbolism of game:

Survival, hunting/stalking skills, adaptability.

Rules of play, including scoring:

Choose one or two players to be "it". Choose a common area to be the goal (a large rock or tree will do). All players line up by the goal to start.

The player who is it hides his or her eyes and counts out loud by 10s to 500. The rest of the players scatter and hide. It is best to discuss boundaries before you begin play.

When the one who is it is finishes counting, he or she yells "Ready or not, here I (we) come!" and then goes to find all the other players. When a player is discovered, the one who is it calls out that player's name really loudly. The player called then has to go to the goal and call out "beckon."

A beckon is given by any other player who is still hiding.* Once the player in the goal gets a beckon, he or she is free to leave the goal area and hide again. But if the one who is it sees the player run off to hide, he or she calls out the running player's name and the player must go back to the goal area again. If you are caught by the player who is it, you become the new it and the game starts over again. All players return to the goal area when the one who is it yells "All ye, all ye urchins free."

Hint: A beckon is an arm or hand movement similar to a wave or a "come here" type of movement. A player cannot save beckons for another round.

BIRTHDAY LINE UP
Eileen Crowley Sullivan
Appropriate for replication.

Players:

Young teens.

Object of game for players:

Creative thinking, alternative communication, strengthening group ties.

Number of players:

Classroom group.

Costume, apparel/equipment required:

None.

Area/arena/field where played—space required:

Classroom, gymnasium.

Time length of game. How is end of game determined?:

When students are lined up from January to December.

Symbolism of game:

Represents understanding nonverbal communication in a variety of situations.

Rules of play, including scoring:

Tell the players you would like them to line up in the chronological order of where their birthday falls in the calendar, and tell them they are not allowed to speak to anyone while playing the game. Do not tell the players to use nonverbal signs or signals; they will figure this out for themselves. Say "Ready? Go." The players will begin to solve the problem and line up from January to December. When they are finished check to see that they are in order.

BOMBARDMENT
Greg Narleski
Appropriate for replication.

Players:

Pre-teens and teens.

Object of game for players:

To hit all of one team with the ball before it bounces.

Number of players:

Eight to 20, in two teams.

Costume, apparel/equipment required:

One to two playground balls.

Area/arena/field where played—space required:

Gymnasium, play area, or field.

Time length of game. How is end of game determined?:

When all of one team is out, or as directed by the teacher.

Symbolism of game:

Represents survival skills in a group and awareness of danger.

Rules of play, including scoring:

The two teams are each in their own half of the playing area. The game consists of throwing the balls(s) back and forth between the two teams, trying to hit each other. Players are out and leave the game if:

a. Hit by the ball before it bounces.

b. Attempts to catch a ball on the fly and drops it.

Any ball first touching the ground or wall may be picked up and thrown. Play for a specified time limit or until all of one team has been gotten out.

Note: Players may run or walk with the ball, but they may not cross over the center line.

BOUNDARY BALL
Eileen Crowley Sullivan
Appropriate for replication.

Players:

Pre-teens and young teens.

Object of game for players:

To throw the ball past opposing players and over their end boundary line.

Number of players:

Eight to 20 in two teams.

Costume, apparel/equipment required:

One playground ball.

Area/arena/field where played—space required:

Gymnasium, play area, or field.

Time length of game. How is end of game determined?:

The first team to win ten points.

Symbolism of game:

Represents the subtleties of negotiations and outcomes.

Rules of play, including scoring:

The playing area is divided into two sections, one team to a section, bounded by the center line and end boundary line. The ball is thrown back and forth between the two teams, the object being to throw the ball past the opposing players and over their end boundary line. Players may bat the ball down or catch it, then throw or pass it, but no player may run or walk with the ball. No player may cross the center line or play behind the end boundary line. Points are scored each time the ball goes over the boundary of the opposing team. Ten points win the game. Each team spreads out informally in its own section, but players should be encouraged to cover and stay within particular areas.

BRING THE BACON HOME
Eileen Crowley Sullivan
Appropriate for replication.

Players:

Pre-teens and young teens.

Object of game for players:

To bring the bacon home without being tagged.

Number of players:

Eight to 20.

Costume, apparel/equipment required:

One playground ball or beanbag (bacon).

Area/arena/field where played—space required:

Gymnasium, play area, or field.

Time length of game. How is end of game determined?:

As directed by the teacher.

Symbolism of game:

Represents food-gathering skills, fitness, and courage.

Rules of play, including scoring:

The class is divided into two groups. Each group counts off and stands behind its own goal line. The bacon is placed on the ground midway between the two groups. The teacher calls a number. The player with that number from each group runs in and attempts to steal the bacon and return to his or her goal line without being tagged by the other player called in. A point is given to a group each time the bacon is brought back safely. Once a player takes the bacon, he or she may be tagged, and may not drop the bacon in order to avoid being tagged. If opposing players reach the bacon at the same time, the best strategy is for them to walk around it, waiting for the right moment to grab it and run for their goal line. The group reaching ten points first, or having the most points at the end of the playing time, wins.

Safety Precautions:

    a. Goal lines should be four feet out from walls or fences.

    b. A ball or beanbag makes a safer bacon than a bowling pin or Indian club.

    c. Place a hoop or several hoops in the center in which to place the bacon to avoid collisions.

Modifications: Call several numbers at a time. Call even numbers, odd numbers, or use a math equation.

HUMAN CHECKERS
Eileen Crowley Sullivan
Appropriate for replication.

Players:

Young teens.

Object of game for players:

Two groups of three students exchange chairs or sides in fifteen moves. Creative thinking, problem solving. Reinforce mathematical concepts and computation skills through games.

Number of players:

Lines of six.

Costume, apparel/equipment required:

Seven chairs or seven papers.

Area/arena/field where played—space required:

Gymnasium, play area.

Time length of game. How is end of game determined?:

As directed by the teacher.

Symbolism of game:

Represents the implementation of rules of society and cultures to achieve a particular result.

Rules of play, including scoring:

Place seven chairs in a row. Three players sit at one end and three sit at the opposite end. There will be an empty chair in the middle. Each group faces the open chair. The object of the game is for the two groups of three students to exchange places, or sides, in fifteen moves. The players on the left will end up on the right and those on the right will end up on the left. Here are the rules:

- Only one move at a time is allowed.
- Students can move to an empty chair or jump another student.
- No one can move backwards at any time.

Examples of two moves might look like this:

1 2 3 X 6 5 4 (The original set up.)

Move #1: Student #6 moves to the empty chair, X.
Move #2: Student #3 jumps over #6 to the now empty chair on the other
side. The end result looks like this:

1 2 X 6 3 5 4 (The end result.)

"INDY" 500 AUTO RACE

Arlene Sequine
Appropriate for replication.

Players:

Children through young teens.

Object of game for players:

To follow directions and move along the "Indianapolis 500" Racetrack;
to sharpen accident awareness and safety education.

Number of players:

Approximately ten to 20.

Costume, apparel/equipment required:

Action wear with safe footwear (be sure sneaker laces are tied).
Flags required: green = go; red = accident; black = report to the pits
(inside track); checkered = race is finished, report to the pit; optional:
white = one lap to go; orange = running with no passing.

Area/arena/field where played—space required:

Use any lines that define a large rectangle in the gymnasium. The racetrack is outside the rectangle and the pit area is inside the rectangle.
The penalty zone (used when black is flagged) is located in the middle of
the pit.

Time length of game. How is end of game determined?:

The action of the game is stopped when the teacher says "pit stop." The players continue running in the direction they are headed until they return to their pit areas. They must stop and slowly proceed into their pit areas and sit down.

Symbolism of game:

Simulates the choreography of the famous Indianapolis 500 Race Car Event, with its dramatic revving up of engines, and time-outs in the pit stops along the race course, with the flagmen signaling drivers around the laps.

Rules of play, including scoring:

1. Players count off by twos and spread out around the racetrack facing the pit.
2. Players take one big step inward and sit. That is their pit area for pit-stops.
3. The teacher selects either number one or number two to enter the track; those players stand up and step out onto the track ready to run.
4. The teacher says "Drivers, start your engines" (the players can drama-tize the sound of the engines), then pauses for a few seconds and says "Go." The players standing on the track all run in the same direction. At any time, the teacher can call "accident." The children stop, change direction, and resume running. The instructor can call "accident" as many times as he or she wants.
5. Now the other number has a turn.

   Rules:

   1. Passing is allowed as long as no touching occurs.
   2. Anyone who falls must report to the pits.
   3. Everyone must run in the same direction.
   4. Players must allow others to pass them on the track or risk being black-flagged.
   5. No sliding into the pit area.
   6. Breaking a rule means reporting to the black-flag area (penalty zone).

   Flag Signals: Use flags to tell the children what to do; green = go; red = accident; black = report to the middle (penalty zone); checker-board = the race is finished, report to the pit.

Variation: More flags could be added to increase the challenge; white = one lap to go; orange = running with no passing.

LAST DETAIL
Shelly Agnew Sweeney
Appropriate for replication.

Players:

Pre-teens.

Object of game for players:

To pick out the six changes in partner.

Number of players:

Groups of two.

Costume, apparel/equipment required:

Players to dress with different clothing parts (like clogs for shoes).

Area/arena/field where played—space required:

Classroom, gymnasium.

Time length of game. How is end of game determined?:

Time set by the teacher.

Symbolism of game:

Represents observant behavior.

Rules of play, including scoring:

Face a partner and memorize everything about their appearance. While one partner turns away (and moves away so they cannot hear) the other partner changes six things about themselves. The first partner then tries to pick out the six changes.

MULTI-BALL

Shelly Agnew Sweeney
Appropriate for replication.

Players:

Pre-teens and teens.

Object of game for players:

To throw an object to a teammate and have him or her catch it in the opposing team's goal.

Number of players:

Classroom group.

Costume, apparel/equipment required:

A ball such as a basketball, football, or lacrosse ball, or a frisbee.

Area/arena/field where played—space required:

Gymnasium set up with a large central play area and a goal zone at either end approximately ten yards deep and wide enough to give ample room to move for the number playing.

Time length of game. How is end of game determined?:

Variable.

Symbolism of game:

Food-gathering experience, throwing skills.

Rules of play, including scoring:

The Players: Two teams, any number per side (as you have more players, add more equipment and make the field larger).

The Game: This game is played much like Ultimate Frisbee, with the goal of throwing an object to a teammate who catches it in the opposing team's goal. To begin the game, each team has two or three (or four or eight, etc.) objects. The team then begins throwing and catching while moving down the field to try and score. If the throws are completed the team keeps moving. (However, a player *must* stand still once she has caught the object. She may not run with it.) If the object is dropped, knocked down, or intercepted, the other team picks it up and moves in the other direction (toward the other goal). Play is *continuous*, with no boundaries *except* on the long ends of the goal zone. (Any object that ends up behind the goal is given to that defending team.)

Scoring: If a player catches an object in the goal zone, she puts it down (she is allowed to spike it). The player then runs and slaps the teacher's hand (which records her score) and then returns to her own goal zone to continue play.

*Players will quickly "show their stripes" in this game by their defensive-offensive midfield preferences.

NASTIES FOUR SQUARE
Shelly Agnew Sweeney
Appropriate for replication.

Players:

Pre-teens and young teens.

Object of game for players:

To eliminate the player in square four. To practice racquet and striking skills.

Number of players:

Four per group.

Costume, apparel/equipment required:

Ball.

Area/arena/field where played—space required:

Four-square box (court), which can be as large as a tennis court.

Time length of game. How is end of game determined?:

The game is over when only one player is left.

Symbolism of game:

Group cohesion.

Rules of play, including scoring:

The squares are numbered 1, 2, 3, and 4. The player in sqaure 1 starts with an underhand serve that must bounce in the corner of the four square box. All hits after that may be any way (the ball cannot be held on the racquet and pulled but must be struck). A ball hitting a line is out. If a ball hits in your square, you must hit it. Anyone playing a ball that hit in someone else's square is out. All is fair after that, with the goal being to eliminate the person in square four (the other three should work together). As a player is eliminated, everyone moves up and the new player comes into square one (you only move up if someone in front of you is out or moves up).

ONE BOUNCE PONG

Shelly Agnew Sweeney
Appropriate for replication.

Players:

Pre-teens and teens.

Object of game for players:

To hit the ball after one bounce on the floor. To practice racquet and striking skills. First player to score 21 wins.

Number of players:

Two, three, or more.

Costume, apparel/equipment required:

Half ping-pong table, ping-pong ball.

Area/arena/field where played—space required:

Gymnasium.

Time length of game. How is end of game determined?:

Variable.

Symbolism of game:

Momentum.

Rules of play, including scoring:

Played on a square table (half a ping-pong table). Players must hit the ball up onto the table top after one bounce on the floor. The ball is allowed to bounce as many times as is necessary on the top of the table. The serve is one bounce on the floor, and an underhand hit to the top of the table. Rotational play requires two players (if three are playing the game) to begin on one side (where the server is) with one on the other. Play the hits in order, which means after you hit, you will have to run to the other side of the table. If a player loses the sequence, misplaces the ball, or allows any error, he or she loses the point. The first player to score 21 is the winner.

PASS THE GLOB

Eileen Crowley Sullivan
Appropriate for replication.

Players:

Young teens.

Object of game for players:

To pass a beanbag to individual players to continue a story. Creative thinking, taking turns, improving verbal communication, strengthening group ties.

Number of players:

A group large enough to form a circle.

Costume, apparel/equipment required:

A ball, beanbag, or small object to pass.

Area/arena/field where played—space required:

Classroom, gymnasium.

Time length of game. How is end of game determined?:

After each player has had a turn.

Symbolism of game:

Represents relaxation, leisure, and story sharing.

Rules of play, including scoring:

Sit in a circle. One player holds a beanbag and starts to tell a story. Any fairy tale or traditional beginning is allowed but use your creative talents to set the scene. One beginning could be, "Once upon a time there lived a King and Queen." After the first player begins the story he or she passes the beanbag to someone else. The second player elaborates and adds to the story, and then passes the beanbag along to another player. Continue in any pattern until everyone has had a turn to add something to the tale. Determine a way to indicate who has had a turn to talk.

PUNCTURED DRUM
Jason Holder
Appropriate for replication.

Players:

Young teens.

Object of game for players:

To fill a small container with water using a punctured can. Creative thinking, cooperation, problem solving in a group through games.

Number of players:

Classroom group.

Costume, apparel/equipment required:

A coffee can or container with punctured holes, pails, water.

Area/arena/field where played—space required:

Gymnasium or play area, but best played while camping, overnighting, or hiking.

Time length of game. How is end of game determined?:

As directed by the teacher.

Symbolism of game:

Represents the ingenuity required to survive in a hostile environment.

Rules of play, including scoring:

Groups are arranged and each is given a can with lots of holes. The goal is to fill a small bucket or wastebasket full of water by carrying water with the punctured can. Players must transport water from one area to another with the can. Only body parts can be used to plug the holes—no other props can be used. Provide time at the beginning of the game for each group to brainstorm how they will solve the problem. Set some guidelines requiring everyone to be involved and take equal time to transport the water.

ROUND UP
Jason Holder
Appropriate for replication.

Players:

Pre-teens and teens.

Object of game for players:

To dribble around the maximum number of different cones in a set amount of time. To improve hand-eye and foot-eye coordination and cardiovascular endurance.

Number of players:

Classroom group.

Costume, apparel/equipment required:

Cones, balls.

Area/arena/field where played—space required:

Gymnasium, play area, or field.

Time length of game. How is end of game determined?:

As directed by the teacher.

Symbolism of game:

Represents rounding-up activities and skills.

Rules of play, including scoring:

Cones are scattered around the playing area. Everyone has a ball. When the activity starts, the challenge is to see how many different cones a player can dribble around in a set amount of time.

SNATCH THE FLAG

Jason Holder
Appropriate for replication.

Players:

Pre-teens and teens.

Object of game for players:

To pull the cloth strip of the other player. To avoid having your own personal strip pulled. To play cooperatively and with consideration.

Number of players:

Classroom group.

Costume, apparel/equipment required:

Cloth strips about two-feet long.

Area/arena/field where played—space required:

Gymnasium, play area, or field.

Time length of game. How is end of game determined?:

As directed by the teacher.

Symbolism of game:

Represents survival experience and courage.

Rules of play, including scoring:

Give one cloth strip to each child. Tuck the cloth strip into a back pocket. *Do not* wrap or tie the strip to a belt loop (they rip off very easily). When the teacher says "Go" each player tries to pull another player's cloth strip without having his or her own strip pulled in return. Once your strip has been pulled, you must sit down and wait until the next round, although you are not entirely out of the game. If you can reach and pull a player's cloth strip as he or she goes by you, this is allowed. Players must play without bumping into others and without being too rough.

SPUD

Eileen Crowley Sullivan
Appropriate for replication.

Players:

Pre-teens and young teens.

Object of game for players:

To catch the ball before it bounces when your number is called.

Number of players:

Six to 20 in a circle.

Costume, apparel/equipment required:

One playground ball.

Area/arena/field where played—space required:

Gymnasium, play area, or field.

Time length of game. How is end of game determined?:

As directed by the teacher.

Symbolism of game:

Represents skills required for responding to dangerous situations.

Rules of play, including scoring:

Each player has a number. One player starts the game by standing in the center, throwing the ball up in the air, and calling out a number. All players run away from the circle except the player whose number is called. If the player whose number is called catches the ball before it touches the ground, he immediately throws the ball up, calls another number, and then runs away. Otherwise the player whose number is called catches the ball after it touches the ground, and then calls "Stop." All players must stop running immediately. If the game is played outside, the player with the ball takes three steps toward any player, and then throws the ball at this player, trying to hit him or her. The target player may try to dodge the ball but may not move either foot to do so. If hit, this player has one point against him and he restarts the game. If the thrower misses, he has one point against him and he restarts the game. After getting four points, a player is out. Each point represents one letter of the word S-P-U-D. If the game is played inside, the thrower is not entitled to three steps before trying to hit another player. In addition, all players may not move until the ball has stopped moving. This permits more than one player to be hit on a single throw.

STATUES
Greg Narleski
Appropriate for replication.

Players:

Pre-teens and young teens.

Object of game for players:

To be touching the statue in two places, each place being a part of a different person's body. To solve problems through movement.

Number of players:

Classroom group.

Costume, apparel/equipment required:

None.

Area/arena/field where played—space required:

Gymnasium, play area.

Time length of game. How is end of game determined?:

When the statue is built.

Symbolism of game:

Loyalty and devotion.

Rules of play, including scoring:

This is a good way to end a class (or a field day). One player starts in the middle, then others join, adding to the statue. The rule is that you must be connected to the statue (touching) in two places and the two touches must be to two *different* people. Once the statue is built, use these variations:

A: Small groups of students leave the statue, not being allowed to disturb the other pieces.

B: The statue moves, or turns in the opposite direction, or changes from high to low, or changes in other ways.

C: Small groups make their own statues and other groups try to guess what they are.

D: On a field day, classes or grade levels can each make their own statue.

STEP-BALL
Tom Jacoby
Appropriate for replication.

Players:

Teens.

Object of game for players:

To hit the step, and then riser, with a ball and then catch it on the fly.

Number of players:

One or two.

Costume, apparel/equipment required:

Street clothes, ball.

Area/arena/field where played—space required:

Street, curb, and steps.

Time length of game. How is end of game determined?:

As directed by the teacher or as decided by the players.

Symbolism of game:

Represents the adaptability of children to play games in their local environment.

Rules of play, including scoring:

The player stands in the street just beyond the curb and throws the ball at a stoop or porch steps (or if there are two sets of steps, stand on the sidewalk below the bottom steps and throw at whichever set is best for game purposes). If the player hits the step and then a riser and then catches the ball on the fly, the player gets one point. If the player hits the edge of the step and then catches it on the fly, he or she gets ten points. If the player misses a catch or does not throw it properly, it becomes the other player's turn. If playing alone, the game is over and a new game begins. The first to reach a predetermined point score is the winner.

STICKBALL
John Cheffers
Appropriate for replication.

Players:

Teens.

Object of game for players:

To hit the ball on one bounce and run the bases.

Number of players:

Any number.

Costume, apparel/equipment required:

"Pinkie" or pimple ball, sawed-off broomsticks. (Pinkie balls are soft rubber balls with a surface of rubber stops.)

Area/arena/field where played—space required:

Adequate space that would ideally accomodate a three-way intersection, with a back-drop wall at the fourth corner. Home plate, the pitcher's rubber, and bases are established utilizing whatever is available and convenient. Ideally set up as a baseball diamond with a wall at home plate.

Time length of game. How is end of game determined?:

Innings are predetermined. If both teams agree, the game can be interrupted if playing at lunch hour and be continued at a later point where the score stands.

Symbolism of game:

Represents the adaptation of certain cultural games to meet the resources of children playing in their home environment.

Rules of play, including scoring:

The pitcher delivers the ball on one bounce, and the batter reacts just as in baseball. Usually, two strikes (including four foul balls) are an out. Balls are not counted. If the ball is hit, baseball rules apply on running the bases. Caught fly balls are an out. "Roofers" (i.e., fair balls hit on a roof) are home runs. There are two or three outs to an inning and games are played any predetermined number of innings.

TEAM TARGET
Elenie Tsarhopoulos
Appropriate for replication.

Players:

Young teens.

Object of game for players:

To move a ball target over an endline by throwing other balls at it.

Number of players:

Eight to 15 per team.

Costume, apparel/equipment required:

Three to ten balls, one different from the rest.

Area/arena/field where played—space required:

Gymnasium, play area, or field.

Time length of game. How is end of game determined?:

When the target ball is moved over the line or as directed by the teacher.

Symbolism of game:

Represents hunting and shepherding skills, and determination.

Rules of play, including scoring:

Teams line up side by side facing each other beyond their own end-lines. Each team starts with half the balls to be used. The target (different colored ball) is placed on the ground in the center of the play space. When the teacher says "Go," both teams throw their balls at the target, trying to move it and keep it moving toward and over the other team's endline. Teams get one point each time the target crosses the other team's endline. No player may stop the target going over his endline except by knocking it out with a ball in play. All players must stay behind their endlines and may not retrieve dead balls in the center. Balls that have stopped in the middle of play may be put in motion again by being knocked by another ball. Any balls going out of bounds cannot be retrieved until a point is made or until there are no balls left in play. When either of these two situations occurs, and all balls are retrieved, the target is again placed in the center, and the game is restarted with the balls evenly distributed between the two teams. Players with balls may not switch places on the endline in order to get in more favorable positions to hit the moving target, but balls may be passed down the line to a player nearer the target.

THUMPA

Arlene Sequine
Appropriate for replication.

Players:

Teens to adults.

Object of game for players:

To perform actions around a circle, first presenting your own action, and then imitating someone else's.

Number of players:

Approximately ten to 20.

Costume, apparel/equipment required:

None.

Area/arena/field where played—space required:

Often played in an outdoor picnic setting, it is easily adaptable to an indoor environment.

Time length of game. How is end of game determined?:

Open-ended; play continues until all players are eliminated from the game.

Symbolism of game:

The original version was a drinking game that grew out of testing the reflexes and memory of the players. In the "spirit of the picnic tradition," player's drank more and more beer as the afternoon wore on with some, though not all, losing their mental sharpness.

Rules of play, including scoring:

Players are seated in a circle. Each player selects an action to pass around the circle, for example, tapping the shoulders or pulling the ears. One player is the leader who begins the game by saying "What's the name of this game?" and everyone answers "Thumpa," while beating the ground. The group starts tapping their knees and asks "How do you play it?" The leader then begins by performing his or her own action and then someone else's action. The next person continues the action of the game by first doing his or her action followed by still another person's gesture. Be sure to always do your own action first. When a mistake is made, the player drops out of the circle and the remaining players must remember not to use the action belonging to the eliminated players. Every time someone drops out, the leader begins the game again. This game is meant to be played sober, not while drinking.

Variation: Amusing sounds may be added to the actions, and they also must be repeated with the corresponding action belonging to each player.

TWO SQUARE AND FOUR SQUARE
Kevin McAllister
Appropriate for replication.

Players:

Pre-teens.

Object of game for players:

To bounce-serve the ball into the opposite square and return it by hitting with one or two hands.

Number of players:

Two or more.

Costume, apparel/equipment required:

One playground ball.

Area/arena/field where played—space required:

Playground, gymnasium, or two squares.

Time length of game. How is end of game determined?:

Until a player misses the ball or there is a foul.

Symbolism of game:

Represents team cohesion.

Rules of play, including scoring:

The game is played in two squares. Opposing players face each other, each standing in a square. The game is started by one player bounce-serving (ball held in left and dropped to the court, then batted with right hand) the ball into the square of the other player. The second player returns the ball after it has bounced once in his or her square by batting it *upward* with one or both hands into the square of the server. Play continues until one player misses or any of the following violations occurs:
- Ball lands on a line or out of playing area.
- Ball is hit with a fist.
- Player holds ball.
- Ball is hit down instead of up.

The player missing the ball or committing a violation leaves the game and a waiting player comes in.

Variation: Played on a four-square court. The same rules apply except that the ball may be hit into any of the other three squares of the court. When a player misses or commits a violation, he leaves the game and the remaining players move up one square toward A. The waiting player enters the game in square D.

WALL BALL
Kevin McAllister
Appropriate for replication.

Players:

Children through pre-teens.

Object of game for players:

To throw and catch a ball three times at progressive three-foot lines.

Number of players:

Four to six per group.

Costume, apparel/equipment required:

One ball per group.

Area/arena/field where played—space required:

Gymnasium, play area, or field. A wall with successive lines drawn near it at three-foot intervals.

Time length of game. How is end of game determined?:

As directed by the teacher.

Symbolism of game:

Represents the skills for hunting and survival.

Rules of play, including scoring:

Players are divided into four or more groups, with one ball to each group. Players take turns throwing the ball against the wall from a designated line, three feet from the wall. Each player must make three consecutive throws and catches at the three-foot line before moving back to the next line for three more throws. Each player continues throwing and catching and moving back. If a player misses, he or she passes the ball to the next player in the group, and goes to the end of the line. When his or her turn comes again, the player resumes throwing from the line at which the last turn ended. Make sure every child takes three throws per turn.

Note: Children like this skill game because of its challenge in working back line by line. In the upper grades, specific throws may be required and different types of balls used, and the distances from the wall may be greater.

WALL BALL RELAY
Kevin McAllister
Appropriate for replication.

Players:

Children and pre-teens.

Object of game for players:

To throw and catch a ball off a wall from a three-foot line five times then return to team.

Number of players:

Classroom group in teams.

Costume, apparel/equipment required:

One playground ball per team.

Area/arena/field where played—space required:

Gymnasium, play area, or field.

Time length of game. How is end of game determined?:

When the winning team has completed the required throwing and catching.

Symbolism of game:

Represents the preparation required for hunting and gathering in a community.

Rules of play, including scoring:

The first player on each team runs to a line drawn three feet from the wall. The player stands toeing this line and throws and catches the ball off the wall five times. The player then returns to the team, hands the ball to the next player, and goes to the end of the line. A player may run over the three-foot line to catch the ball, but all throws must be made from behind the line. If any one of the five throws is made with feet over the line, it must be repeated.

Variations: Specify kind of throw: underhand, overhand, chest.

THE WEB EXCITE
Eileen Crowley Sullivan
Appropriate for replication.

Players:

Teens.

Object of game for players:

To travel through the web without touching a rope (or band). To solve problems while working as a team.

Number of players:

Classroom group.

Costume, apparel/equipment required:

Jump rope, or jump band (cloth, like a rope).

Area/arena/field where played—space required:

Gymnasium, play area, or field.

Time length of game. How is end of game determined?:

When team passes through the web.

Symbolism of game:

To develop teamwork and problem solving abilities.

Rules of play, including scoring:

Two teams, evenly split, one team with jump ropes (or jump band) for each person (add more ropes or bands as the players become more skillful). The team with jump ropes forms two facing lines. This team creates a web by holding the ropes across the middle in either straight lines or angles (from foot to hand or waist to above head, etc.). The players should make the web as tricky as possible, with many levels covered. The second team must then travel through the web to the other side *without* touching a band or rope.

WIRE-BALL

Tom Jacoby
Appropriate for replication.

Players:

Pre-teens and young teens.

Object of game for players:

To throw the ball at wires so that it cannot be caught.

Number of players:

Two to six is best, though it can be any number.

Costume, apparel/equipment required:

Solid pinkie or pimple ball.

Area/arena/field where played—space required:

A good cross-street intersection, not too heavily traveled, with a fine array of overhead telephone wires.

Time length of game. How is end of game determined?:

As directed by the teacher or as decided by the players.

Symbolism of game:

Represents the creative use of the environment for games.

Rules of play, including scoring:

There are two teams with equal numbers (one, two, or three on each side are best—more can become boring). The object is to throw the ball at the wires, attempting to deflect the ball in such a way that it cannot be caught. Caught balls are an out. Balls bouncing once are singles, twice are doubles, and so on.

PART III

Asia

China

BLOWING A PING-PONG BALL

Shen Xun-zhang
Appropriate for replication.

Players:

Teens.

Object of game for players:

To heighten vital capacity, develop lung function, and increase flexibility.

Number of players:

Eight.

Costume, apparel/equipment required:

Table and ping pong balls.

Area/arena/field where played—space required:

Half a table-tennis table or an 80 x 80 centimeter desk.

Time length of game. How is end of game determined?:

When the ball is blown off the table.

Symbolism of game:

Coolness and skill under stress of competition.

Rules of play, including scoring:

Players are divided into two groups of equal number and stand along opposite sides of the table. A ping-pong ball is placed in the center of the table. Players blow hard on the ball, doing all they can to make the ball roll toward the opposite side and to prevent the ball from rolling back toward themselves. A group loses a game as soon as the ball falls off their own side of the table. The player with the highest total score of direct blow offs wins. No part of a player's body, including mouth and hands, may touch the table.

BOAT TUGGING
Charlie Song
Not appropriate for replication.

Players:

Traditionally, young male adults, but also anyone who is interested in participating.

Object of game for players:

Two boats head in opposite directions with equal numbers of oarsmen on each boat. A water game played during the Lotus Festival, and first played by fishermen in the Lake South area of Jiazin, Zhejing, since the Song Dynasty (960 A.D.), on 24 June of the Chinese lunar calendar.

Number of players:

Ten to 20.

Costume, apparel/equipment required:

Two boats, oars for each person, a drum, comfortable exercise clothes, and lotus leaves, or the equivalent.

Area/arena/field where played—space required:

An open area of water without a strong current. Two lotuses symbolically placed 50 meters apart, one meter above the water. The distances may vary depending on the ability level of players and water conditions.

Time length of game. How is end of game determined?:

The game ends when one boat picks up a lotus. A time frame may be set for each contest. If no one picks up a lotus, a tie is awarded.

Symbolism of game:

The game symbolizes the power of the fishermen and their desire for hope, beauty, and happiness.

Rules of play, including scoring:

Two boats facing opposite directions are tied together with a rope from the end of each boat. A drum beat signals oarsmen on each boat to paddle hard to pull the other boat. Each boat must use an equal number of oarsmen plus a head person, who keeps the paddles in rhythm. The winner is determined by the head person picking up a lotus placed in the direction the boat is facing.

BUMUGA

Charlie Song
Not appropriate for replication.

Players:

Young teens, or those interested in playing.

Object of game for players:

Kicking a ball inside a round field with six rings. Started by cowboys and shepherds in Inner Mongolia.

Number of players:

Eight to 16.

Costume, apparel/equipment required:

A soccer ball (originally, people used a ball made of animal bladder and cloths). A flag on a post five to seven meters high. The costume is similar to a soccer uniform or any comfortable exercise uniform.

Area/arena/field where played—space required:

Open area. Six marked circles form the center point (like a bull's eye) where the flag stands, within the smallest ring of two meters' radius. Rings with radii increasing by two meters surround the smallest center ring. The largest ring has a radius of 12 meters. The numbers 1, 2, 3, 4, 5, and 7, are marked on each ring from the outside in.

Time length of game. How is end of game determined?:

Twenty minutes to one hour.

Symbolism of game:

The game was played by the cowboys as a joyous celebration of happiness and health.

Rules of play, including scoring:

Usually the game is played between two teams with equal numbers of players on each. There are one or two referees. The players may start playing at any spot outside the third ring and inside the field by kicking the ball into the air. Three to five kicks are allowed for each play depending on the skill level of the players. The ball must be kicked above the top of the flag for each kick. The next kick must follow the first rebound after the ball hits the ground. Each rebounding spot is marked by the referee. If the ball falls outside the field, the play is dead and the player must leave the field. Any points earned before the dead kick are counted into the final score of the player or the team.

Scoring: The points for each kick area are earned by matching the number marked for the ring where the ball is rebounded. The game is decided by the individual players' or the team's total points. The game may be played with multiple rounds such as preliminary, semifinal, and final. If two players have scored the same number of points after the competition is over, the referee judges the winner by comparing the points earned from the first kick(s). If a tie still exists, first the second, and then the third kicks will be compared. The highest score wins.

CATCHING PEARLS
Charlie Song
Not appropriate for replication.

Players:

Males and females of all ages; typically pre-teen and older.

Object of game for players:

Catching a ball with a net basket. Young pearl farmers of Manchurian nationality invented the game hundreds of years ago by simulating the work of catching pearls.

Number of players:

Twelve.

Costume, apparel/equipment required:

- Ball: any air-inflated rubber ball, junior volleyball, or junior soccer ball.
- Racket: a wood paddle in the shape of a clam shell 40 centimeters in width, with a handle 18–20 centimeters long connected to the base of the "shell."
- Basket: a net basket with an opening 30 centimeters in diameter, 30 centimeters in depth, with a handle 15 centimeters long connected to the ring at the top of the basket.

Area/arena/field where played—space required:

An open area about the size of a basketball court. It should have the following:
- Two side lines 28 meters long.
- Two base lines 15 meters long.
- A center line dividing the field into two halves.
- Scoring lines two meters from each base line. The zone between the scoring line and the base line is called the scoring zone.
- Defensive lines four meters from each base line. The zone between the scoring line and the defensive line is called the defensive zone.

- Restricted lines five and a half meters from each base line. The zone between the defensive line and the restricted line is called the restricted zone.
- A circled area one meter in radius in the center of the field called the starting zone, where the play starts.

The area between the two restricted lines is called the water zone.

Time length of game. How is end of game determined?:

The game lasts until there is a winner.

Symbolism of game:

Traditionally, the game has been a celebration for the harvest of pearls. It symbolizes the cooperation, unity, and happiness of the pearl farmers.

Rules of play, including scoring:

Two teams play against each other, with six players at a time on each team. In offensive play, two players with baskets stay in the scoring zone of the opponents' side of the court to catch the pearl (ball) from their teammates. In defensive play, two players stay in the water zone to interfere with opponents' play and get the pearl back. Four players stay in the defensive zone to break the offensive play and keep the opponents from catching the pearl.

CHAI WONG DAI OR CHAI LAU TAI (THE EMPEROR OF THE STAIRS)
Charlie Song
Appropriate for replication.

Players:

Pre-teens and young teens.

Object of game for players:

There are two versions of the game, one on a staircase and the other on flat ground. The object in either version is to be the first one to reach the throne (the throne is the top of the stairs or a specified place when played on flat ground).

Number of players:

Usually two when played on a staircase, but at least three when played on flat ground.

Costume, apparel/equipment required:

None.

Area/arena/field where played—space required:

Stairs or flat ground.

Time length of game. How is end of game determined?:

No time limit.

Symbolism of game:

The winner is the emperor and players queue up for their turns to challenge the emperor. The game teaches players to respect authority, which is central to Chinese Confucian thinking.

Rules of play, including scoring:

Each player on the count of three makes his or her hand into a "box," a "scissors," or a "handkerchief." A box is shown by a closed fist, a scissors by fingers one and two open, and a handkerchief by an open palm. In the hierarchy of the game, the box "breaks" the scissors, the scissors "sever" the handkerchief, and the handkerchief "wraps up" the box, leaving a clear winner for each play. In case of a tie, the play is restarted.

Stairs: When playing on stairs, players who win the box-scissors-handkerchief contest advance one step up the stairs. The first player to reach the top of the stairs is the emperor.

Flat Ground: When playing on flat ground, the winner of the box-scissors-handkerchief contest is the emperor, who defends his or her throne from other challengers, who line up for their turn to challenge the emperor.

CHASE THE DRAGON'S TAIL
Christine M. Conboy
Appropriate for replication.

Players:

Pre-teens and young teens.

Object of game for players:

To run and tag one player while holding onto another. To learn about Chinese culture and tradition through games.

Number of players:

Classroom group.

Costume-Apparel/Equipment required:

None.

Area/arena/field where played—space required:

Gymnasium, play area, or field.

Time length of game. How is end of game determined?:

When there are only two players left, or as directed by the teacher.

Symbolism of game:

Represents the dragon and dragon legends that are still told in China. The game portrays the dragon as a fearsome fire-eating reptile that carries off fair maidens and destroys farmers' crops with fiery breath.

Rules of play, including scoring:

The players line up one behind the other. The player at the front of the line is the head. The player at the end is the tail. Each player puts his or her arms on the shoulders of the player in front and the line of players becomes a dragon. The head runs in a big circle, trying to the catch the tail while the dragon twists and turns and does everything possible to prevent the head from catching the tail. Players must be careful not to break the line. Every time the head catches the tail the line becomes shorter because the tail must drop out. When a break in the line occurs, the player who was supposed to hold on also drops out.

CHINA'S 'EIGHT BASIC EXERCISES'
Myrna Schild
Appropriate for replication.

Players:

Pre-teens and young teens.

Object of game for players:

To improve muscular coordination, flexibility, and tone and also to warm up for other activities. To learn the mass exercises required of all Chinese people.

Number of players:

Classroom group.

Costume, apparel/equipment required:

Music.

Area/arena/field where played—space required:

Gymnasium, play area, or field.

Time length of game. How is end of game determined?:

When exercises are completed.

Symbolism of game:

Represents the culture of China in its socialist period. In schools, the Eight Basic Exercises are performed en masse (200–300 students) once or twice daily to music piped through an ever-present public address system. Games have been devised to compliment these exercises and competitive activities are de-emphasized. Much of the program was militarily inspired, but some sports, dance, and acrobatic-gymnastics endure.

Rules of play, including scoring:

All of the exercises begin and end in a standing position of attention with arms down at sides.

Exercise #1

a. Side-stride position, arms in "W" position.

b. Arms straight up in "H" position.

c. Same as (a), "W" position.

d. Arms out to side, "T."

Exercise #2

a. Walking with same arm as leg forward, first left arm and leg, then change to right arm and leg. Exercise is done slowly, with control.

Exercise #3

a. Moving forward, first with forward-stride position, arms straight forward.

b. Forward lunge with arms extended out to sides.

c. Repeat (a) and (b).

d. Deep knee bend (turn both to the side and to the front).

Exercise #4

a. Arms up, right foot back (turn both to the side and to the front).

b. High kick with right foot, arms touch foot.

c. Same as (a).

Exercise #5

a. Side lunge to left, left arm up, right arm on waist.

b. Bend farther to left each time.

Exercise #6

a. Arms in "T," feet astride.

b. Left hand touches left foot, right arm is straight up.

c. Swing up to face reverse direction; both arms reach backward and head turns.

Exercise #7

a. On toes, arms up.

b. Touch toes.

c. Left leg lunge.

Exercise #8

a. "T" position, jump, feet astride.

b. Jump left, feet together, arms overhead.

c. Same as (a).

COCKFIGHTING

Shen Xun-zhang
Not appropriate for replication.

Players:

Males and females of all ages.

Object of game for players:

To increase physical strength of legs; to temper will power.

Number of players:

Two to ten.

Costume, apparel/equipment required:

None.

Area/arena/field where played—space required:

A smooth, neat place.

Time length of game. How is end of game determined?:

- The game is over when one player falls or lets both feet touch the ground.

Symbolism of game:

Direct confrontation.

Rules of play, including scoring:

Raise the opposing player's right leg (or his or her weak leg) and wind it toward the inside. Use the opposing player's left hand to hold your own anklebone or instep, and use his or her right hand to hold your own thigh. A player responds to an opposite player with kneecap fighting, so as to attack and make the opponent unable to stand firmly on his or her feet. Pushing with hands or kicking with feet is not allowed. If the raised leg is let go, the player letting go is defeated.

Method:
- A cockfighting duel.
- Group relay cockfighting: Divided into two groups of equal numbers, the group that keeps a greater number standing after the match wins.
- Circle cockfighting: Within a drawn circle four meters in diameter, players cockfight. If a player steps on the line or jumps out of the circle, the player loses the match.

DOING IN THE OPPOSITE DIRECTION
Shen Xun-zhang
Appropriate for replication.

Players:

Teens.

Object of game for players:

To decrease reaction time.

Number of players:

Ten to 16.

Costume, apparel/equipment required:

None.

Area/arena/field where played—space required:

Playground or vacant lot.

Time length of game. How is end of game determined?:

A predetermined count such as "ten errors" ends the game.

Symbolism of game:

The "briar patch" philosophy. The rabbit says to the fox "Throw me, kick me, hit me, but please don't throw me in the briar patch" (which is the rabbit's haven).

Rules of play, including scoring:

Two teams stand facing each other, two meters apart. A judge stands at the center of both teams. One player is the judge, who shouts commands and instructions. The players' actions in response must be the opposite of what was demanded. If a judge shouts "Stand at attention," players must stand at ease at once. If a judge shouts "Right face," players must stand left face. If the command is "Onwards a step," players must move backwards a step; if it is "bend over," players must stand upright; "Both hands cover own head" means players place their arms akimbo; and so on. Players are ordered off the field for foul play, or as soon as their actions are inconsistent with the commands of the judge. The team that fouls out least and keeps more people in the game wins the match.

DRAGON BOAT
Charlie Song
Not appropriate for replication.

Players:

Male and female teens and adults.

Object of game for players:

To win the boat race. The race is between teams of people canoeing boats with sculpted dragon heads and tails and decorated bodies. Dragon boat racing can be traced back to the Han Dynasty (206 B.C.). Zhejiang and Hunan are the provinces recorded as the earliest places where dragon boats were made and raced for ceremonial events.

Number of players:

Traditionally, young male adults participated in the race. Now the race attracts diversified groups of people who are interested in and capable of participating.

Costume, apparel/equipment required:

Traditionally, bright-colored sleeveless garments and loose pants made of either cotton or silk are worn by players. Boats, drums, and gongs.

The Boat: Traditionally, dragon boats came in a wide variety of designs, shapes, and sizes, small boats holding only five to six people and large ones accommodating over 100 oarsmen. In order to make it a fair competition, the optimum boat size now is 15.5 meters long (excluding the head and tail) with a width of 1.1 meters and weighing 1.2 to 1.4 tons. The boat requires 20 oars. A triangular or rectangular boat flag flies at the head of the boat and a rudder is installed at the end.

Area/arena/field where played—space required:

Water for boating.

Time length of game. How is end of game determined?:

When race finishes.

Symbolism of game:

The dragon is the symbol of China. The dragon boat was thought to be a sacred vehicle, allowing people requesting merciful offerings and protection for their lives access to the Dragon God, who was regarded as the ruler of the universe. The ceremony of boat racing also symbolizes the love of homeland, justice, and peace.

Rules of play, including scoring:

A 1,000-meter long race lane is divided by lane markers. Each team has one helmsman, one drummer, one gonger, twenty oarsmen, and three back-up oarsmen. Teams compete in elimination heats (two boats at a time) with the winner advancing to the next round; in round-robins (two boats at a time), crews advance to the next round by having the highest number of wins; and in timed races (a multiple number of boats at a time based upon the availability and capacity of the racing lanes) the winner is the boat finishing in the least amount of time.

DUCK HUNTING
Charlie Song
Appropriate for replication.

Players:

Teens.

Object of game for players:

Throwing a sandbag to hit your opponent's lower legs below the knees. Hunt the ducks in the pond by throwing a sandbag at the ducks below their knees.

Number of players:

Two to ten.

Costume, apparel/equipment required:

A sandbag weighing three to four ounces and a watch.

Area/arena/field where played—space required:

An open area with two six to eight meter parallel lines drawn ten to 15 meters apart from each other. The exact distance between the lines depends on the age of the players. The area between the lines is called the pond and the areas behind the lines are banks.

Time length of game. How is end of game determined?:

Switch roles of hunter and ducks every two to five minutes, depending on the age of the players. The game may be decided by:

1. Setting a certain amount of playing time and the team with more ducks alive at the end of the playing time wins.

2. Recording the amount of time a duck or team of ducks stays alive in the pond; the individual or the team who stays alive longest wins.

3. The number of times a duck is hit within a certain time period when individuals play against each other; the duck that is hit the least number of times wins.

Symbolism of game:

The game provides a variety of benefits to the health, fitness, and courage of children and indicates the happiness, joy, and innocence of children.

Rules of play, including scoring:

The game may be played by individuals against each other or by two teams with an equal number of players on each team.

Rules: Only one bag is thrown at a time. The hunters must stay behind the line (on the bank) when throwing the bags. The ducks must stay in the pond at all times, but may run around any area of the pond. Ducks may use running, jumping, or any movement to avoid being hunted. If winners are chosen according to the amount of time a duck or a team of ducks can stay alive in the pond, once a duck is hit, he or she must leave the pond immediately.

EAGLE AND CHICKENS
Charlie Song
Appropriate for replication.

Players:

Pre-teens and young teens.

Object of game for players:

One person tries to catch another at the end of a line of people. The eagle tries to catch the chicken at the end of the line by touching him or her to score a point.

Number of players:

Six to 16.

Costume, apparel/equipment required:

Comfortable exercise clothes and shoes.

Area/arena/field where played—space required:

An open play area about 20 x 20 meters.

Time length of game. How is end of game determined?

Each game is played in a timed period and the scores are recorded. Each game lasts one to two minutes depending upon the age of the players. After each catch, the play restarts. If the line is broken apart, the eagle earns a point and the play restarts. The game ends after a preset amount of time or when the eagle has accumulated a preset number of points.

Symbolism of game:

The game inspires the spirit of team unity, courage, strategy, and fair play.

Rules of play, including scoring:

One person is chosen to be the eagle and another group to be chickens. The chickens form a line by each one holding the waist of the person in front of him or her. The first person in the line is the chicken mom, who may extend her arms wide to protect the rest of her chickens. The game starts with the eagle facing the chicken mom with the line of chickens behind her. The eagle may run around freely to catch the chickens by touching them, but is not allowed to go under the arms of the chicken mom. The game may be played with two teams of players competing against each other by choosing two or three eagles from each team.

FIRECRACKER RINGS
Charlie Song
Not appropriate for replication.

Players:

Usually young adult males.

Object of game for players:

A firecracker is used to send a ring into the air and two teams compete to catch it and place it in a basket. The game has been popularly played by the Dong, Miao, Shund, and Molao people for more than 500 years.

Number of players:

Twenty.

Costume, apparel/equipment required:

Uniforms similar to those worn by soccer or rugby players, metal rings 50 millimeters in diameter covered by red ribbons, and firecrackers used to fire the rings approximately 20 meters into the air.

Area/arena/field where played—space required:

An open grass field that is surrounded by a line 50 x 60 meters. A 5-meter diameter circle called the firing zone is drawn in the center of the field. A box zone of 6 x 4 meters is drawn and connects to the base lines at each end of the field. A decorated basket is placed in the center of each box zone. A red flag 0.5 to 0.6 meters high is placed at each line intersection on the field.

Time length of game. How is end of game determined?

A game lasts 40 minutes with a 10-minute half-time intermission.

Symbolism of game:

Originally, the game was only played with three rings and three firecrackers. Catching the first ring symbolized prosperity of life and good fortune to come. The second catch indicated another harvest, and the third ring forecasted a peaceful life and wishes coming true. Today this is a beloved game played by many young people and it is an official competition in China's National Peasants' Games.

Rules of play, including scoring:

Two teams compete against each other with ten players on each team. Players try to catch the ring after it's fired into the air. The team possessing the ring may use passing, throwing, rolling, or any necessary skills and team effort to place the ring into the basket of their own side. The defensive players try to stop the opponents' action and gain possession of the ring. Substitution is allowed at any time during the game and there is no limit to the number of substitutions that can be made. One point is awarded for placing the ring into the basket. Another ring is fired after the previous one is placed into the basket. In places or countries where fire crackers are banned, throwing flash lights can be substituted.

HO CHAI KUNG (MASTER HO CHAI)

Charlie Song
Appropriate for replication.

Players:

Teens.

Object of game for players:

To pay tribute to Master Ho Chai Kung.

Number of players:

No limit.

Costume, apparel/equipment required:

None.

Area/arena/field where played—space required:

No space limit.

Time length of game. How is end of game determined?:

No time limit.

Symbolism of game:

Master Ho Chai is a historical Chinese monk who helped others to cope with their difficulties, especially their illnesses. Master Ho Chai (Ho Chai Kung) is one of the supernatural figures the Chinese worship and rely on to help them solve their problems.

Rules of play, including scoring:

One player is a chaser who catches other players. The other players have to say Master Ho Chai (Ho Chai Kung) before they are caught (touched or grabbed) by the chaser. If a player fails to say the name, he or she loses and becomes the chaser. To rescue a player, other players have to do two things: (1) touch the frozen player and (2) say "Chee Tong Shan" (the happy medicine).

JINGLUO (HEALTH BALLS)
Rosabel S. Koss
Not appropriate for replication.

Players:

Males and females of all ages.

Object of game for players:

To strengthen the hand and improve general health. Several hundred years' practice has proven that regular use of health balls can strengthen the hands and arms, promote good blood circulation, improve the central nervous system and the memory, coordinate the functions of different parts of the body, and even prolong life. The Chinese believe that doing hand exercises with the balls can also help prevent or cure problems such as numbness or tremors in the hand, arthritis, high blood pressure, and diseases related to the nervous system. They believe they can help the aged to build up physical strength.

Number of players:

One.

Costume, apparel/equipment required:

A pair of special balls that have tones, with one sound pitched high and the other sound pitched low. These special balls make sounds as they are moved around in the hand.

Area/arena/field where played—space required:

Anywhere.

Time length of game. How is end of game determined?:

Each game ends when one or more balls are dropped.

Symbolism of game:

For a longer, more balanced life, one must wear off sharp defensive edges and become more like a ball, well-rounded, able to roll with ups and downs, no matter what happens.

Rules of play, including scoring:

Place two balls on your palm, crook and stretch the five fingers in sequence to cause the balls to rotate and revolve either clockwise or counter-clockwise. When doing this, all the joints of the hand are always in motion. Crooking and stretching the fingers involves the forearm muscles, which are contracted and relaxed harmonically. At first you may select balls of small size, but when skilled, you can select larger balls. Smaller hands require smaller balls. The two hands may practice one at a time, in alternation, or in unison. Three or four balls may be put on the palm at one time when skilled. The balls may clash in an unskilled hand, however, they move freely with practice. Some people can even rotate three or four balls with one hand with ease.

LAYING A RAILWAY TRACK
Shen Xun-zhang
Not appropriate for replication.

Players:

Pre-teens and young teens.

Object of game for players:

To improve running speed.

Number of players:

Sixteen.

Costume, apparel/equipment required:

Surveyor's poles and gymnastic bars.

Area/arena/field where played—space required:

Vacant lot, one gymnastic bar for each player, and four surveyor's poles. Two parallel lines are drawn at intervals of 20 meters on the playground, one as a starting point, the other as a terminus point, which has the four surveyor's poles set at intervals of two meters.

Time length of game. How is end of game determined?:

When the railway track is completed.

Symbolism of game:

Teaching means of construction.

Rules of play, including scoring:

Competitors are divided into four groups with equal numbers. With a gymnastic bar in hand, each person stands at the back of the starting line in columns. The first person runs out when the starting gun goes off. Players run toward the surveyor's pole (one pole to each group), go around the pole, and put the gymnastic bars down against it. Players run back quickly and clap the next person's hand. The second player runs out in the same way. He or she also puts his or her bar down close to the first person's bar at intervals of one meter so as to form a railway track. Then the player quickly returns and claps the third player's hand. Players continue as above. A player waiting to be clapped on the hand must stand behind the starting line. If the surveyor's pole is knocked down the player who knocked it has to straighten it up. The group that makes a better railway track wins the game.

RIDING A BICYCLE AT A SLOW PACE
Shen Xun-zhang
Not appropriate for replication.

Players:

All ages.

Object of game for players:

To improve equilibrium.

Number of players:

One per bicycle.

Costume, apparel/equipment required:

Bicycles.

Area/arena/field where played—space required:

A 20-meter runway in a track-and-field venue.

Time length of game. How is end of game determined?:

When a player or group of players wins a match.

Symbolism of game:

Teaching control and balance.

Rules of play, including scoring:

Players sit on bicycles waiting for the starting sound; one leg may be propped on the ground. After the starting sound, each player begins riding his or her bicycle straight ahead, the slower, the better. Going in turns, the player who spends the most time getting to the terminus point wins the match. Also, the group with the longest time wins the match. Riders cannot go backwards or place feet on the ground, they cannot interfere with other riders, and they cannot leave their assigned lanes.

SHUTTLECOCK
Charlie Song
Appropriate for replication.

Players:

All ages.

Object of game for players:

Tossing a shuttlecock and keeping it from falling to the ground by using a variety of tossing skills. Shuttlecock was initially played by the ancient Chinese during the Han Dynasty around 200 B.C. as a leisure activity. By the time of the South and North Dynasty (420–581 A.D.), the game reached its highest popularity in China.

Number of players:

One player per shuttlecock.

Costume, apparel/equipment required:

A shuttlecock, which traditionally was made by sewing a few goose feathers to a money coin that had a hole in the center. Shuttlecocks can also be made from a piece of round metal glued with some paper or cloth tassels on it, or it can be manufactured from plastic.

Area/arena/field where played—space required:

Any indoor or outdoor area where there is enough space to play.

Time length of game. How is end of game determined?:

Variable.

Symbolism of game:

Overcoming gravity with agility.

Rules of play, including scoring:

Skills: A wide variety of skills are used to toss a shuttlecock and they involve many parts of the body. The main tossing techniques are performed by using the legs and feet such as:

1. Knocking: bending the knee and knocking the shuttlecock with the top surface of the knee.
2. Kicking: kicking the shuttlecock with the top front area of the feet or the heels in the back (some elite players can do this).
3. Bouncing: using either the interior or exterior sides of the feet to bounce the shuttlecock up into the air.

Other parts of the body such as the forehead, shoulders, chest, or even the abdominal area are used to toss the shuttlecock.

Rules: Few rules are established other than the universal agreement that the upper limbs are not allowed to toss the shuttlecock. Competition may be judged in terms of:

1. The length of time the shuttlecock is kept from falling to the ground.
2. The complexity of using combinations of skills to toss the shuttlecock (need experienced judges).
3. The cooperation between players during a team competition.

Benefits: Participation in the game of shuttlecock may improve balance, cardiovascular capacity, body-eye coordination, and agility.

SUB TSE KAR TAU FU
(THE CROSS AND THE BEAN CURD)
Susanna Chow
Appropriate for replication.

Players:

Pre-teens and young teens.

Object of game for players:

To trick the other players out of their corners and to take that space.

Number of players:

Five.

Costume, apparel/equipment required:

None.

Area/arena/field where played—space required:

A space with four corners.

Time length of game. How is end of game determined?:

No time limit.

Symbolism of game:

Conveys the importance of having a space or home of your own, teaches directional concepts (east, south, west, north, cross, or middle), and develops creativity.

Rules of play, including scoring:

One player at each corner (north, east, south, west), and one player in the middle. The middle player requires the other players to perform a number of difficult tasks necessary to take over one of the corners. For example: players are asked to hop on one foot (imagining they are hopping barefooted on a hot sandy beach) until the middle player says stop, and then they all run to take up a corner. The player who is last becomes the middle player.

TIN HA TAI PING (PEACE IN THE WORLD)
Susanna Chow
Not appropriate for replication.

Players:

Pre-teens and young teens.

Object of game for players:

A pencil and paper task in which the players build a castle, weapons, and military defenses before attacking another player's castle.

Number of players:

Two.

Costume, apparel/equipment required:

Paper and pencil.

Area/arena/field where played—space required:

Anywhere.

Time length of game. How is end of game determined?:

When one of the players' castles is destroyed.

Symbolism of game:

The irony of peace and war.

Rules of play, including scoring:

Every time a player wins in the game of "box, scissors, and handkerchief" (played like rock-paper-scissors), he or she can build his or her castle, weapons, and defenses step by step. The player first writes the four Chinese characters meaning Peace in the world (Tin Ha Tai Ping) one stroke at a time within a four-square castle. This is followed by the building of cannons, and then the defense shield. Ironically, once these are written, the player can proceed to destroy the defense shield, weapons, and castle (in that order) of the other player by winning and systematically destroying the other castle. This is achieved through continued rounds of "box, scissors, handkerchief." Players continue until one of the players loses everything.

TONG CHI DUL
(SUGAR STICKING TO THE BEANS)

Susanna Chow
Appropriate for replication.

Players:

Pre-teens and teens.

Object of game for players:

The players need to stick together to avoid being tagged by the chaser.

Number of players:

At least three.

Costume, apparel/equipment required:

None.

Area/arena/field where played—space required:

Can be played anywhere with a space large enough for players to run freely.

Time length of game. How is end of game determined?:

No time limit.

Symbolism of game:

To reflect the Chinese use of physical properties of objects to describe human relationships. When cooking beans with sugar, they stick together; when mixing oil with water, they do not mix. This game teaches children that they can turn to a friend when they are in trouble.

This is used to describe the existence or absence of closeness or bonding between two people.

Rules of play, including scoring:

Another version of the tag game in which the chaser has to catch a player to replace him- or herself as chaser. Catching is accomplished by the chaser touching a player who is alone. Any player standing alone can be caught by the chaser. If one player is in danger of being caught, another player can come to the rescue. If the player is caught, however, the player will lose and become the chaser.

TUNG NAM SAI BUCK
(EAST SOUTH WEST NORTH)
Susanna Chow
Not appropriate for replication.

Players:

Male and female young teens.

Object of game for players:

To find out specific messages or follow specific instructions.

Number of players:

Two or more.

Costume, apparel/equipment required:

An origami "toy" that is handmade by the players and inscribed with personal messages or instructions.

Area/arena/field where played—space required:

Any location.

Time length of game. How is end of game determined?:

No time limit.

Symbolism of game:

To educate children in the directions, east, south, west, and north, and create and carry out new tasks or ideas.

Rules of play, including scoring:

Players first fold an origami toy and write eight tasks or messages on the inside flaps of the folds. The first player manipulates the folded origami to reveal a message or an action according to the direction and number of times the other player specified. The player who does not follow the required actions will lose his or her turn.

WA TZE (LITTLE RICE BAGS)
Susanna Chow
Appropriate for replication.

Players:

Male and female young teens.

Object of game for players:

To use fine dexterity skills that involve picking, throwing, and catching small rice bags with the hand. Progressively more difficult levels of play.

Number of players:

No limit.

Costume, apparel/equipment required:

Usually five small bags filled with rice, either 2-inch cubic squares or cubic rectangles.

Area/arena/field where played—space required:

Any location.

Time length of game. How is end of game determined?:

No time limit.

Symbolism of game:

A traditional Chinese game often played indoors by girls. Because they are of food, the handmade rice bags reinforce gender stereotyping.

Rules of play, including scoring:

Simple Level: A player throws one rice bag in the air while picking up another from the ground. The player then puts that rice bag down and proceeds to the next. This is done one at a time until five bags are collected. The first player to collect five bags wins the round; several rounds are played.

Intermediate Level: This is similar to the first level except that the player retains two rice bags in his or her hand while picking up and catching the next rice bag.

Next Levels: A player picks up two or three bags at a time and then follows the same pattern.

Please Note: Players can invent their own rules such as catching the rice bag with the back of the hand instead of the palm.

India

KABADDI

A. K. Banerjee, S. Dhabe, and Myrna Schild
Appropriate for replication.

Players:

Male and female teens.

Object of game for players:

To learn a popular raiding game from India for improving agility and the ability to breathe while running.

Number of players:

Classroom group in two teams of 10 to 20.

Costume, apparel/equipment required:

Palla, or center line.

Area/arena/field where played—space required:

Playing field.

Time length of game. How is end of game determined?:

Two 20-minute halves with a five-minute rest period between halves.

Symbolism of game:

The influence of the Colonial British custom of physical education that is taught through universal, compulsory, and free education to students up to 14 years of age.

Rules of play, including scoring:

Captains toss to determine the first raiding team. Teams take positions on each half of the playing area. The teams alternate raids and only one player raids at a time. The raiding player assumes a position on or near the palla (center line). The raider, taking a deep breath, repeats loudly "Kabaddi," while advancing into the opponents' area to tag as many opponents as possible before running out of breath. The raider must return to the Palla before running out of breath or risk capture by the opponents. Points are accumulated for the number of opponents tagged by each raider and for the number of raiders that are caught. The game should be supervised by a referee.

Korea

ARROW-THROWING GAME

Ok Soo cha

Not appropriate for replication.

Players:

Male and female children and teens.

Object of game for players:

To strengthen and improve the balance of the body, for the purpose of serving guests.

Number of players:

Usually two.

Costume, apparel/equipment required:

Traditional Korean clothes, arrows, and a large, bronze, conical pot.

Area/arena/field where played—space required:

Outside area.

Time length of game. How is end of game determined?:

No limit.

Symbolism of game:

This is one of the games enjoyed by the former royal families and nobles. This game was played to show the hospitality of good manners from Dang time. This game was played in Korea from early Chosun times.

Rules of play, including scoring:

Place a bronze pot at the center of a grass field or a floor. Divide the players into East and West teams, and start throwing the arrows into the pot from 10 steps away. In throwing arrows care must be taken to balance both shoulders.

The winner is the player who throws the most arrows into the pot. Winning is called *Hyun* and losing is called *Pulseoug* (no winner). *Ilho* (one arrow) refers to only one arrow making it into the pot. If throwing in a palace the king can give the prize to the winning team.

DAH RAM JUI UI SOH POONG
(SQUIRREL'S PICNIC)
Myrna Schild
Not appropriate for replication.

Players:

Male and female teens.

Object of game for players:

To improve coordination, timing, and dance skills. To learn about the culture of Korea through dance.

Number of players:

Classroom group.

Costume, apparel/equipment required:

The Jae Hoon Park composition "Dah Ram Jui" with lyrics by Young Il Kim.

Area/arena/field where played—space required:

Gymnasium or school hall.

Time length of game. How is end of game determined?:

As directed by the teacher.

Symbolism of game:

Represents the Koreans love of music and dance and their unique music and dance traditions. This dance represents happy Korean children portraying the joyful outing of a squirrel's picnic.

Rules of play, including scoring:

Form a single circle with dancers facing the center of the circle, hands clasped.

The music is in a slightly fast 2/4 beat. There is a four-measure introduction. The following list explains what to do during each measure after the introduction.*

Measure

1–2	1 schottische step forward, starting with right foot
3–4	1 schottische step backward, starting with left foot
5–6	2 step-hops forward, starting with right foot
7–8	2 step-hops backward, starting with right foot
9–10	1 grapevine schottische (right back, right hop)
11–12	1 grapevine schottische (left back, left hop)
13–16	While jumping, clap hands at the same time
13	1 jump with plié forward
14	1 jump with plié backward
15	2 jumps right and left
16	1 jump in place with pli[e-acute] and hold

Repeat the dance from the beginning

Notes on Style: On all hops, the lifted legs have the following shape: leg is bent about two degrees (about 130 degrees). Knees face outside, lower leg faces outside, too (somewhat like the forward attitude shape in

*Choreography by Moon Ja Minn Suhr, 1984

ballet), and the foot is flexed. The hop step is modified from a Korean traditional farmer's dance.

Rhythm and Word Cues

1–4	Three steps forward, hop, three steps back, hop
5–8	Forward step, hop, forward step, hop, back step, hop, back step, hop
9–12	Right back, right hop, left back, left hop
13–16	Jump forward, jump back, jump right, jump left, jump in place

FOX-FOX GAME

Ok Soo cha
Appropriate for replication.

Players:

Males and females of all ages.

Object of game for players:

To foster a spirit of cooperation in a game to enjoy anytime, anywhere.

Number of players:

Usually six to seven.

Costume, apparel/equipment required:

None.

Area/arena/field where played—space required:

Any location.

Time length of game. How is end of game determined?:

The playing time varies.

Symbolism of game:

The enjoyment of old Korean songs that have been passed down in an oral tradition.

Rules of play, including scoring:

Using a rock-scissors-paper game, the players decide who will be the tagger. The tagger (the fox) squats 3 to 4 meters away. The rest of the players hold hands to form a line. They walk closer and closer to the tagger while singing this song:

> *Went over a first hill, oh! My legs!*
> *Went over a second hill, oh! My legs!*
> *Went over a third hill, oh! My legs!*

Then they approach the tagger and ask:

> *Fox! Fox! What are you doing?* (all together)
> *Sleeping* (the tagger answers)
> *Sleepyhead* (all together)
> *Washing my face* (the tagger)
> *Dandy* (all together)
> *Eating rice* (the tagger)
> *What kind of rice* (all together)
> *Maggot rice* (the tagger)
> *What food?* (all together)
> *A frog* (the tagger)
> *Alive or dead?* (all together)
> *Dead (or alive)* (the tagger)

If the tagger says "dead," the players may not move. If anyone moves, he or she will be the next tagger. If the tagger says "alive," the players must quickly run away. While running away, if the tagger says "Stand there," the players must stop where they are. Again, if a player moves, he or she will be the next tagger.

GATE GAME
Ok Soo cha
Appropriate for replication.

Players:

Males and females of all ages.

Object of game for players:

To understand how words and sentences are joined through songs.

Number of players:

No limit.

Costume, apparel/equipment required:

Comfortable style.

Area/arena/field where played—space required:

A wide open place such as a playground.

Time length of game. How is end of game determined?:

No limit.

Symbolism of game:

All fences can be scaled.

Rules of play, including scoring:

Koreans play this game any time with unlimited numbers of participants. Two players hold their hands together to make a gate. The rest of
the players stand in a line by holding the waist of the person in front of
them with both arms. Players then go in and out of the gate bent at their
waists. The object is to sing the gate-opening words, which are prechosen.
When the right words are sung the two players forming the gate open the
gate and let the line pass through.

SEE-SAW
Ok Soo cha
Not appropriate for replication.

Players:

Usually female pre-teens and teens.

Object of game for players:

For women to see outside beyond a fence in the Chosun Dynasty, when
women were forbidden to go outside.

Number of players:

Usually three.

Costume, apparel/equipment required:

Seesaws and *Hanbok* (traditional Korean clothes).

Area/arena/field where played—space required:

Open area outdoors.

Time length of game. How is end of game determined?:

No limit.

Symbolism of game:

This is a representative play for women, enjoyed nationwide on the Great Holidays such as Dan-O in May and Chuseok in August, including the first day of the Lunar New Year.

Rules of play, including scoring:

Two players, each standing on one end of the seesaw, begin to jump up slowly by turns, holding the handle. A person at the center of the board stabilizes it with his or her hands for support. Two players jump up in turns, pushed up by the power of the other's gravity, and they soar higher and higher as they continue jumping.

This is too strenuous to play for a long time without a break. It is desirable, therefore, that a number of people participate in this game. And it is good sportsmanship for subsequent players to wait their turns.

SSIRUM WRESTLING
Jong-Hoon Yu
Not appropriate for replication.

Players:

Male wrestling partners of any age matched by weight.

Object of game for players:

Two wrestlers each try to throw the other to the ground.

Number of players:

Two.

Costume, apparel/equipment required:

Korean traditional pants (*satpa*).

Area/arena/field where played—space required:

Played on a round sand mat nine meters in diameter.

Time length of game. How is end of game determined?:

The game ends when one wrestler touches the ground with any part of his body other than his feet.

Symbolism of game:

Competing strength. Involves a variety of skills, including gripping, tripping, and throwing. This game has been popular in Korea since ancient times and dates back at least 1,500 years. It is a major event of the festive programs of Tano (the fifth day of the fifth lunar month). The winner is awarded the title Super Strong Man, and Ox. Competitions are now held in divisions based on weight.

Rules of play, including scoring:

Each wrestler binds his loins and the upper thigh of his right leg with a two-foot long cloth called satpa. One uses a red satpa and the other blue. Each wrestler grasps the other's satpa in the right hand at the loins and in the left hand at the thigh. At the referee's signal, the two wrestlers stand, pushing, pulling, and employing a variety of tactics.

STONE-THROWING GAME
Ok Soo cha
Not appropriate for replication.

Players:

Males and females of all ages.

Object of game for players:

To feel achievement and pride. To improve running ability and control within a limited space. To improve consciousness and the ability to understand rules. To improve spatial awareness and judgment through trial and error by throwing.

Number of players:

Usually two to eight.

Costume, apparel/equipment required:

A stone for each team. Comfortable, casual wear. A *mozka*, which is like a small weight or cloth.

Area/arena/field where played—space required:

Any designated area indoors or out.

Time length of game. How is end of game determined?:

It varies.

Symbolism of game:

There are two stories of the origin of this game. The first is that it originated in the people's resentment toward Songduk Monument, which was a traditional relic of the feudalistic bureaucratic system. The other is that it originated in a stone-throwing fight as the first act of self-protection since the appearance of the first human beings.

Rules of play, including scoring:

Using the rock-scissors-paper game to determine who goes first, the losing team must draw a line at three to four meters' distance and place a ten-centimeter stone on it. The player going first then does the following:

1. The player going first hits the other's stone on the line with the mozka from his or her line.
2. The player throws his mozka at a distance and jumps up three times with just one leg, and then hits it with his stone.
3. The player puts the mozka on his or her right foot, jumps up one time on the left leg, and then hits the stone with the mozka on the foot.
4. The player holds the mozka with the right hand and hits it by throwing it through the right leg.
5. The player puts the mozka on his stomach and walks forward.
6. The player puts the mozka on his or her shoulder and walks forward.
7. The player puts the mozka on his or her cheek and walks forward.
8. The player puts the mozka on his or her forehead and walks with hands folded behind his or her back.
9. The player puts the mozka on his or her buttocks and walks backward.

TAEKWONDO*

Willy Pieter

Not appropriate for replication.

Players:

Males and females of any age. Typically, however, those in the age range of about six to about thirty years will be engaged in so-called free-sparring competition.

Object of game for players:

The game consists of attacking with arms and legs. The techniques used include punches with the fists, blocking with the arms, and kicking with the legs. In some cases players may choose to execute jump kicks. There are two broad categories in which players may participate. One is in forms (*p'umse*) and the other is in free sparring (*gyorugi*). In forms, the player will go through a predetermined set of attacking and blocking techniques. In many cases, the player will perform the skills in four different directions: forward, backward, left, and right. However, there are also forms in a straight line (left to right) or even with steps taken diagonally. In free sparring, the players kick and punch each other with the aim

*This game is best played with a qualified Taekwondo instructor in charge.

of scoring points. Those with the most points at the end of the game, win. It is also possible to win by causing a knock-out or technical knock-out.

Number of players:

Forms are usually done individually, but during competition players will also have the option of performing as part of a team. There is no set rule for the number of participants on a team for forms competition. Most often a team will consist of three members, but it is possible to have four- or even five-member teams. The team members perform the forms all at the same time in a synchronized fashion. Free sparring is a bout between two players. Although it is possible to have team competition in free sparring, the bouts can only be between two players at any one time.

Costume, apparel/equipment required:

For forms, a standard two-piece white uniform, which is similar to but lighter than a judo uniform, is worn with a black-rimmed V-neck in the top if a player has reached the so-called black-belt level. Those who have not yet attained this level wear all-white uniforms. A belt, indicating the rank of the player, complements the attire. In free sparring, protective equipment is worn in addition to the aforementioned uniform. In addition to from a foam rubber helmet, the players also wear a chest protector, forearm and shin pads, as well as a groin cup for both genders. For both forms and free sparring the players are barefoot.

Area/arena/field where played—space required:

The competition area is a 12 meter x 12 meter ring, which usually is not matted. Some countries have adopted the safety measure of matting the ring to help reduce injuries, but as of this writing the official international rules have not yet followed suit. Within the larger 12 meter x 12 meter ring, there is a smaller 8 meter x 8 meter area within which the actual free-sparring competition takes place. Forms competition is not necessarily restricted to this smaller area, however. The aforementioned requirements are for competition purposes only. When training, any flat-surfaced area will suffice. Indoor training usually takes place in a gymnasium. Outdoor training may be done on a beach or on a grass field. Competition, however, is always indoors.

Time length of game. How is end of game determined?:

Training may vary, depending on local circumstances. A typical training session may be from one to two hours. Forms competition is also

variable, depending on the length of the form, but all forms can be performed within two to three minutes each. Free-sparring bouts are three
rounds of three minutes each with a one-minute break between rounds.
If pressed for time, tournament organizers may decide to shorten the
bouts to three rounds of two minutes each with a 30-second break in
between rounds.

Symbolism of game:

Taekwondo is a twentieth-century sport, but is based on older martial
symbolism that is characteristic of the society in which it originated.
Similar to other combative games, taekwondo free-sparring competition
may be thought of as combat between two individuals. Instead of killing
the opponent, out-scoring him or her is now the objective. Forms training
or competition, however, is rooted in a more complicated symbolism. In
this case, a form may be considered as communication between the individual and nature. The performer has to transcend his or her physical self
beyond the dichotomizing boundaries of the mind. The player will have
to become one with the form to achieve a state where subject and object
are one. Since taekwondo is a new and competition-oriented game, the
symbolism of its forms is not immediately clear to the participants.

Rules of play, including scoring:

There are eight weight divisions for each gender according to the
following breakdown:

Division	Males	Females
Fin	less than or equal to 50kg	less than or equal to 43kg
Fly	> 50–54 kg	> 43–47 kg
Bantam	> 54–58 kg	> 47–51 kg
Feather	> 58–64 kg	> 51–55 kg
Light	> 64–70 kg	> 55–60 kg
Welter	> 70–76 kg	> 60–65 kg
Middle	> 76–83 kg	> 65–70 kg
Heavy	> 83 kg	> 70 kg

Legitimate techniques and targets include punches and kicks to the trunk
covered by the chest protector and to the face and side of the head.
To help prevent injuries as a result of falls after a kick, the players wear
helmets covering the top, back, and sides of the head. One point is
awarded for each accurate and powerful technique to legal target areas of
the body. The player with the most points accumulated at the end of the
bout, wins. No score will be awarded (a) if the player falls on purpose

after the delivery of his or her technique; (b) if the player commits an illegal act after delivering a blow, or (c) if he or she incurs a penalty.

Penalties are divided into warnings and deductions. Two warnings are counted as one deduction point, but the last odd-numbered warning will not count toward the grand total of points. If the player incurs three deduction points in one round he or she will be declared the loser. The following table displays the warnings and deductions.

Warnings	Deductions
Grabbing the adversary	Attacking the fallen opponent
Pushing the fellow participant with the shoulder, body, hands, or arms	Intentionally attacking after the referee has declared a break up
Holding the other player with the hand or arms	Attacking the back or the back of the head on purpose
Intentionally going out of bounds	Excessive contact of the face with the hands or the fists
Avoiding an attack by turning one's back to the other player	Butting
Falling down on purpose	Throwing the fellow participant
Pretending to have sustained an injury	Violent or abusive remarks or behavior on the part of the participant or the coach
Attacking the knee	
Intentionally attacking the groin of the other player	
Intentionally stepping on or kicking the legs or feet of the other player	
Hitting or punching the adversary's face with the hands or fists	
Gesturing to indicate a score or a deduction point by raising one's hand	
Any undesirable remarks or misbehavior on the part of the participant or the coach	

In the case of a tie, the head referee will decide who the winner is based on superiority as evidenced by the initiative taken by the players. Winning can be accomplished by:

- Effecting a knockout (K.O.).
- Referee stopping the contest (RSC).
- Accumulated scores.
- Withdrawal of the other player.
- Disqualification of the other player.
- Referee's decision based on number of penalties sustained by the other player.
- Knockdown.

TOAD'S HOUSE GAME
Ok Soo cha
Not appropriate for replication.

Players:

Male and female children.

Object of game for players:

To strengthen hands by playing with soil, and making a "toad's house."

Number of players:

Usually two to three.

Costume, apparel/equipment required:

Wet sand or soil.

Area/arena/field where played—space required:

Under the eaves in the shadow or at the main entrance of the house.

Time length of game. How is end of game determined?:

No limit.

Symbolism of game:

This originated from a play with soil called "toad's house game," which two or three boys sat and played under the eaves, in the shade, or at the main entrance of the house in summer.

Rules of play, including scoring:

Players collect wet sand or soil. While singing a song, they put their left hands on a mound of sand or soil and pat it with their right hands until it is strong enough to remain standing. Players then pull out their left hands carefully. If a cave remains, the player wins the game. If it is destroyed, the player loses the game. The song that is sung while making a toad's house is as follows:

> *Toad! Toad! I build your house. Give me my house.*
> *With a cow foot on it, with a magpie's foot on it, it is okay.*
> *No worry about falling down, just be built well.*

Songs sung while making a toad's house vary according to region.

Philippines

LUKSONG TINIK
(HURDLING SPANS OF HANDS
OR HURDLING THORNS)

Edna B. Reyes
Appropriate for replication.

Players:

Male and female teens of the Tagalog Region, playing separately.

Object of game for players:

To build human hurdles with hands and feet that jumpers will try to hurdle without touching.

Number of players:

Variable, split evenly into two teams.

Costume, apparel/equipment required:

None.

Area/arena/field where played—space required:

Outdoors, preferably in a grassy area.

Time length of game. How is end of game determined?:

Not available.

Symbolism of game:

Filipinos like to play games because of their sociability. Games serve to bring members of the family together after chores have been done in the home and neighborhood. Games strengthen the ties that bind families.

Rules of play, including scoring:

Two members of the team sit on the ground facing each other. Around six to ten meters away from them, a line is drawn and the jumping team falls into line.

The two players on the ground extend their right feet forward and press their soles against each other. One by one the members of the opposing team jump over the right feet of the players on base, then return to the back of the line. The two seated players then press the soles of their left feet together and put them on top of the two right feet. The jumpers take turns in jumping and returning behind the line again. One of the seated players stretches one hand and puts it on the toes of the left feet. Each member of the opposing team jumps over the hand. The other seated player adds a hand to the "hurdle." The opponents jump one after the other. (Note: the two seated players keep on adding hands until what is known as the "hurdle of thorns" is completed, with four hands stacked on top of four feet. The opponents jump every time a hand is added).

For Three or More Players to a Team: A third player joins the two seated players on base. This player stands or kneels behind one of the seated players then adds one more hand to the top of the hurdle. The opposing team jumps. Optional: Another player stands behind one of the seated players and stretches an arm to cover the side gap between the head of the seated player and the tip of the hurdle.

Note: If a child touches any part of the hands while jumping, the seated player whose clothes or body was touched shouts *"Nasaleng"* (touched!), and the mother comes forward to save the touched child. The mother jumps again on behalf of the child touched. Should the mother fail, the two teams exchange places and the game starts all over again.

When none of the jumpers touches, the game starts all over again with the same teams performing the same roles.

- Players must clear obstacles without touching them with any part of their bodies or clothing.
- Obstacles can go as high as four feet above the ground.
- Players are divided into two equal groups.
- Leaders are called *"nanay"* (mother), and are supposed to be the best high jumpers in the group; the rest of the players are the *"anak"* (children).

PALO SEBO (GREASED BAMBOO CLIMBING)
Francis D. Magno
Not appropriate for replication.

Players:

Young male teens.

Object of game for players:

To climb a greased pole and seize the prize at the top.

Number of players:

Two or more.

Costume, apparel/equipment required:

Long, stout, well-polished bamboo poles, each around four inches in diameter. The poles are lavishly greased to make them slippery.

Area/arena/field where played—space required:

Outdoors in a wide open area like a town plaza. Played during town fiestas or on special occasions.

Time length of game. How is end of game determined?:

No limit.

Symbolism of game:

The long practice of climbing rough tree trunks.

Rules of play, including scoring:

This game takes place against a background of music provided by the town brass band playing such seemingly out of place tunes as "The William Tell Overture." The music is reduced to the brass and drums when the spectators start screaming and shouting as they root for a young friend or relative slipping and sliding every inch of the way as he tries to climb a greased pole. Experience climbing rough tree trunks is no guarantee of winning. The last two or three feet to the top of the pole are practically dripping with tons of fat and grease. Many an expert tree climber finds himself slipping and falling helplessly to the ground.

Pre-Game:
Ground Preparation: A small bag containing a prize (money or gift) is tied to the top of a pole before it is planted securely in the ground. Colorful strips of rice paper or ribbons are usually used to decorate each pole.
Formation: For older players a pole is assigned to each player. The player stands at the foot of the pole assigned to him. Other volunteers stand behind him ready to play if the first player drops from the pole.
Objective: To climb a slippery pole and get the prize hanging at the top.
Movements:
1. At a given signal, the boys attempt to scamper up the poles. (Note: In a situation where the first player to climb the pole slides down, he is immediately replaced by the second player behind him. Unless the player slides down, no one else is supposed to climb after him.)
2. If a player is able to reach the top of the pole, he unties the prize and then slides down to the ground.
3. The first player to reach the ground with the prize in his hand is declared the winner. In addition to the pole prize, he receives an extra prize from the town officials.

Alternate Version (For Young Boys)
Pre-Game:
About three to four players form a team at the foot of each bamboo pole. The best climber is first in the line.
Movements:
1. The first player climbs the pole. As soon as his feet are off the ground the second player starts climbing after him. The third player follows the second, and so on.
2. As soon as the first player starts slipping, the second player makes him stand on his shoulders. The third player makes the second player stand on his shoulders. The whole team inch their way up in this way, climbing to the top of the pole.
3. When the first player reaches the top, he gets the prize and the whole team slides down the pole to the ground.

4. The first team to get the prize from the top of their pole wins first prize in the competition. They receive sizable gifts, money, or toys from the game committee of the town fiesta.

Occasionally, a whole team slides down the pole without reaching the prize. This is the reason why some players hang around near the bamboo poles while a team is trying to climb. Players are allowed to use ashes or sand on their hands, legs, and feet to help them climb. However, no rope is allowed.

Alternate Regional Version:

Players try to climb a greased coconut tree to get a prize at the top.

PATINTERO

Francis D. Magno
Not appropriate for replication.

Players:

A group of male and female pre-teens. From ten years and above, males and females tend to group themselves according to sex.

Object of game for players:

A team of invaders attempts to cross over a line into enemy territory while a defensive team tries to stop them from succeeding in their mission.

Number of players:

Six to eight players is best.

Costume, apparel/equipment required:

Chalk or charcoal to draw the rectangular figure used in the game if playing on cement. If playing on the ground, a stick or poured water will work.

Area/arena/field where played—space required:

A designated rectangular area.

Time length of game. How is end of game determined?:

No limit.

Symbolism of game:

There are several regional variants of the patintero game in the Philippines but the structural pattern remains the same for all. When a guard tags an invader on any part of his body, this is symbolic that the invader has been caught and stopped. *Tubig* (water) is an element that plays a major role in this game, hence such names as *Tubig-Tubig, Tubigan,* or *Tubiganay* in many regions. Players pour water from coconut shells or cans to draw the rectangle and its lines on the dry baked ground. The use of water in games has been associated by nineteenth-century folklorists of the ritualistic schools, like Lady Alice Bertha Gomme, with water worship. Among many examples, Gomme points to Hindu brides who sprinkle their groom and the court of the new house with water by way of exorcism.

Rules of play, including scoring:

Pre-Game:

Assignment of roles: Two leaders are chosen or the two oldest or most aggressive players appoint themselves. The two leaders choose their members alternately from among players.

Deciding turns: The leader of each group fills his or her mouth with water. The two leaders stand side by side and each spits out the water in his mouth as far as he or she can. The one who spits farthest wins and his or her team plays first. The loser and his or her team are on base. Other methods popularly used to determine who plays first are: 1. *Tao o Ibon* (heads or tails) 2. *Tihaya o Taob* (right side or bottom's up) 3. *Jack En Poy* (finger flashing).

Ground preparation: A rectangle, about 5 x 6 meters, is drawn on the ground. Parallel lines are drawn inside the rectangle, the number of lines depending on the number of players. (Note: The player guarding line one is called *patoto* [leader]. This player has more power and privileges than anyone on his or her team. Only the patoto can guard the middle line [perpendicular to all the parallel lines]; the patoto stands guard from the outset and the patoto alone can come to the rescue of any of his or her players on any line.)

Objective: The object of the runners is to get through all the lines (1, 2, and 3) and then return without being tagged; the taggers try to block (*harang*) and tag the runners as they get near them or as they cross their lines.

Movements:

1. The leader of the team on base shouts "Game" and the taggers of his or her team stand with outstretched hands, ready to tag any member of the invading team. The members of the rival team all together try to penetrate the defenses of the guards on base by distracting and confusing the tagger on line one. (Note: As one by one the invading team gets inside the rectangle, all the guards run back and forth blocking with outstretched hands.)

2. As soon as one of the runners crosses line three, he or she turns around and tries to trace his or her way back and out through line one. The taggers concentrate on stopping the runner. (Note: This is because this player is about to finish *isang gabi* [one night] and will score a point for his team.)

3. When the runner gets out of the rectangle without being tagged he or she calls out *tubig!* (water!).

4. The same team runs in the second game if it scores three consecutive nights. The rival team stays on base for the second time. If a runner is tagged while trying to cross a line, the two teams exchange roles.

Penalties:

The following are some of the punishments imposed by the winners on the losers:

a. *Suot lungga* (enter the mouse hole): The members of the winning team form a line with their legs wide apart. The losing team is made to crawl between the legs of the winners in one direction then back in the other direction.

b. *Baba* (piggy-back ride): The winners are each given a ride on the backs of the losers.

c. *Bantilan* or *pitikan* (flicking knuckles of losers): This is done ten or 20 times to the losers.

d. Blow-out: Usually done during festivals, this requires the losers to treat the winners to some soft drinks or food after the game.

Regional Versions:

Harangang Taga: Tagalog (nueva Ecija)

Lumplumpas: Igorot (Bontoc)

Sabatan: Kapampangan (Bacalor, Pampanga)

Sinibon: Ilokano (San Jose, Nueva Ecija)

Tadlas: Tadlas (for four players), Birus-Birus (for six players), Visayas (Ormoc, Leyte)

Tubigan: Tagalog (Quezon City)

Tubig-Tubig: Visayan (Cebu)

Taiwan

WOOD BALL

David Chang Szn-Min
Not appropriate for replication.

Players:

Males and females of all ages.

Object of game for players:

Each team includes two to four players who, taking turns at hitting the ball, complete 12 fairway competitions (or two six-fairway cycles).

Number of players:

Eight to ten.

Costume, apparel/equipment required:

The equipment, made of wood, includes ball, mallet, and wicket. The ball is about 9.5 centimeters in diameter and weighs about 400 grams. The mallet has a T-shaped rubber-covered head for easy hitting. The wicket contains a two-bottle-shaped wooden frame from which a wine-glass-shaped wooden cup is suspended. The inside width of the wicket is

16 centimeters, and the bottom of the wooden wine-glass cup is seven centimeters above the ground.

Area/arena/field where played—space required:

A Standard Wood Ball course consists of 12 fairways. The length of each fairway is from 20 meters to 80 meters (including four short fairways, four middle fairways, and four long fairways); the width of the fairways is from two to ten meters; the total length of all the fairways together should be over 500 meters. Among the 12 fairways, there are two that are left-curve and two that are right-curve.

Time length of game. How is end of game determined?:

Variable.

Symbolism of game:

Hand-eye coordination.

Rules of play, including scoring:

1. Hitting: The player swings the mallet and hits the ball with the mallet head. Moving the ball a second time or hitting the ball with the side of the mallet head are prohibited.
2. Passing the wicket: While near the wicket, the player moves the ball with the mallet head and hits it to make the ball pass the gate successfully.
3. Fairway cycle: To complete one fairway contest, the player must hit with the mallet head, punching the wine-glass-shaped cup causing it to pass through the wicket.
4. Out of bounds: When the ball is hit outside the fairway, the new hitting point is a semicircle the distance of two mallet heads extended from the point where the ball went out of bounds. When scoring, an extra stroke is added as a penalty.
5. Score: The winner is the one who takes the fewest total strokes. If there is a tie, the winner is the one who took the lead in most fairways, or a tie-breaking game is held.

Thailand

NGU KIN HUNG (THE SNAKE EATS THE TAIL)

Myrna Schild

Appropriate for replication.

Players:

Male and female pre-teens.

Object of game for players:

To improve chasing and tagging skills.

Number of players:

Classroom group. One player is Father Snake, one is Mother Snake, and the rest are Baby Snakes.

Costume, apparel/equipment required:

None.

Area/arena/field where played—space required:

Outdoors or indoors.

Time length of game. How is end of game determined?:

Variable.

Symbolism of game:

Represents Thailand's education, which is free and compulsory for students from the ages of eight to 15 years and includes physical education for every grade.

Rules of play, including scoring:

Mother Snake stands with hands on her waist. First Baby Snake stands with hands on Mother's waist. Each Baby Snake stands with hands on waist of Baby in front. This pattern follows with all babies in a straight line.

1. Father asks Mother:

   "Where have you been, Mother?"

   Mother answers:

   "We have gone to drink water"

   Father asks:

   "To which pool did you go?"

   Mother answers:

   "To the sad pool"

   Mother and babies begin to sway from side to side crying. Father tries to grab the last baby in the line. Mother Snake extends her arms to protect her babies. The line of babies is allowed to move in order to flee from Father. If the last baby is caught or touched, that player is out of the game. The babies must try to hold fast to the waist of the baby in front of them or the line will break and it will be easier for Father to catch them.

2. In the second round, Father Snake asks the same questions. The Mother answers the last question: "To the *bird* pool." The Mother and all her babies wave their arms like birds in flight and then grab waists as before.

3. Other answers can be devised, for example, "To the *happy* pool" or "To the *elephant* pool," or some other pool that would be easy for the students to portray.

Vietnam

DRAGON STORY TAIL

Ken Hawkins

Appropriate for replication.

Players:

Male and female pre-teens and young teens.

Object of game for players:

To write, tell, or act out a story using the words or story starters written on "tails." Raise awareness of oral and written communication through games.

Number of players:

Unlimited.

Costume, apparel/equipment required:

Socks, streamers, or tags with story starters or topics.

Area/arena/field where played—space required:

Gymnasium.

Time length of game. How is end of game determined?:

When all of the tails are removed.

Symbolism of game:

Represents the rewards associated with perseverance.

Rules of play, including scoring:

Players tuck tails into their clothes on their backsides. The tails must be accessible and easy to pull off. Players begin in a circle formation and call out, "Dragon Story Tail!" Players run away and each one tries to pull off the tails of the other players as they protect their own tails. When someone's tail is snatched that player remains in the game and continues to try to pull tails. Play continues until all the story tails have been pulled. It is not a contest to see who pulls the most tails. The tails have words or story starters on them and individuals or groups are then asked to write, tell, or act out a story using the content from the tails.

PART IV

Europe

Austria

BIRD CATCHER
(ALSO CALLED DOG CATCHER)
Eileen Crowley Sullivan
Appropriate for replication.

Players:

Male and female pre-teens.

Object of game for players:

To avoid being tagged by the bird catcher.

Number of players:

Fifteen to 25, divided into four groups.

Costume, apparel/equipment required:

None.

Area/arena/field where played—space required:

Gymnasium, play area, or field.

Time length of game. How is end of game determined?:

As directed by the teacher.

Symbolism of game:

Represents hunting and survival, fitness, and courage.

Rules of play, including scoring:

Children are divided into four groups, each group named after a different bird. One child, the bird catcher, stands in the middle, and another, the mother bird, stands in a large area. The bird's nest is at the opposite end of the playing space from the birds. The mother bird calls one group of birds home. This group tries to run to the nest, past the bird catcher, without being tagged by him or her. Those tagged are out and go to an area outside the game, called the bird cage. After all four groups have been called home, the bird catcher's score is determined by the number of birds in the bird cage. *All* birds return to the starting line, and a new game starts with a new bird catcher and new mother (or father) bird. The bird catcher with the highest score wins. Those in the bird cage can pay a penalty such as doing 20 jumping jacks, then be let free.

Safety Precaution: Bird's nest should be a large enough area to accommodate all children running into it.

Belgium

MAKING RAIN IN THE RAIN FOREST

Erik De Vroede

Appropriate for replication.

Players:

Male and female young teens.

Object of game for players:

To make a "rainstorm" by making a sequence of motions, to work cooperatively in a group, and to raise environmental awareness through games.

Number of players:

Classroom group.

Costume, apparel/equipment required:

None.

Area/arena/field where played—space required:

Classroom.

Time length of game. How is end of game determined?:

As directed by the teacher.

Symbolism of game:

Represents understanding the weather patterns of the local environment.

Rules of play, including scoring:

Turn out the lights and start a rainstorm right in the classroom. With everyone seated in a circle, players remain quiet until a leader passes a movement behavior to the player on his or her left. Each player will imitate the sound and behavior of the player on his or her right and continue that sound until a different one is passed to him or her. The leader rubs his or her palms together, then the student on the left joins in, and the player on that player's left joins in, until everyone in the circle is performing the same movement. The leader starts a new motion but people in the circle continue the past motion until the new one is passed on to them from the player on their right. The second motion travels around the circle. The sequence of motions for the leader are as follows:

Rub palms together
Snap fingers
Clap hands
Slap thighs
Stomp feet

The rainstorm disappears by reversing the sequence of motions. When everyone is stomping their feet, the leader slaps his or her thighs and passes the motions in reverse order. Soon the rainstorm stops completely and there is peace in the rain forest.

STRUIFVOGEL
Erik De Vroede
Not appropriate for replication.

Players:

Male and female adults.

Object of game for players:

The struifvogel player takes his or her place in a marked square on the ground.

Number of players:

Variable.

Costume, apparel/equipment required:

The struifvogel is often an artistically sculptured wooden bird, suspended from the ceiling or from a cross beam by rope. An iron or steel pin is put in the beak of the bird. The bird is held by a leather strap fixed under the bird's tail. The target is similar to that used in archery.

Area/arena/field where played—space required:

An open area.

Time length of game. How is end of game determined?:

No limit.

Symbolism of game:

A target game emphasizing accuracy and integrity.

Rules of play, including scoring:

After putting a pin in the bird's beak, the struifvogel player takes the tip of the leather strap, aims, and launches the bird. If the bird hits the target, the pin in its beak gets stuck in the disc while the bird flies backward to the player. The bull's eye counts for 25 points, and the value of the surrounding circles decrease outwards: 20, 15, 10, 5, and 1 point for the outside zone. The struifvogel game can be played in several ways: bull's eye contest, one contest (as often as possible in the outside circle), or in any other way players choose.

Different kinds of shooting contests: In addition to weekly shooting contests, every struifvogel association organizes its own yearly king's shooting contest. The winner of this contest is called the king, and the runner up is called the prince. Struifvogel is an old contest, and traditionally every year the associations organize an Alliance Shooting Contest. On the occasion of the yearly fair in one of the towns, all existing struifvogel associations are invited to participate in the Fair Shooting Contest. Struifvogel is also played in the Belgian region of Flanders.

Denmark

TRUST IN PAIRS
John Cheffers
Appropriate for replication.

Players:

Male and female young teens.

Object of game for players:

To promote cooperation and trust while working in pairs. To raise awareness of players' abilities and disabilities through movement.

Number of players:

Any even number.

Costume, apparel/equipment required:

A grocery bag for each player, and an obstacle course.

Area/arena/field where played—space required:

Gymnasium or open field.

Time length of game. How is end of game determined?:

As directed by the teacher.

Symbolism of game:

Trust and cooperation when working in a team.

Rules of play, including scoring:

Each player brings in a large paper bag for this activity. Younger players will enjoy decorating and drawing facial features on the bag. Players will then work in pairs. Prior to the activity a simple obstacle course needs to be set up in the gymnasium. In each pair, one of the players puts the bag over his or her head and the other player becomes the guide. Safety issues should be stressed here, particularly reviewing some of the safe ways to assist unsighted individuals. The player guide leads the student with the bag over his or her head to the gymnasium. Players are led through a series of obstacles such as around cones, under tables, and over steps. Each player should attempt to kick a ball, throw a ball, and use a manipulative instrument like a hockey stick, or a bat. Players switch roles so that each one has a turn guiding and moving through the obstacle course without sight.

England

GROUP JUGGLING
Bernard Smith
Appropriate for replication.

Players:

Male and female young teens.

Object of game for players:

To juggle as many objects as there are players and to improve eye contact, and passing skills while strengthening group ties.

Number of players:

A large enough group to form a circle.

Costume, apparel/equipment required:

A variety of different-size balls or objects.

Area/arena/field where played—space required:

Classroom, gymnasium, or play area.

Time length of game. How is end of game determined?:

When a set number of objects has been juggled, or as directed by the teacher.

Symbolism of game:

Represents management in day-to-day activities and more complex situations.

Rules of play, including scoring:

In circle formation, have player #1 start passing a ball to another player across from him or her. Player #2 passes the ball to player #3, and so on, until each player has caught and thrown the ball to another player. Everyone must catch and throw the ball once. The last player to complete the pattern passes the ball back to player #1. Player #1 starts the same pattern again by passing to the same second player he or she passed to the first time. (Make sure the players know who they pass to and receive from before complicating the game.) As soon as the players understand who they pass to and receive from, player #1 can start to add additional objects into play one at a time. The goal is to have as many objects being passed as there are players. Stress eye contact and good passing skills for all age levels.

HILL DILL

Bernard Smith
Appropriate for replication.

Players:

Male and female pre-teens.

Object of game for players:

To avoid being tagged while calling out set words.

Number of players:

Eight to 20.

Costume, apparel/equipment required:

None.

Area/arena/field where played—space required:

Gymnasium, play area, or field.

Time length of game. How is end of game determined?:

As directed by the teacher.

Symbolism of game:

Represents survival techniques and an awareness of danger.

Rules of play, including scoring:

One player is chosen to be it, or the tagger, and stands in the middle of the play area. The rest of the players stand side by side on one endline facing the one who is it. The one who is it calls, "Hill Dill, come over the hill, or else I'll catch you standing still!" Immediately, all players run across the play area, past the tagger, to the opposite endline. The tagger chases them, and those tagged join him or her in the middle and help him or her tag the rest.

Safety Precautions: "Hill Dill" was originally played with players evenly divided on both endlines and both groups crossing over to opposite lines at once. However, too many collisions result from the crossing over and the many taggers chasing in different directions. Therefore, it is suggested that all players run to the opposite line to be safe, then back to the original line on the second call by the one who is it.

ONE VS. FIVE TAG
Bernard Smith
Appropriate for replication.

Players:

Male and female pre-teens.

Object of game for players:

To make it to the opposite side of the floor without being tagged.

Number of players:

Classroom group.

Costume, apparel/equipment required:

Something to identify one-sixth of the players, like pinnies, or nerf balls.

Area/arena/field where played—space required:

Gymnasium, play area, or field.

Time length of game. How is end of game determined?:

The number of times that the floor has been crossed in one minute.

Symbolism of game:

Effort, especially when the odds seem overwhelming.

Rules of play, including scoring:

A large area needs to be divided in half, with sidelines and endlines designated. Two teams are assigned to either side of the playing field. The runners should be on one half; five times as many taggers occupy the other half (the taggers need some type of visible designation, like pinnies, or carrying a nerf ball, for example). Put another way, if there is a class of sixty, ten will be taggers and fifty will be runners. Players must make it to the opposite side of the playing area without being tagged. If they make it, they walk up one side of the field (out of play) and tag the teacher on the sideline to register their score—one for each successful crossing. These players then return to their side and try again. If tagged, they go to the other sideline, perform a quick exercise (two sit-ups, two push-ups, or four jumping jacks, for example), and then return to their side to continue. The goal is to score as many times as possible in one minute. After one minute allow time to strategize. Then each group will try to break the previous game's record (taggers under the number, players over the mark).

PUMPKINS AND WITCHES
Bernard Smith
Appropriate for replication.

Players:

Male and female pre-teens and young teens.

Object of game for players:

To avoid being caught by the opposite team.

Number of players:

Eight to 20, divided into teams of two.

Costume, apparel/equipment required:

None.

Area/arena/field where played—space required:

Gymnasium, play area, or field.

Time length of game. How is end of game determined?:

As directed by the teacher.

Symbolism of game:

The "chase."

Rules of play, including scoring:

Players are divided into two groups, Witches and Pumpkins, and stand at opposite ends of the play space. Each group chooses a leader. The Witches turn their backs while their leader watches the Pumpkins sneak up on them. When he or she thinks they are near enough, the leader calls "The Pumpkins are coming!" The Witches turn around and chase the Pumpkins back to the Pumpkins' goal. Any Pumpkin caught counts as a point for the Witches. Next the Pumpkins turn their backs while their leader watches, and the Witches sneak up on them. When the Pumpkin leader calls, "The Witches are coming!," the Pumpkins turn around and chase the Witches back to the Witches' goal. Any Witch caught counts as a point for the Pumpkins. Both leaders play as well as watch for their group. If leaders are tagged, new ones are chosen.

Safety Precautions:
a. Children should spread out in their group to avoid collisions when running.
b. Goals should be four feet from walls or fences.

QUICK HAND—SIT-UP POSITION
Bernard Smith
Appropriate for replication.

Players:

Male and female pre-teens and teens.

Object of game for players:

To improve abdominal strength, listening skills, reaction time, and lateral movement while manipulating a beanbag; to work cooperatively in small groups.

Number of players:

Classroom group divided into groups of three.

Costume, apparel/equipment required:

Beanbags representing bacon.

Area/arena/field where played—space required:

Gymnasium, play area, or field.

Time length of game. How is end of game determined?:

As directed by the teacher.

Symbolism of game:

Represents survival skills and food gathering experience in challenging situations.

Rules of play, including scoring:

Group divides into smaller groups of three. Two players face each other in a sit-up position, and then lay down on their backs. The third player dangles the beanbag (bacon) directly above the center of their feet. The third player gives the command "right," "left," or "both," signifying which hand (or both) the players must use. Partners then sit up to grab the beanbag. Positions rotate after a designated number of repetitions.

QUICK HANDS—PUSH-UP POSITION
Bernard Smith
Appropriate for replication.

Players:

Male and female young teens.

Object of game for players:

To manipulate an object while in the push-up position; to increase upper body strength, listening skills, reaction time, and lateral movement.

Number of players:

Classroom group divided into groups of two.

Costume, apparel/equipment required:

Beanbags.

Area/arena/field where played—space required:

Gymnasium, play area, or field.

Time length of game. How is end of game determined?:

As directed by the teacher.

Symbolism of game:

Represents strength and survival experience.

Rules of play, including scoring:

Partners face each other while in their version of the *up* position of a push-up. A beanbag is placed directly in the center between the partners. Only use the commands, "right hand" or "left hand" in the push-up position. Players can also hold their right or left leg up while waiting for the command to grab the beanbag.

ROBINSON CRUSOE
Bernard Smith
Appropriate for replication.

Players:

Male and female young teens.

Object of game for players:

To find items on a list, work in pairs, and reinforce curriculum through games.

Number of players:

Groups of 20, sometimes divided into pairs.

Costume, apparel/equipment required:

A list of requirements for the groups.

Area/arena/field where played—space required:

Play area, or field.

Time length of game. How is end of game determined?:

As directed by the teacher.

Symbolism of game:

Represents the means of survival when marooned in a foreign territory.

Rules of play, including scoring:

An area is designated as the playing field and groups are arranged in a designated area. The game works well in pairs, too, with one player representing Robinson Crusoe and the other Friday. On signal, the groups begin a search for the items on their lists, which are hidden throughout the area. The list could include: something edible, something to use as a tool or utensil, water, or shelter, for example. Players return to the starting area after a designated time period or when they complete their lists.

A second version of the game has the shipwrecked crews or groups working toward a specific problem. The same open-ended problem could be presented to each group or different problems could be provided. An example of this version is, What type of shelter can you create given these four sticks, a sheet, and a heavy rock?

TRIANGLE TAG
Bernard Smith
Appropriate for replication.

Players:

Male and female teens.

Object of game for players:

To tag one of the people in the group; to work cooperatively in a small team.

Number of players:

Groups of four.

Costume, apparel/equipment required:

None.

Area/arena/field where played—space required:

Gymnasium, play area, or field.

Time length of game. How is end of game determined?:

As directed by the teacher.

Symbolism of game:

Represents care and protection.

Rules of play, including scoring:

Three people form a hand-in-hand circle (or triangle). The fourth person is on the outside of the circle and is the tagger. The object of the game is for the tagger to touch one of the three designated people in the group. The other two people in the circle work together to protect the third "tagee" by moving the circle to block the path. The circle may not break, and the tagger may not reach across the two protectors.

Finland

CHAINS

Risto Telama

Appropriate for replication.

Players:

Male and female pre-teens and young teens.

Object of game for players:

To tag all of the players so that a chain is formed.

Number of players:

Eight to 20.

Costume, apparel/equipment required:

None.

Area/arena/field where played—space required:

Gymnasium, play area, or field.

Time length of game. How is end of game determined?:

As directed by the teacher.

Symbolism of game:

Represents conscription and survival.

Rules of play, including scoring:

One player is chosen to be it, or the tagger. When he or she tags some-one else, the two join hands and chase someone else. When another player is tagged, he or she also joins them, making a chain of three. The game continues with each tagged player joining the end of the chain. Chained players must keep hands joined. Only the first and last players on the chain may tag. Boundaries of play must be set beforehand.

Safety Precautions:

a. Limit the chain to four or five and then have the chain split into two groups.
b. Caution the chain to cooperate, to curb roughness.
c. Limit playing time and give all players the opportunity to rest.

France

BOX-BALL

Maurice Pieron
Appropriate for replication.

Players:

Male and female pre-teens and young teens.

Object of game for players:

To return the ball after it has been hit into the box.

Number of players:

Two per team.

Costume, apparel/equipment required:

A ball.

Area/arena/field where played—space required:

Two sidewalk squares representing the court. The baselines are the outer limits of the concrete. The joint between the two squares is the "net."

Time length of game. How is end of game determined?:

The first player to get 21 points wins. Games must be won by two points. The game can be suspended and resumed later.

Symbolism of game:

Represents the creativity and resourcefulness in using the natural environment for games.

Rules of play, including scoring:

Players figure out a method of determining the first server. The ball is hit with an open palm into the opponent's box. After one bounce, it is returned by slapping it with an open palm or by some specially personalized cutting technique. (Cutting describes a short, sharp chop with the hand or racquet designed to produce a backspin.) A point is scored when the opponent fails to return a shot into the server's box or if the opponent misses the ball entirely. The winner of the point continues to serve.

CLUBS ROYALE
Maurice Pieron
Appropriate for replication.

Players:

Males and females of all ages.

Object of game for players:

To advance a ball or puck through a goal using soccer and/or hockey skills.

Number of players:

Variable.

Costume, apparel/equipment required:

Hockey sticks, ball or puck, cones for goals, team color bands.

Area/arena/field where played—space required:

Outdoor field, gymnasium, or large multiservice room.

Time length of game. How is end of game determined?:

Variable. Two fifteen minute halves.

Symbolism of game:

Represents an adaptation of two traditional games—hockey and soccer—adapted to suit different cultures. Also cultivates fitness and ball hitting skills. Hockey and soccer tend to be played in different countries, but here they are combined.

Rules of play, including scoring:

Depending on the size of each team, distribute hockey sticks to one half or one third of each team. Those players using the hockey sticks play the game like floor hockey, without high sticks. The ball or puck can be advanced with the sticks or according to soccer rules. Each team attempts to advance the ball into their own goal area, which can be modified according to the players' ages.

Play begins with a hockey face-off in the center of the playing area. Team members either kick the ball, if they do not have a stick, or hit the ball with the hockey stick. The teacher specifies how a goal can be made for a specific amount of time. Following is a list of suggestions for ways of scoring goals:

a. Females can score the next three minutes.*
b. Males can score during the next play time.
c. Only those with hockey sticks can score.
d. Those without sticks or using their feet can score.
e. Males with hockey sticks can score.
f. Females with hockey sticks can score.
g. Males playing according to soccer rules can score.
h. Females playing with their feet can score.

Modify the game by providing more than one goal for each team. In "Four Goal Club Royal," players can score at four goals, placed at each side as well as at the end.

---

*Calling on players according to gender is done without prejudice, merely as a way of structuring the game.

DECK TENNIS

Maurice Pieron
Appropriate for replication.

Players:

Male and female teens.

Object of game for players:

To return deck tennis ring over the net while preventing opponent from returning it.

Number of players:

Two to four.

Costume, apparel/equipment required:

Two seven-foot posts, 3 x 3 inches thick, stuck in two feet four inches deep at the center of the sidelines; four eyelets on posts for net ropes; net stretched tightly so top is four feet eight inches high for entire length; deck tennis ring of spliced rope or rubber with air vents to permit "give" when caught, or of a length of rubber hose with a wooden stopper joining the ends.

Area/arena/field where played—space required:

Playground, gymnasium, or singles court, 12 x 40 feet; doubles court 18 feet wide, divided into two nine-foot courts. Neutral area three feet from the net on each side.

Time length of game. How is end of game determined?:

Game is played to 15 points.

Symbolism of game:

A net game emphasizing territory.

Rules of play, including scoring:

The deck tennis ring is thrown back and forth over the net in an effort to prevent opponent from returning it. The ring must be caught with one hand only, and must be returned immediately with same hand. Ring must travel in an upward direction. A down stroke is always a foul on either the service or rally stroke.

For a singles game, one player plays on each side of the net. For doubles, two players play on each side of the net as partners.

The server standing outside of right court, tries to throw the ring with an upward toss beyond the neutral area and into the diagonally opposite half court. If the server or teammate makes a point, the ring is thrown again by the server from the left court. The server continues to alternate between left and right courts until his or her side makes an error or foul. Points are awarded when the ring is dropped or thrown foul (outside the boundaries or into the net).

Following service, the ring is thrown back and forth over the net until a player misses or fouls. If the serving side misses or fouls, the serve is lost. The entire area of the court from net to backline and both sidelines may be used for rally play. The neutral area is disregarded except for service.

In a doubles game, the retiring server takes position in the right court and becomes the first receiver; the partner takes the next service sent by the opponent. The partner of the first server takes the third service, and so on, until the game is won or lost.

Fouls include catching the ring with both hands, changing the ring from the catching hand before throwing, stepping on or over rear boundary line while serving, making a downward stroke when throwing the ring, or permitting ring to touch any part of the body other than the catching hand. If a foul is committed by the server or the server's partner, loss of service occurs and ring is given to the opponent. No score is made on loss of serve. If the foul is committed by the receiving side player, one point is credited for the serving team and the ring continues in service.

Notes:

1. Practice catching and throwing equally well with either hand.

2. Practice catching the ring at short and long distances.

3. Let hand "give" when catching the ring.

4. Use volleyball or net ball rules when teams play (four or more players on a side).

FOUR-WAY BOX BALL
Maurice Pieron
Appropriate for replication.

Players:

Male and female pre-teens and young teens.

Object of game for players:

To return the ball after it bounces into the appropriate box.

Number of players:

Four per team.

Costume, apparel/equipment required:

A ball.

Area/arena/field where played—space required:

Four sidewalk squares arranged in a 2 x 2 meter box to form a court.

Time length of game. How is end of game determined?:

Play continues until only one player is left.

Symbolism of game:

Represents the creativity and resourcefulness of using the natural environment for games.

Rules of play, including scoring:

The rules are essentially the same as for Box-Ball. The first server is selected by throwing fingers, or being out, or some such method. The first serve is to the box on his or her right, and after the first bounce, the receiver may return the ball to any box. The ball continues in play until one of the four players misses. Points are scored *against* the player due to misses. After ten misses, a player is eliminated. Once a player is out, his or her box becomes a dead box and cannot be used. Balls hit into the dead box count against the hitter.

PADDLE TENNIS
Maurice Pieron
Appropriate for replication.

Players:

Male and female young teens.

Object of game for players:

To hit the ball over the net and within the court using an underhand serve.

Number of players:

Two for singles, four for doubles.

Costume, apparel/equipment required:

Tennis or rubber ball (6-inch playground ball may be used), two to four wooden paddles, badminton net (piece of line with white strips of cloth tied to it may be used).

Area/arena/field where played—space required:

Gymnasium or outside area with hard surface such as cement, asphalt, wood, or clay. Net 2 feet 10 inches high at center, 3 feet 1 inch at posts (for younger players, 2 feet 2 inches at posts).

Time length of game. How is end of game determined?:

When a game is won (points are scored as in tennis: 15, 30, 40, Game). The game can also be scored as in table tennis, and the game ends when a player makes 21 points. When the game is scored in this manner, the serving alternates after every five points.

Symbolism of game:

A net game of striking and territoriality.

Rules of play, including scoring:

The game is played and scored like lawn tennis except for the serve, which is underhand. Only one serve is allowed to put the ball into play for each point. (Beginners may have two serves if needed.)

The server stands in the right corner behind the baseline and serves the ball over the center line to the player diagonally opposite on the other side. Then the opposing player returns the ball, and the game continues until one of the players or teams fails to return the ball. The server then changes to the left side of the court and serves. When a player or team fails to return a ball, a point is made by the opponents. If a ball is hit out of bounds or fails to cross the center line, a score is also made by the opponents.

Variation: May be played with the hands instead of paddles, in a game called Hand Tennis.

Germany

THE WANDERER
Herbert Haag
Appropriate for replication.

Players:

Male and female pre-teens and young teens.

Object of game for players:

To follow a routine accompanied by music.

Number of players:

Classroom group.

Costume, apparel/equipment required:

Recorded music of "The Wanderer," by Celine Dion, or any even beat music (new, country, oldies, etc.).

Area/arena/field where played—space required:

Gymnasium.

Time length of game. How is end of game determined?:

As directed by the teacher.

Symbolism of game:

Represents folk festivities.

Rules of play, including scoring:

4 counts	Right foot touch to the side, feet together, to the side, together.
4 counts	Left foot touch to the side, feet together, to the side, together.
4 counts	Right foot touch to the side, touch front, touch side, touch behind.
4 counts	Grapevine right (right, left, right—R, L, R) then hop 1/4 turn to the right on count 4.
4 counts	Back up left, right, left then hop (or run in place) right, left—also could be called a quick step. (The right–left is done on the 4th count after the run in place.)

Holland

PICTURE THIS . . . THE PAINTER'S DANCE
Arlene Sequine
Appropriate for replication.

Players:

Male and female teens.

Object of game for players:

To imagine oneself an artist who can draw with every part of the body.

Number of players:

Five to 25 or more, as space provides.

Costume, apparel/equipment required:

Loose fitting clothes with either dry paint brushes or paint rollers (improvised) and maybe a painter's hat.

Area/arena/field where played—space required:

A clear space large enough to permit "painters" to stretch out while moving around. Another option is to have floor mats (a variation in which players paint while lying on their backs).

Time length of game. How is end of game determined?:

The duration of the game is determined by the number of variations introduced.

Symbolism of game:

The actions of the players simulate artists painting masterpieces by using all of their body parts. They paint in space.

Rules of play, including scoring:

Organization of the game:

1. Set the scene by telling the players they are going to pretend to paint a huge picture on the side of a wall. It will be a beautiful picture, but they only have five minutes to paint it, so they have to use both hands and other body parts.

2. Motivate players by asking what kind of picture they would like to paint (animals, forest, lake, etc.).

3. Have players paint the theme in the air with one hand, and after 10–20 seconds, have them switch to other ways of painting: with the forehead, nose, jaw, ear, other ear, shoulder, other shoulder, elbow, other elbow, stomach, hips, knee, other knee, both knees; one foot, other foot, and both feet.

4. Players can discover other ways of painting faster, such as by painting with both hands and nose, both elbows and jaw, both hands and stomach, both elbows and knees, both shoulders and hips, nose and knees, jaw and hips, one ear and one foot, one ear and the other foot, both hands and one foot, and both hands and the other foot.

5. Each player lies down on his or her back and paints with both feet, both hands, and nose. After about five minutes, the players' bodies should be warmed up and they will have created a masterpiece in their mind's eye.

RED LIGHT, GREEN LIGHT
Arlene Sequine
Appropriate for replication.

Players:

Males and females of all ages.

Object of game for players:

To move without being detected.

Number of players:

Any number.

Costume, apparel/equipment required:

None.

Area/arena/field where played—space required:

Sidewalk with defined squares.

Time length of game. How is end of game determined?:

When the one who is it is tagged.

Symbolism of game:

Represents resourcefulness in playing games in a simple environment.

Rules of play, including scoring:

The player who is it stands at one end of the playing area while all other players stand at the opposite end. The player who is it turns her back to the others, and when she calls "Green Light," they move forward as rapidly as possible. When the player who is it turns around and calls "Red Light," all the movers must stop. Any moving players are returned to the starting line. The winner (and next player to be it) is the player who manages to get close enough to the one who is it without being detected and tags her.

Ireland

GAELIC FOOTBALL
Howard Darbon
Appropriate for replication.

Players:

Typically played by young male teens.

Object of game for players:

To score as many points as possible by kicking the ball through the uprights, or goal posts. The ball can also be fisted through, but only by the goalkeeper, who is the only one permitted to pick up the ball from the ground.

Number of players:

Two teams of 15 players each.

Costume, apparel/equipment required:

Shorts, jerseys, and boots. Soccer ball.

Area/arena/field where played—space required:

An area 140 x 160 yards long and between 84 and 100 yards wide. The goal posts are 21 feet apart and 16 feet high. A crossbar is set at 8 feet high.

Time length of game. How is end of game determined?:

Two 30-minute halves.

Symbolism of game:

Extremely competitive position of a single instrument with the purpose of moving that instrument to a set goal.

Rules of play, including scoring:

Gaelic football is a keep-away game with the teams attempting to score goals. It starts with a free kick from the opponents goal line that is disputed by the opposition team. Players can pass to each other using their heads or feet, but cannot run with the ball. Tackling is legal and scores are plentiful because there is no offside rule. A goal is worth three points if kicked underneath the crossbar and one point if kicked above the crossbar. Both teams are expected to play hard but are not expected to tackle high or low. The game features teamwork in order to score the necessary goals to win the game.

PASS THE ORANGE
Christine M. Conboy
Appropriate for replication.

Players:

Male and female teens.

Object of game for players:

To pass an orange from chin to chin.

Number of players:

Classroom group.

Costume, apparel/equipment required:

An orange or any object that can be passed from chin to chin.

Area/arena/field where played—space required:

Classroom, gymnasium, play area.

Time length of game. How is end of game determined?:

When the orange has been passed to the end of the line.

Symbolism of game:

Represents friendly cooperation, which is part of the culture of Ireland and the forms of entertainment and games played by children.

Rules of play, including scoring:

Two team leaders are selected who alternately pick players for their side. An extra player becomes the judge. The two teams line up with the leaders at one end. The leaders tuck oranges under their chins. At the signal from the judge, the leaders try to pass the oranges to the next players on their team. Each player must grasp the orange with chin only; no hands or elbows are allowed. If the orange is dropped, it must be returned to the leader, who starts it again. The team that passes the orange to the end of the line first without dropping it is the winner.

SHINTY

Howard Darbon
Not appropriate for replication.

Players:

Male and female teens, played separately.

Object of game for players:

To score goals.

Number of players:

Two teams of 12.

Costume, apparel/equipment required:

Sticks (like hockey sticks), a ball, and players dressed in boots, shorts, and jerseys. The stick is stout and the ball is made of cork covered with leather.

Area/arena/field where played—space required:

An area 200 yards x 100 yards. The goal is 12 feet wide and 10 feet high with a 12-foot-long line ten yards in front of the goals. The center circle is ten yards in diameter.

Time length of game. How is end of game determined?:

Typically the game lasts 90 minutes.

Symbolism of game:

The game is highly competitive and features heavy physical contact and speed of play. This game is played in Scotland, particularly in Glasgow and Edinburgh, and throughout Ireland. (Game is also known as "Hurling" in Ireland.)

Rules of play, including scoring:

The game starts with a hit from center field by the team that wins the toss. Teams hit the ball towards their respective goals. Both sides of the stick may be used but obstruction, holding, tripping, kicking, and dangerous play are fouls. The game is played similarly to field hockey. Only the goalkeeper may stop the ball with his or her hands and no player may use hands to ground the ball. Players may pass without the ball touching the ground by long and hard hits but they must not use hands.

Italy

BOCCE

Jean Roberts

Appropriate for replication.

Players:

Males and females of all ages.

Object of game for players:

To position personal bocce as close to the jack as possible by knocking away opponents' balls or knocking jack away.

Number of players:

Two to four.

Costume, apparel/equipment required:

Eight croquet balls, four painted red, four blue, and one white golf ball, the jack (*palino*).

Area/arena/field where played—space required:

Playground, gymnasium, or corridor. The court is 50–75 feet in length, and 8–12 feet in width.

Time length of game. How is end of game determined?:

When 15 points are reached in singles, or 18 points are reached in doubles or team play.

Symbolism of game:

The game is a leisure activity with competitive overtones.

Rules of play, including scoring:

Bocce is played like "Bowling on the Green." It is Italy's most popular outdoor recreation, and is now being played throughout the United States.

The object of the game is for the first player to roll his large bocce (croquet) ball as close to the jack (golf ball) as possible, to knock the opponents' balls away from the jack, or to knock the jack away from the opponents' balls. The second player then tries to get his or her ball closer to the jack than the first player, and they continue in turn until all the balls have been played.

A point is scored for each ball of the same player or team that is closer to the jack than all of the opponents' balls. The winning score is 15 points in singles and 18 points in doubles or team play. In case of a tie, an additional round is played until the tie is broken.

SHADOW DRIBBLE
Jean Roberts
Appropriate for replication.

Players:

Male and female pre-teens and young teens, played separately.

Object of game for players:

To have one partner follow the other partner. To work cooperatively with a partner.

Number of players:

Unlimited, divided into groups of two.

Costume, apparel/equipment required:

Balls.

Area/arena/field where played—space required:

Gymnasium, play area, or field.

Time length of game. How is end of game determined?:

As directed by the teacher.

Symbolism of game:

This game represents hunting experience and stalking.

Rules of play, including scoring:

Partners both have a ball. One partner follows the other partner. Both dribble a ball around the playing area. On the signal "Switch!," given by a third person (teacher), the pair stops and switches directions (about face). The new leader takes over while both continue to dribble. The third person assesses how well the pair stalk each other, and assigns one point for each successful turn.

Norway

TOGETHER SAVE

Jean Roberts
Appropriate for replication.

Players:

Male and female pre-teens and young teens.

Object of game for players:

The group stands on a small platform for a set period of time. Cooperation and small group problem solving through games is stressed.

Number of players:

Groups of 12 to 15 or larger.

Costume, apparel/equipment required:

Sturdy wooden crate or an oaktag square taped to the floor.

Area/arena/field where played—space required:

Gymnasium.

Time length of game. How is end of game determined?:

When all are aboard safely.

Symbolism of game:

Represents the need for organization, leadership, and trust in the face of disaster.

Rules of play, including scoring:

A wooden crate, block of wood, or piece of paper taped to the floor is needed to play this game. Size depends on the number in each group and the grade level. The size of the block should make it just a bit difficult for the group to all stand on the platform together. Create a story to coincide with the game. Perhaps there has been an explosion at a molasses factory and to be saved everyone must be on the crate. Set a time limit that the group is required to hold its pose. Ten or fifteen seconds works well for most groups. Everyone must work together and all must make it aboard safely. The task is for the group that is not on the wooden crate to get on successfully, all together without falling off, in the time allowed.

Poland

FLOWERS AND WIND
Jean Roberts
Appropriate for replication.

Players:

Male and female pre-teens.

Object of game for players:

To belong to the group with the most players. To learn about the natural environment through games.

Number of players:

Eight to ten, divided into two groups.

Costume, apparel/equipment required:

None.

Area/arena/field where played—space required:

Gymnasium, play area, or field.

Time length of game. How is end of game determined?:

As directed by the teacher.

Symbolism of game:

Nature and the elements.

Rules of play, including scoring:

The class is divided into two groups, flowers and wind. Each group stands along their own goal line. The players in the flower group choose the name of a flower, then walk up to the wind group, and stand still while the wind tries to guess the name chosen. When the wind guesses correctly, the flowers call "Yes!" and turn and run back to their goal, while the wind group chases them and tries to tag them. The tagged players join the wind group, and the two groups switch names. The new flower group decides on a name and walks up to the new wind group. The group with the most players at the end of the playing time wins.

Portugal

SHIPWRECK

Jean Roberts
Appropriate for replication.

Players:

Male and female pre-teens and young teens.

Object of game for players:

To quickly follow a variety of commands.

Number of players:

Ten to 30.

Costume, apparel/equipment required:

Bases for each station.

Area/arena/field where played—space required:

Gymnasium, play area, or field.

Time length of game. How is end of game determined?:

As directed by the teacher.

Symbolism of game:

Represents requirements of work and ability to adapt quickly to varying conditions.

Rules of play, including scoring:

The teacher is the captain who gives orders to the shipmates (players) who must promptly obey. Areas in the gymnasium are designated as play areas; when the commands "Bow," Stern," "Port," or "Starboard" are given, shipmates run and touch the line in the appropriate area. "Hit the Deck" means shipmates lie on the floor with at least one hand within the circle area. "Man the Lifeboats" means sit in a line in groups of three, "Captain's Coming" means salute, and "Man Overboard" means get in a piggy-back position. After trying out the commands a few times, play the game. Continue to add commands relating to ships and sailing. The players can create new commands.

Safety Precaution: Make sure there are several bases at each station for students to run to in order to avoid collisions.

Russia

KOROBUSHKA
(A FOLK DANCE FROM RUSSIA)
Myrna Schild
Appropriate for replication.

Players:

Male and female children and teens.

Object of game for players:

To improve coordination, timing, and dance skills, and to learn a Russian-style dance.

Number of players:

Classroom group.

Costume, apparel/equipment required:

Recorded music of the Korobushka folk song.

Area/arena/field where played—space required:

Gymnasium or school hall.

Time length of game. How is end of game determined?:

As directed by the teacher.

Symbolism of game:

Dance and folk dance represent aspects of the cultural heritage of the former USSR and the surrounding countries and regions. Intermarriage and movement of people reflect many different cultures, including that of the Turks, Slavs, Mongolians, and Ugrian tribes. This dance is characterized by emotional expressiveness, and the music is similar to Eastern (or Slavic) music. Korobushka means little basket or peddler's pack.

Rules of play, including scoring:

Form a double circle with partners facing each other and males with backs to the center. Females place their hands on their hips and males cross their arms on their chests. Directions given are for males; females' part is the reverse.

Part 1: Schottische Step Forward

Beginning with the left foot, take one schottische step forward, away from the center of the circle. Hop, and extend foot. Then reverse direction, beginning with the right leg. Take one schottische step backward toward the center. Repeat forward schottische step. Break step (cross, apart, together) with right foot up and working. Click heels on "together."

Part II: Schottische to Side

Beginning with the right foot for both males and females, move away from partner with a schottische step. Then repeat with other foot starting so that both dancers return to place. Join right hands, begin with right foot, and balance together and away. To complete phrase, male and female exchange places by female turning inward under male's right arm (4-step turn).

Repeat Part II

Three-step turn for male to end with left foot up.

Mixer

On repeat of part II, take one schottische step to right, then take second schottische step in place with new partner and complete sequence.

Scotland

BARNYARD GOLF
Brian Devaney
Appropriate for replication.

Players:

Male and female pre-teens and teens.

Object of game for players:

To get beanbag or ball in hole #1 and remaining holes with the least number of tries.

Number of players:

Two to four.

Costume, apparel/equipment required:

Beanbag or ball per player; nine #10 tin cans or bicycle tires scattered in irregular formation. The cans or tires are numbered.

Area/arena/field where played—space required:

Playground, gymnasium, or corridor.

Time length of game. How is end of game determined?:

The player who makes nine holes in the fewest strokes.

Symbolism of game:

A target game of hand-eye coordination.

Rules of play, including scoring:

Players follow one another in sequence, each trying to get the beanbag or ball in hole #1 with as few throws as possible. Play continues in like manner for the remaining holes.

The winner is the player who makes nine holes in the fewest throws (strokes).

Notes:

1. Make the course more difficult by introducing various obstacles or by increasing the distance between holes.

2. Use as a hot weather game.

3. Make up "golf" score cards.

Serbia

SAVE THE SNOWBALLS

Elenie Tsarhopoulos
Appropriate for replication.

Players:

Male and female pre-teens and young teens, played separately.

Object of game for players:

To prevent snowballs from melting and get them into the freezer. Creative play through games.

Number of players:

Classroom group in pairs or small groups.

Costume, apparel/equipment required:

Boxes and an abundance of snow balls (homemade wads of newspaper or small soft balls).

Area/arena/field where played—space required:

Gymnasium or play area.

Time length of game. How is end of game determined?:

As directed by the teacher.

Symbolism of game:

Represents survival through teamwork and trust in a hostile environment.

Rules of play, including scoring:

This is a cooperative game that is amusing to play any time of the year. The goal of the game is to save the snowballs from melting and get them into the freezer. Working cooperatively with a partner, players must determine a way to carry a snowball from one end of the room to the other. Players must both be involved in the process and hands cannot be used to carry the snowballs. One player must have at least one part of his or her body touching the snowball. Players can carry the snowballs back to back or stomach to stomach without using their hands, for example. A new method of carrying must be used with each snowball. How long will it take the whole class to save the snowballs?

Slovakia

CELEBRATION DANCE
Elenie Tsarhopoulos
Appropriate for replication.

Players:

Male and female teens.

Object of game for players:

To follow a movement routine accompanied by music.

Number of players:

Classroom group.

Costume, apparel/equipment required:

Recorded music. The teacher may choose traditional or popular music.

Area/arena/field where played—space required:

Gymnasium.

Time length of game. How is end of game determined?:

As directed by the teacher

Symbolism of game:

Represents folk activities.

Rules of play, including scoring:

The teacher comes up with a dance pattern that the children have to follow along and dance to with the music. An example follows:

Beats:	Action:
1 & 2	Pump hands in the air up and to the right 2x.
3 & 4	Pump hands in the air up and to the left 2x.
5 & 6	Pump hands down and to the right 2x.
7 & 8	Pump hands down and to the left 2x
9	Pump hands up to the right 1x
10	Pump hands up to the left 1x
11	Pump hands down to the right 1x
12	Pump hands down to the left 1x
13	Slap right hand on left shoulder
14	Slap left hand on right shoulder (arms are crossed)
15	Slap right hand on right hip
16	Slap left hand on left hip
17 & 18	Jump forward with both feet (hands remain on hips)
19 & 20	Jump 1/4 turn to the right

Slovenia

TARGET

Elenie Tsarhopoulos
Appropriate for replication.

Players:

Male and female young teens.

Object of game for players:

To hit the target (player) with a ball below the waist.

Number of players:

Six to 20.

Costume, apparel/equipment required:

One soft playground ball.

Area/arena/field where played—space required:

Gymnasium, play area, or field.

Time length of game. How is end of game determined?:

As directed by the teacher.

Symbolism of game:

Represents the skills required for hunting and historic games.

Rules of play, including scoring:

One child, the target, stands in a small circle drawn on the floor in the center of a circle of players. Circle players try to hit the target below the waist with a playground ball. The target may duck, turn, dodge, or jump to avoid being hit, but may not leave the small circle. The player who hits the target at waist level or below, becomes the next target.

Variation: With the older teens, the emphasis is on accuracy in throwing. How few throws does it take to hit a target? How many throws can the target dodge before being hit?

Sweden

HOT SUN
Jean Roberts
Appropriate for replication.

Players:

Male and female pre-teens and young teens.

Object of game for players:

To spell the words Hot Sun while listening to music. Raise awareness of the physical and earth sciences through games.

Number of players:

Unlimited.

Costume, apparel/equipment required:

A ball or object that represents the sun.

Area/arena/field where played—space required:

Classroom, gymnasium, or play area.

Time length of game. How is end of game determined?:

As directed by the teacher.

Symbolism of game:

Represents the experience of and understanding the environment and the associated culture.

Rules of play, including scoring:

Players sit in a circle and a ball is passed around the circle as music is played or a song is sung by the class. The passing ceases when the music stops. The entire group receives the first letter in the words Hot Sun. H is given to the entire group but the person holding the sun must give a characteristic or attribute about the sun. The music starts again and the game continues until Hot Sun is spelled by the group.

NO MAN'S LAND
Jean Roberts
Appropriate for replication.

Players:

Male and female pre-teens and young teens.

Object of game for players:

To catch the ball on the full (in the air) when a number is called.

Number of players:

Eight to 20, in two teams.

Costume, apparel/equipment required:

One playground ball.

Area/arena/field where played—space required:

Gymnasium, play area, or field.

Time length of game. How is end of game determined?:

Teacher specifies time limit.

Symbolism of game:

Represents setbacks and consequences encountered in community living.

Rules of play, including scoring:

Each team numbers off. If there are eight players on each team, one team numbers off from one to eight, and the other team from nine to sixteen. The game starts with players on one team calling a number, then throwing the ball over a "no-man's-land" to the opposite team. Anyone on the opposite team may catch the ball, but if the ball is dropped or allowed to touch the ground, the player whose number was called is out, and he or she goes to prison (is out of the game). The player receiving the ball may run or walk with it except into no-man's-land. The player calls a number of the opposite team and throws the ball. The game continues for a specified time limit. The team with the most players left in the game wins.

Variation: The game may be played by throwing the ball over a net 6 feet high, instead of over no-man's-land.

Switzerland

CLOCK BALL
Kevin McAllister
Appropriate for replication.

Players:

Male and female young teens.

Object of game for players:

To run around the circle as many times as possible while the ball is tossed around once.

Number of players:

Ten to 20 per circle.

Costume, apparel/equipment required:

One playground ball per circle.

Area/arena/field where played—space required:

Gymnasium, play area, or field.

Time length of game. How is end of game determined?:

As directed by the teacher.

Symbolism of game:

Represents pitting one's wits against the elements.

Rules of play, including scoring:

On the signal "Go" from the teacher, the ball is tossed around the circle from player to player while one player runs around the outside of the circle. The object of the game is to see how many times a runner can go around the circle while the ball is tossed around just once.

NAME THE ANIMAL

Christine M. Conboy
Appropriate for replication.

Players:

Male and female pre-teens and young teens.

Object of game for players:

To toss the ball while calling the first letter of the name of an animal and to learn about the Swiss culture through games.

Number of players:

Classroom group, lined up and facing the leader, all either standing or sitting.

Costume, apparel/equipment required:

Ball or sock filled with rags.

Area/arena/field where played—space required:

Indoors.

Time length of game. How is end of game determined?:

As directed by the teacher.

Symbolism of game:

Represents the environment of Switzerland, its long periods of snow, and the Swiss children's love of playing in the snow. Indoor games have developed for the times the children cannot play outside, perhaps because of a snowstorm.

Rules of play, including scoring:

First the players choose a leader who stands in front of the others with a ball. Tossing the ball up in the air, the leader appears to think. Suddenly, he or she tosses the ball to the first player on his or her left, shouting "Name the animal. The first letter is W." The player catches the ball and tosses it back, saying "It's a Wolf," or some other animal whose name starts with a W. If the animal is correctly guessed that player becomes leader, and the old leader moves to the end of the line. If incorrect, the first leader continues to toss the ball on down the line. If the end of the line is reached without anyone guessing, the leader starts at the head of the line again, this time shouting "Name the animal, the first letter is R," or whatever letter. (Animals include birds and fish.) Other topics can also be used such as countries or cities.

Wales

MOUSE TRAP

Eileen Crowley Sullivan

Appropriate for replication.

Players:

Male and female pre-teens and young teens.

Object of game for players:

To avoid being caught in the trap.

Number of players:

Eight to 20.

Costume, apparel/equipment required:

None.

Area/arena/field where played—space required:

Gymnasium, play area, or field.

Time length of game. How is end of game determined?:

Game ends when all mice are caught in the trap.

Symbolism of game:

Represents survival and hunting and gathering experience.

Rules of play, including scoring:

Half the players join hands and make a circle called the mouse trap. The rest of the players, called mice, make a circle around the mouse trap without holding hands. A teacher calls the signals. On the signal "Go," the two circles move in opposite directions, the trap to the left and the mice to the right. On "Stop," both circles stop moving, and the trap raises its arms. The mice *walk* in and out of the trap. On "Snap," the trap lowers its arms and the trap is shut. All the mice caught inside the trap become part of the mouse trap. Play continues until all the mice are caught. The game is played again with the mice becoming the trap and the trap becoming mice.

Safety Precautions:

a. Mice should *walk* in and out of the trap to avoid collisions in a limited space.

b. Mice should run wide of the trap when the two circles move to avoid colliding with trap players.

Variation: Game starts with two mouse traps, each trap made of two players holding hands. The two traps stand at opposite ends of the playing area, and the rest of the players move around the play area, going under the raised arms of both traps. When the instructor calls "Snap," the two traps lower their arms. Players caught in the traps form a trap of their own. When playing this way, be sure to repeat the game, choosing four new players as starting traps.

PART V

The Middle East

Ancient Egypt

SENET

Arlene Sequine
Appropriate for replication.

Players:

Male and female pre-teens and young teens.

Object of game for players:

The object of the game is to take as many of your opponent's tokens, called kelbs, as possible. Kelbs are small circular discs no more than one inch in diameter. To take an opponent's kelbs, a player must get two of his kelbs in the squares on either side on a game board.

Number of players:

Two.

Costume, apparel/equipment required:

Five-by-five square game board scored on the ground or on a table, and twenty-four kelbs. Twelve kelbs should be one color and twelve should be another.

Area/arena/field where played—space required:

The game board is scored with 5 x 5 squares and has an overall dimension of 10 x 10 inches.

Time length of game. How is end of game determined?:

Whoever captures the most kelbs, or whoever's opponent cannot or will not move, is the winner.

Symbolism of game:

African version of board games.

Rules of play, including scoring:

1. Toss a coin or roll a die to see who plays first.
2. The winner of the toss places two kelbs on two different squares, which are called oyoons. The center oyoon is left open.
3. The second player then places two kelbs on the board.
4. The players continue to alternate, each placing two kelbs on the board until it is covered except for the center oyoon.
5. The first player moves one kelb into the center oyoon. Kelbs can be moved up, down, and sideways, but not diagonally. This is how the game is prepared. If a player cannot move then his or her turn is skipped.
6. Kelbs are taken when they are trapped by an opponent between two opposing kelbs after the game has begun. If a kelb is captured, it is removed from the board.
7. Each time a player takes a kelb, he or she earns another turn. However, if more than one kelb is captured at a time, the capturer only receives one additional move.

Israel

RELEASE
Margalith Akavya
Appropriate for replication.

Players:

Male and female teens.

Object of game for players:

To escape the opponents' circle and to discover the unnumbered player.

Number of players:

Variable.

Costume, apparel/equipment required:

A ball.

Area/arena/field where played—space required:

Open area.

Time length of game. How is end of game determined?:

The game continues until all players are in their home circles and the unnumbered player has been discovered.

Symbolism of game:

Agility, deception, and discovery.

Rules of play, including scoring:

The players are in foreign or opposite circles. A leader throws the ball to one circle. When the player to whom the ball is directed catches the ball, he or she throws it to the opposite circle and runs to his or her home circle. The receiving player does likewise. During this action an unnumbered player (preselected) must be challenged and discovered. When that happens, the game is declared won.

When one of the players standing in a circle catches the ball without dropping it, he must throw it to the player standing in the second circle and only then can he leave the circle in which he is standing and return to his side. He returns to his side whether or not this player catches the ball without dropping it.

If the second player in fact catches the ball without dropping it, he too must return to his side. This player cannot release the player who has just arrived in the first circle. The implication is that only two players can be released at a time.

SHELTER
Margalith Akavya
Appropriate for replication.

Players:

Male and female pre-teens and teens.

Object of game for players:

To survive being hit by the ball as it is thrown in the active zone.

Number of players:

Six or more.

Costume, apparel/equipment required:

A ball.

Area/arena/field where played—space required:

A field.

Time length of game. How is end of game determined?:

15 minutes.

Symbolism of game:

Endurance and agility.

Rules of play, including scoring:

A neutral area one meter wide is marked out in the middle of the field. On both sides three to six meters from the neutral area, a circle is drawn so that if the two circles were to be joined up by an imaginary line it would run diagonally through the neutral area. The diameter of each circle is 1.6 meters.

There are two teams. When the whistle is blown the first team must try to throw the ball to player #1 standing in the circle on the opposite side of the neutral area. Player #1 must try and catch the ball without dropping or losing it. The player stands in a circle. All players must return the ball then run through the neutral zone to safety without being hit by the opponents throwing a ball from their circle.

THE WALL
Margalith Akavya
Appropriate for replication.

Players:

Male and female teens.

Object of game for players:

Throwing and catching a ball. Throwing the ball toward a specific target.

Number of players:

Six or more.

Costume, apparel/equipment required:

A ball.

Area/arena/field where played—space required:

In the middle of the field a neutral area one meter wide is marked out. No player from either team may enter this area. At the end of each team's area a line is drawn that represents a wall. The distance between each wall and the neutral area is determined by the age of the players and the distance they can throw a ball. Normally this distance is three to five meters.

Time length of game. How is end of game determined?:

The game continues until one of the two teams has had all its members stand behind the wall of the opposing team or until the time allotted for the game has expired, usually 15 minutes.

Symbolism of game:

Agility and teamwork.

Rules of play, including scoring:

- Each team lines up on their side of the field.
- Each team member is given a number.
- Each team sends their first player to a spot behind the wall situated in the opposing team's area.
- The team winning a toss starts (team #1). The team losing the toss is team #2.

When the whistle is blown team one must try and throw the ball to their team member standing behind the wall. This player must try and catch the ball without dropping or losing it. Once he or she catches the ball, this player must bounce it once and then rush back to his or her half and shout "Number 2." Player #2 must then run to team #2's side and stand behind the wall. Like player #1, he or she must try to catch the ball thrown to him by members of his or her own team without dropping it. And so the game continues.

If the player drops or loses the ball in any way, then the ball reverts to team #2 who must then try to throw the ball to their player #1, who is standing behind the wall of team #1.

A player standing behind the wall of the opposing team can only return to his or her team if:

1. he or she does not drop the ball, or

2. one of the members of the opposing team crosses the line representing the wall.

The ball must be handed over to the opposing team if:

1. the player loses the ball after catching it,

2. the player drops the ball after catching it,

3. in catching the ball the player crosses the line representing the wall into the opposing team's area,

4. any player enters the neutral area between the two sides,

5. any player holds on to the ball for longer than three seconds, or

6. if the player holding the ball moves forward with it or dribbles with it in any way.

Under certain circumstances a player can also earn advantages for his team.

Jordan

TARA AL HAMAM
(THE PIGEON FLEW)
Tom Sharpe
Appropriate for replication.

Players:

Male and female young teens.

Object of game for players:

Players are seated around a table (or their desks) with both hands on the table, palms down. One player acts as the leader and says "The pigeon flew up." The players raise their hands quickly. When the leader says "The pigeon flew down," the hands are placed on the table again. The leader calls out another animal and players follow instructions. The leader tries to catch players who move their hands in the wrong direction. A marker is given to those who are caught. The player who has the least amount of markers after all players have had a turn is the winner.

Number of players:

Twenty or more with one leader.

Costume, apparel/equipment required:

None.

Area/arena/field where played—space required:

Classroom, desks, or tables.

Time length of game. How is end of game determined?:

The game ends when all players have been the leader once.

Symbolism of game:

Dramatization of birds and animals.

Rules of play, including scoring:

Players should follow the animal depicted by the leader and admit if they move in the wrong direction. Keeping a tally of the markers earned is how to keep score.

Palestine

THE SEVEN STONES
Abdel Naser Qadomi
Appropriate for replication.

Players:

Young male teens.

Object of game for players:

Team A must try to rebuild a pile of stones without being hit by the ball. If a member is hit on any part of the body, except the head, he is disqualified and cannot continue to assist his team in rebuilding the pile of stones. Team B tries to hit all the members of Team A before they can rebuild their pile of stones.

Number of players:

Eight, divided into two equal teams.

Costume, apparel/equipment required:

Seven thin, roundish or square stones. A small, soft ball, about the size of a tennis ball.

Area/arena/field where played—space required:

An open field. Played on spring evenings and on mornings during holidays.

Time length of game. How is end of game determined?:

Game ends when one team wins two our of three games.

Symbolism of game:

Develops physical strength, speed, and coordination. Fosters coopera-tion and friendship among the players. Allows for fun and recreation. Develops attention span and concentration.

Rules of play, including scoring:

The players are divided into two equal teams, Team A and Team B. The teams toss a coin to determine which team will build the pile of stones (heads), and which team will try to knock the stones down (tails). If heads, Team A piles seven stones on top of each other and then moves aside.

Team B stands at a distance of about three yards from the pile of stones. Each member of Team B takes a turn trying to knock the stones down from the pile, each player getting one chance to throw the ball. If Team B fails to knock down all the stones with the ball, them Team A gets the ball and each of its members takes a turn at trying to knock the stones from the pile. If Team B succeeds in knocking off all the stones with the ball, then Team A scatters about the field, away from the pile of stones, and Team B takes the ball and tries to hit the members of Team A with the ball. If Team A succeeds in rebuilding the pile of stones without all its mem-bers being hit with the ball, then Team A wins the game. If Team B hits all the members of Team A before they can rebuild the pile of stones, then Team B wins the game. The game begins again and the team that wins two out of three games wins the match.

Saudi Arabia

AD-DA
(SEARCH FOR A MISSING OBJECT)
Adnan D. Jallon
Not appropriate for replication.

Players:

Male and female pre-teens and teens.

Object of game for players:

The main object of the game is to look for hidden objects in one of the players' palm.

Number of players:

Two to six or more, divided into two groups.

Costume, apparel/equipment required:

Casual wear. The equipment needed is a piece of plain cloth, blanket, or sheet; a small marble, stone, or similar object, such as a pistachio nut or almond; and a twisted turban head dress called a *mi'kara*.

Area/arena/field where played—space required:

An area 2 x 2 meters indoors or out.

Time length of game. How is end of game determined?:

Players may start and end the game any time they want.

Symbolism of game:

This is a game of looking for an object hidden in a player's hands. The turbinate piece of head cloth, shell or *ghutra*, called *mi'kara* represents a stick for the punishment of the team who will not be able to identify the place of the hidden object.

Rules of play, including scoring:

Players sit facing each other in a kneeling or squatting position. A coin toss is made to choose the starting team that gets the marble or stone, the blanket or sheet, and the mi'kara. The starting team begins the game by moving their hands under the sheet. To trick their opponents, they may exchange the stone between their hands while making a continuous "zziii" sound. Suddenly, all hands stop moving and appear from beneath the blanket. The backs of all hands should be facing up and remain in that position. The other team tries to guess in which hand the stone is hidden. If they figure out where it is, they get all the equipment and start the game again in the same manner. If they fail, each member of their team is hit with the mi'kara one, two, or three times, depending on previous agreement. The game ends when both teams feel fed up and want to move on.

AD-DABB (THE LIZARD)
Adnan D. Jallon
Appropriate for replication.

Players:

Male and female pre-teens and teens.

Object of game for players:

To improve the player's knowledge of different types of animals and things. To teach players to practice line drawings.

Number of players:

Classroom group.

Costume, apparel/equipment required:

Traditional costumes. A stick for drawing a lizard on the ground or a piece of chalk for drawing and an eraser, either made of wood for cleaning the picture on the ground, or made of cloth, for cleaning the blackboard.

Area/arena/field where played—space required:

Outdoor area, 10 x 10 meters, or indoors, using a classroom blackboard.

Time length of game. How is end of game determined?:

The game lasts for five to ten minutes or until each player gets a turn.

Symbolism of game:

Ad-Dabb, the lizard, is a drawing game that has been practiced in Arabia for more than 1,500 years and represents guessing accuracy.

Rules of play, including scoring:

Draw a picture of an animal. Choose a first player by coin toss. All players sit around the picture in a circle. One player should sit with his or her back to the picture and puts one hand on it, touching some part of the lizard. The player is then questioned by a player in the circle, "On which part of the lizard are you placing your hand?" If the player answers correctly, the two players exchange places. If the player answers incorrectly, he or she must carry the questioner a certain distance on his or her back.

Note: Both girls and boys may play the game together.

AD-DAHW (THE ARABIAN GULF)

Adnan D. Jallon
Not appropriate for replication.

Players:

Male and female teens.

Object of game for players:

Using a stick to drive a ball into a hole in the ground, with the lowest possible number of strikes.

Number of players:

Two or more. The game may be played as individuals or teams.

Costume, apparel/equipment required:

No specific costume needed.

Area/arena/field where played—space required:

The game needs an open area about 30 x 30 meters or more.

Time length of game. How is end of game determined?:

No time limit. Players can play for a set amount of time, or until a set score is reached.

Symbolism of game:

It is a form of an old traditional stick and ball game. In al-Madinah during the time of the Prophet, around 633 A.D., Al-Hassan and Al-Husain, the Prophet's two grandsons, played the game of ad-Dahw with other children using wooden sticks and a wooden ball. It represents traditional, historic, and sacred activities.

Rules of play, including scoring:

Preparing the equipment and field: Prepare and make the bats Middha or Maddrab, the playing sticks, which should suit the players in length and weight. Prepare the ball, which should be light, strong, and able to withstand lifelong hitting. Prepare a dusty or sandy hill, small, and higher than the surrounding ground. Dig a hole in the ground, making it a little larger than the ball.

Method of playing: The winner of the toss: Put the ball at the top of the dusty hill. Strike the ball sharply toward the dusty hole. If the ball goes into the hole, the player wins a point. If not, the player tries again, until the ball does go into the hole. Then the next player takes his or her turn, and so on.

Method of winning in ad-Dahw game: The real method of playing ad-Dahw is not clearly explained in any of the available references so it is suggested that winner of the game can be determined as follows: (a) Figure the number of plays according to the number of repetitions necessary to get the ball in the dusty hole, and (b) the player who gets the ball into the hole with the lowest number of strikes is the winner.

AL-ARDDA AN-NAJDIYYA (THE NAJDIYYAH DANCE)
Adnan D. Jallon
Not appropriate for replication.

Players:

Male teens through adults.

Object of game for players:

To receive the highest score as determined by judges who watch contestants dance and award points for specific aspects of the dance.

Number of players:

Two teams, evenly divided. Up to 100 people or more can be organized into a square or circle and can dance in the same location.

Costume, apparel/equipment required:

The Saudi national dress is worn, including the white or red headdress, called *shshall*, *ghutrah*, or *shshmagh*, topped with the Saudi *iqal*, a cord or headband made of black wool or cotton. Dancers also wear an embroidered vest for this occasion, and in some regions they surround their waists and shoulders with belts filled with empty bullets, as signs of traditional war costume.

The equipment needed is a large national Saudi Arabian flag, erected vertically in the middle of the performance arena, ten to 20 middle-sized tambourines on each side of the arena, and a sword in the hand of each dancing player of both teams. (Some dancers used to hold a piece of long bamboo as a sign of the sword.)

Area/arena/field where played—space required:

The Najdiyyah dance needs a large space such as a large open air arena or stadium, or a large indoor sports hall.

Time length of game. How is end of game determined?:

According to the occasion, the game or dance lasts for one to two hours.

Symbolism of game:

Saudi folk dancing is colorful, lively, and unique. Similar dancing and performances are held in various parts of Saudi Arabia, but the Najdiyyah dance is the most famous nationwide, as well as in the Arabian peninsula, and other Arab and European countries. In the old days, the main purpose of performing the game or dance was to encourage the dancers and show the power and strength of the tribe, which gathered to fight in the wars. In contemporary, more peaceful Saudi Arabia, the dance is performed in different regions and on various types of occasions to show the unity, happiness, and recreational spirit of the Saudi people.

Rules of play, including scoring:

The dance begins and ends as follows:
a. The carrier of the national flag stands in the middle of the arena and spreads the flag around his shoulders. Both teams stand facing each other in two rows with tambourines in their hands and swords hanging from their belts. They are ready to start the dance.
b. One of the teams' leaders starts singing some of the verses and then players of the same team start beating the tambourines and repeat the verse. Next, the other leader does the same, and so on. The dance starts with both dancing leaders introducing, exchanging, and repeating with the spectators different verses until the end of the dance or festival.

c. While dancing, players of both teams raise their swords and start moving the swords between fingers and exchanging sword play with both hands.

d. During and after the dance, both leaders come closer to the most honored guest and invite him and some of his guests to dance. They all surround the national flag and go on singing and dancing in rows or circles for ten to 20 minutes or more. A sign is given, finally, to end the dance.

e. Scoring of the Najdiyyah dance concerns some of the following aspects of the dance:

1. the general coordination of the dance performances
2. the beauty of the traditional clothes
3. the appropriateness to the occasion of the verses chosen
4. ability to coordinate the dance with the music, i.e., keeping to the rhythm of the tambourines' beats

AL-KAYRAM (THE CAROMS)

Adnan D. Jallon
Not appropriate for replication.

Players:

Male and female pre-teens and older.

Object of game for players:

To drive one's disk in any hole of the playing board before any other player does so.

Number of players:

Two or four playing singles or doubles.

Costume, apparel/equipment required:

Casual wear. A kayram board and 32 rounded disks made of wood, plastic, fiberglass, or any other light strong material. There need to be 15 white disks, 15 black disks, one red disk, and one disk a little larger in size and different in color from the others. This is used as a striker during the game.

Area/arena/field where played—space required:

Open area or indoor area at least 3 x 3 meters.

Time length of game. How is end of game determined?:

The game's end is determined by the first player to get the score chosen by all the players at the beginning of the game. The results are be determined by scoring the highest points first, according to the values and methods of playing.

Symbolism of game:

This is a well known game in Saudi Arabia and the Arabian Gulf area. India, Burma, and Pakistan each claim the game originated in their land, and as far as we know, Caroms was introduced to the Saudi people in the middle of the nineteenth century. Caroms represent years of life.

Rules of play, including scoring:

There are many types and methods of playing the kayram. The main idea is to drive disks into any hole of the board before any other player or players. Below are the most famous methods.

Method I: In the normal method of kayram play, singles or doubles players challenge each other to get the most disks into the holes first. The disks are on the board in a triangle shape. The values of the disks are:
a. One point for any of the white or black disks.
b. Five points for the red disk.
c. One point lost and one of the disks on the board retained when the striker al-Maddrab is driven into any hole during playing; five points lost if the red disk is driven into any hole before a player gets one of his or her own disks into a hole.
d. A player or doubles team wins the game by reaching the prechosen score first.

Method II: This method is called the trade and is similar to the method mentioned above except that the values of the disks are weighted differently. The values of the disks are:
a. Five points for each of the black disks.
b. Ten points for each of the white disks.
c. Fifty points for the red disk.

In both methods, a player is penalized and loses his or her turn when:
- he or she fails to hit or drive a disk into any of the four holes.
- he or she hits and drives the red disk into a hole before hitting his last disk.
- he or she drives the striker al-Maddrab into any hole before hitting or driving one or more of his or her disks into a hole.

AL-MIQLA (THE SLING)
Adnan D. Jallon
Not appropriate for replication.

Players:

Male and female pre-teens and teens.

Object of game for players:

To shoot pellets from a sling at targets to score points.

Number of players:

Any number.

Costume, apparel/equipment required:

Traditional costume. The equipment needed is a sling, which is usually made of interwoven strands of wool, cotton, or any strong, flexible, non-stretchable material; a small rectangular piece of the same material as the sling; some stones or steel pellets, which might be of the same or different sizes; and, when using the sling in sports competitions, targets that are made with sheets of strong wood covered with heavy sheets of tin.

Area/arena/field where played—space required:

A field anywhere in size from 30 x 50 meters to 30 x 70 meters, facing north-south. Targets must be placed on the target lines at 30 to 70 meters.

Time length of game. How is end of game determined?:

In competition, the game generally lasts one to two hours, with players shooting about 15 to 30 pellets in three rounds. The game ends when a player reaches a predetermined score.

Symbolism of game:

The *miqla*, or sling, is an old Arabian traditional device used for recreation, hunting, war, and driving birds out of farms. It has been used traditionally worldwide by different nations, including the Egyptians, Greeks, and Romans. The sling is also mentioned in the Holy Qur-ran and in the Old Testament. A famous Old Testament mention of the sling is in the story of David and Goliath, where a giant is knocked down and killed by the smooth pebbles thrown from David's sling.

Rules of play, including scoring:

In contemporary sports games, slings can be used as follows: From a shooting line, slingers shoot a number of pellets toward their own targets. Shooting starts and ends under the direction of a judge. Target judges use white flags for showing acceptable hits and red flags for pellets hit out of a target's range. The player with the highest score after a certain amount of time is the winner of the competition.

AL-MUSSARA'A AL-ARABIYYA (ARAB WRESTLING)
Adnan D. Jallon
Not appropriate for replication.

Players:

Older male teens.

Object of game for players:

To put the opponent's shoulders on the ground.

Number of players:

Two, or two teams.

Costume, apparel/equipment required:

Shorts, similar to those long shorts used in swimming. Wrestling costumes should be strong, wide, comfortable, not transparent, and not stretchable.

Area/arena/field where played—space required:

A wide, large indoor arena or an area outdoors, which must be at least 10 x 10 meters square. The ground should be soft and covered with a modern wrestling mat, or filled with sand.

Time length of game. How is end of game determined?:

The Arab traditional wrestling game has no time limit, but ends when someone wins.

Symbolism of game:

To build up one's strength, prepare youth for manhood, and show the standard of strength and manpower ability necessary for battling a foe.

Arab wrestling is an old, traditional game. From an early age, Arabs practice wrestling, which shows the strength and ability to struggle for life, and against the danger of the desert. Among Arabs, and in Makkah al Mukarramah, Rukanah was one of the strongest and well-known wrestlers. In the beginning of the seventh century A.D. at al-Battha, Rukanah tried to challenge the Prophet Mohammed, saying "I challenge you, and I want to have a wrestling round with you. If you win, you will get three of my goats." The Prophet won the first time and Rukanah asked for another round. By the third round, after losing three goats in each of the first two, Rukanah said, "No one put my side *janbi* (shoulder) to the ground," and he immediately converted to Islam. The Prophet returned the three goats to Rukanah saying, "It is not our habit to win against you and take your goats."

Rules of play, including scoring:

For contemporary Arab wrestling, these main following points apply:
- Arabian traditional wrestling starts and ends from a standing position. It also may be ended from a sitting position, but only when one wrestler tries to put the opponent's shoulder(s) on the ground to win the game.
- The wrestling game, or match, consists of three rounds, lasting three minutes each, with a minute of rest in between each round.

- Wrestlers may fight other wrestlers of different categories, but not if more than three categories away from his own. Wrestlers win when they pin their opponents (that is, place their shoulders on the ground).

AL-MUZZMAR
(THE OBOE DANCE)
Adnan D. Jallon
Not appropriate for replication.

Players:

Older male teens through adults. In schools, and for special performances, children as young as six also play.

Object of game for players:

To perform the use of the al-Nabut stick, or *Asa.*

Number of players:

Two groups of ten to 20 each.

Costume, apparel/equipment required:

Each player wears the national Saudi dress, consisting of a *thubb* (turban), *immah* (cloth belt), *buqqsha, hizam,* or *zinnar* (dress), and *madas* (Arabian sandals). Players need the stick (the *asa* or *nabut*), an echo drum (the *naqqrazan*), another echo drum (the *marrad*), and a tambourine (the *tarr*). Also, some dried pieces of wood are lit during the dancing.

Area/arena/field where played—space required:

The teams face each other on either side of the field (*maydan*) and by the end of the dance most of the spectators join in as well. The dancing ground needs to be an open area 30 x 30 meters, and there must be a larger area for the spectators to watch from. In the dancing area, three circles, each one inside the other, are drawn as follows:

A small circle 50 centimeters in diameter is drawn within a larger circle, 8 meters in diameter, which is drawn within the largest circle, 12 meters in diameter.

Time length of game. How is end of game determined?:

The game normally lasts at least one to two hours. When the game ends the guests, or spectators, continue dancing for up to half an hour. They generally leave the dance within an hour after that.

Symbolism of game:

The Muzzmar game or dance is the second most important national Saudi game, but the most important in the Southern region of Saudi Arabia. The history of the game goes back more than 1,400 years, when during the Ead's festival, some Abyssinian children danced in Madinah at the Prophet's mosque. Prophet Mohammed, along with his wife 'A'isha and some of his companions, watched the dance. Since that time, the Muzzmar dance, which derives from the same old Abyssinian dance, has become very famous. The dance is sacred to Mohammed's memory.

Rules of play, including scoring:

A flame is set in the inner circle. Then the game begins with the playing of the drum and the other musical instruments. Players stand in two rows facing each other. A leader of one team enters or jumps into the second circle and starts dancing, showing his talents and skills in playing with the nabut stick. A few minutes later, the other leader does the same. Then the rest of the players enter the circles dancing in pairs, each player showing his abilities. Before dancing, each of the players tries to get a handful of dust or sand that is available to throw into the middle of the smallest circle, where the flame is. They then walk in the middle circle and perform dancing and playing with the stick. The spectators dance into the circle one by one or in pairs. Ultimately, a celebration and competitive gathering is held to show the best performing and dancing team in the country.

AL-QALL (ARABIAN HOCKEY)
Adnan D. Jallon
Not appropriate for replication.

Players:

Males of any age, although the game is most successful with older teens and adults. Sometimes a mixture of different age groups is used when one village plays against another village.

Object of game for players:

To score as many goals as possible.

Number of players:

Ten or more customarily play the game.

Costume, apparel/equipment required:

No special costume is required, but it is necessary to tuck in clothes so they do not interfere with play or cause injuries. The equipment needed is a cloth ball filled with wool, plant fibers, flax fibers, coco fibers, or any similar materials, strongly threaded in a curricular shape. A palm tree stump (Jaridat Nakhla) sharply bent at the end. Goals made from four middle-sized stones, with two stones fixed in the middle of each of the far ends of the field.

Area/arena/field where played—space required:

The field is limited to the boundaries between two villages. In some cases the goal of one team is fixed at the edge of one village and the goal of the other is fixed at the edge of the other village. Both goals can be fixed on a hockey, football, or soccer field.

Time length of game. How is end of game determined?:

One whole day.

Symbolism of game:

The *qall* or palm tree stump-hockey is a similar game to ancient Egyptian Al-Hoksha, which is known now as field hockey. A long time ago the qall was played in al-Madinah al-Munawwarah and other villages. In 1975, Tabya secondary school celebrated the foundation of the first Saudi qall's team and in 1985 physical education students of the Faculty of Education at King Abdul-Aziz University started practicing the qall game in a traditional way. The game symbolizes history and adaptation to other world games.

Rules of play, including scoring:

The winner of a coin toss starts the game from the middle of the field. He then competes with the other team running, attacking, and defending between both goals or villages. The team with the highest scores will win the game.

Two teams play throughout an entire day. Some villages play the game in the moonlight. The game is limited and controlled according to the agreement of both teams and by one of two methods:

a. Scoring the highest numbers of goals throughout the limited times wins.

b. The first team to score the highest scores, for example, five or ten points, wins.

KUM KUM (THE COWRY SHELLS)
Adnan D. Jallon
Not appropriate for replication.

Players:

Females of all ages; sometimes males play the game, too.

Object of game for players:

To score points depending on the way shells land when tossed onto a rug.

Number of players:

Two or more.

Costume, apparel/equipment required:

A piece of rug or thick cloth 50 x 50 centimeters or more. It should be a different color than the cowry shells. Four cowry shells.

Area/arena/field where played—space required:

The game requires an area 2 x 2 meters, either indoors or out.

Time length of game. How is end of game determined?:

No time limit, however, the game ends as soon as the first player reaches a score of 50, 100, or 150 points, depending on what was decided by the players before the game started. The game normally lasts between 30 and 60 minutes.

Symbolism of game:

Building and strengthening good relations between young and old generations. A traditional game played by young girls and women, especially old women.

Rules of play, including scoring:

Methods of playing Kum Kum:
a. Individual method: one player plays against another, or a group of players all play, individually, one against the other.
b. Team method: two teams of two players play against each other.

Rules and winning of the game:
A coin toss determines who starts. Each player throws the four shells three times. Winning, losing, and playing may be continued as follows:
1. If the shells land in different positions of faces and backs, the player has another chance to go.
2. If the player fails to win a point, she passes the shells to another player.
3. When the shells land on backs or faces, the player is allowed to enter the game and make as many throws as possible. At the same time, he wins points.
4. Points are won as follows:
   - One point for each strike of two shells in a row.
   - Four points for having all the shells land on their backs.
   - Twenty points for having all the shells land on their faces. This is the only case in which a player is allowed to snatch one shell or more. Five points will be given for each snatched shell.
5. The first player, or team, to reach 50 points (or 100 or 150, depending on the prechosen amount) is the winner.

UZAM WAD-DAH
(THE BRIGHT BONE)
Adnan D. Jallon
Appropriate for replication.

Players:

Male pre-teens and young teens.

Object of game for players:

To encourage young children to search for missing objects at night under the moonlight.

Number of players:

Four or more.

Costume, apparel/equipment required:

Traditional costumes and a bone.

Area/arena/field where played—space required:

Outdoors.

Time length of game. How is end of game determined?:

The game ends when the bone is found, although usually more than one game is played in a row. The game begins when a player starts searching and ends when he finds the bone. Sometimes when the players fail to find the bone, they get a second bone or another object and begin again (otherwise, they have to give up playing the game).

Symbolism of game:

Encouraging boys and adolescents to practice games at nighttime, which supports and strengthens their abilities, personalities, and capabilities when facing future life adventures. The white bone is usually the scapula of a goat or lamb. The game has been played in Makkah Al-Mukarrama (in the southern part of Saudi Arabia) for more than 1,500 years. At an early age the Prophet Mohammed played this game with some of his young colleagues. The bone is the sacred symbol of the warrior.

Rules of play, including scoring:

Divide the players into two teams. All players face the leader who won the toss. The leader throws the bone as far as possible. A few seconds after the bone lands on the ground, the leader gives the signal to search for the bone. When a player finds the bone, points are determined in the following way:

- If the player is from the leader's team, his team gets one point and the game starts again. Each game is one play.
- If the player is from the other team, his team gets the bone and has a turn to make a starting throw and try to win points.
- The team with the highest point score wins.

Turkey

MAGIC CARPET
Hambdi Urkundt
Appropriate for replication.

Players:

Male and female pre-teens and teens.

Object of game for players:

To stop when the whistle is blown and avoid being caught on a "poison" spot.

Number of players:

Eight to ten.

Costume, apparel/equipment required:

None.

Area/arena/field where played—space required:

Gymnasium, play area, or field.

Time length of game. How is end of game determined?:

As directed by the teacher.

Symbolism of game:

Represents awareness of danger, and sharpens survival skills.

Rules of play, including scoring:

Four circles at least three feet in diameter, "poison spots," are drawn on the floor or ground around the play area. On "Go," players walk, run, skip, or hop, as designated by the instructor, to the right around the play space, being sure to go in and out of every poison spot. No player may jump over or skirt around a spot. When the whistle is blown or "Stop" is called, all players stop immediately. Those standing with one or both feet in a spot find a partner to move with for the next round. The pairs of players may grow larger. If, in a subsequent round, either of the players in the pair freezes on a poison spot they must find another player to join them.

Variation: Music or an instrument can be used. When music stops, players stop.

PART VI

Oceania

Australia

AUSTRALIAN RULES FOOTBALL
Howard Darbon
Appropriate for replication.

Players:

Males and females of all ages.

Object of game for players:

To score more points than the opponent by kicking the ball through the tall posts at the scoring end or by rushing the ball through any of the four goal posts. A goal scored is worth six points and a behind scored is worth one point. The team with the highest point tally at the end of play is the winner.

Number of players:

Two teams of 18.

Costume, apparel/equipment required:

Boots, shorts, and jerseys are the apparel, and the football is similar to a rugby ball.

Area/arena/field where played—space required:

The grass arena is a large oval about 150 x 180 yards, and the grandstands are large. Crowds in excess of 100,000 gather at the Melbourne Cricket Ground, which is the senior football venue in Australia.

Time length of game. How is end of game determined?:

The game is played in four quarters, 25 minutes each. Time is added to the clock each time the ball is dead, which means each quarter is usually 30 minutes in length.

Symbolism of game:

Begun in 1835 about the time Melbourne was founded as a city, this game is a remarkable example of ribald, competitive youth seeking out the ball and attempting to move it toward the goal. There is ample opportunity for individual brilliance but few teams succeed without a combination of players working together. Restrictions to natural body functioning are observed, as they are in most football games. A player can catch or pick up a ball with his hands, but cannot throw the ball. New skills are required, in that the ball is punched from one hand by the other.

Rules of play, including scoring:

The game begins with the umpire bouncing the ball. Possession is then gained by one team or the other and the ball is moved toward the goal. Players may not run more than ten yards with the ball without bouncing or grounding it and may pass the ball on either by hitting, punching, or kicking it. A mark, catching the ball in the air or on the full, results in the freedom to take time to kick the ball. Penalties result from tackling on the shoulders and above, on the hips or below, and by pushing in the back. Unsportsmanlike conduct also results in a penalty when elbows, fists, or legs are used to knock down a player. Players must not delay the flow of the game. This can result in a 50-yard penalty and an almost certain goal for the opposing team. Chewing, fighting, biting, punching, tripping, elbowing, and cursing result in free kicks and sometimes a report, which is taken to a tribunal and usually results in such penalties and fines or missed games in the future. The game is enormously popular, inviting huge crowds on a weekly basis. The final is always played before a crowd in excess of 100,000 people.

BEACH FLAG RELAY
Ken Edwards
Not appropriate for replication.

Players:

Male and female teens.

Object of game for players:

To complete the assigned voyage and be on the team to cross the line first.

Number of players:

Two teams of four.

Costume, apparel/equipment required:

Small flag (beach flag) or baton.

Area/arena/field where played—space required:

A level beach area with a number of lanes marked between 75 and 100 meters long. Starting and finish lines are marked on the sand at each end of the course.

Time length of game. How is end of game determined?:

Upon termination of the relay.

Symbolism of game:

Team competition.

Rules of play, including scoring:

1. Each member of the team runs about 75 meters with flag unfurled.
2. Teams take up positions on the beach indicated by the check starter or beach judges.
3. At the start the players' fingers and feet must not be over the starting line.

4. A player waiting for the flag must toe the line and not move off until he or she has received the flag from the incoming runner.

5. Any player finishing without the baton, or any player jostling, or going over the line while waiting for the flag, causes his or her team to be disqualified.

6. Flags or batons that are dangerous to players must not be used.

   Variations:

- Use a flag or baton held in either hand.
- Each player runs between 95 to 100 meters.
- Players taking the baton on the second, third, and fourth legs stand on a line five meters behind the start and finish line. They can move while taking the baton, but will be disqualified if any part of their bodies or hands cross the front line, or if they are not in possession of the baton.
- Run in marked lanes.

BEACH FLAGS (BATONS)

Ken Edwards

Appropriate for replication.

Players:

Male and female teens.

Object of game for players:

To gain a baton and not be eliminated from the competition.

Number of players:

Many, although each Beach Flag heat, quarter-final, semifinal, and final should contain up to a maximum of 15 starters.

Costume, apparel/equipment required:

Beach Flags (batons) 30 centimeters long with an external diameter of 2.5 centimeters, made of flexible material (for example, plastic hose).

Area/arena/field where played—space required:

An outdoor sand course approximately 20 meters in length and wide enough to provide a minimum spacing of 1.2 meters between each of up to 15 competitors. (An easy and accurate way to attain this result is to place a piece of rope, knotted at 1.2-meter intervals, in front of competitors.)

Time length of game. How is end of game determined?:

Usually 15 minutes.

Symbolism of game:

Competitive nationalism.

Rules of play, including scoring:

The event is started with a whistle blast.

Procedure: Players take up their positions as drawn on the starting line (their bodies should be separated by 60 centimeters, about one arm's length). Players lie face down, with their toes on the starting line, heels together, hands on top of each other, and heads up. Elbows must be extended forward so that the chest lies flat on the sand, and the body must be at right angles to the starting line. (Players are allowed to level the sand but no scooping or digging is permitted.) On the command "Heads down," players stretch their chins forward, placing them on their hands, and await the start. At a signal from the starter, the players rise to their feet as quickly as possible and race to obtain a baton.

Willful jostling or obstructing another player so as to impede his or her progress results in disqualification. If disqualification occurs, points or medals awarded from the previous elimination still stand. Any competitor picking up two batons is disqualified. Caps must remain on the head, securely fastened under the chin, until judging is complete.

Start: The start line is designated at each end by a green flag on a 1.5 meter pole. The batons are positioned in a line parallel to the starting line so that a perpendicular line between any two adjacent competitors passes approximately through a baton.

The starter must be unseen by the players when placing the *shiste* (chin strap) in his or her mouth. If a player delays the start by taking an unnecessarily long time to level the sand, or by not putting his or her head down on command, the player will receive a warning. A second infringement results in disqualification. The starter gives the command, "Heads Down," and after waiting between two and five seconds, signals the start with a whistle blast. Any player lifting any part of the body from the sand prior to the starting signal must be warned that they have made a break. A second infringement results in disqualification.

Competition: The sectional referee determines the number of players to be eliminated in each round of each heat or semi-final, with the condition that in any one heat no more than three players can be eliminated, and in a semi-final, no more than two players can be eliminated on one run. In the finals, when the number of contestants has been reduced to six or eight, as determined by the sectional referee, there shall be a draw for positions after each run, and players shall be eliminated one at a time to determine first, second, and third place, as well as any other required placings.

Each run or re-run is judged as a separate segment of the overall event and an infringement in one run or re-run is not carried over or counted against a player in any subsequent runs or re-runs. Should the circumstances arise, because of breaks, all remaining players' runs or re-runs shall be commenced afresh. Should a player in a run or re-run be disqualified for breaking who would otherwise but for that disqualification have been awarded points and/or a place medallion, that player shall be awarded the points and/or medallion that would have been awarded had he or she been eliminated in that run or re-run.

Judging: The sectional referee positions him- or herself at one side of the course to maintain overall supervision. Two break and/or course judges, one at either end of the starting line, are positioned to observe any infringements, false starts, or willful jostling. Two or three finish judges are positioned a few meters behind the line of batons to reclaim the batons from the successful competitors and set them up for the next run. In the event two or more players hold the same baton (regardless of the hand position on the baton), the finish judges declare a dead-heat, decide the winner, or conduct a run-off between the players involved.

BRAMBAHL (SKIPPING)

Ken Edwards
Not appropriate for replication.

Players:

Older men of the Juwalarai people of the Narran River in New South Wales.

Object of game for players:

To vary the performance of the skipping and to have fun while enjoying the outdoors.

Number of players:

Any number.

Costume, apparel/equipment required:

A number of skipping ropes four to six meters long.

Area/arena/field where played—space required:

Any designated area.

Time length of game. How is end of game determined?:

Variable.

Symbolism of game:

A favorite game of the old men of the Juwalarai people. Men more than 70 years old were often the best players. Depicting age as a nonvariable.

Rules of play, including scoring:

A player stands at each end of a long rope. When it is in full swing, a player moves in as the skipper. After skipping in the usual way for a few rounds the player begins to mime variations. These consist, among other things, of:

- Taking thorns out of the feet.
- Digging as if for the larvae of ants.
- Digging for yams with a digging stick.
- Grinding grass-seed.
- Jumping like a frog.
- Doing a type of dance.
- Appearing to be looking for something in the distance.
- Running out, picking up a child (or object), and skipping with it in their arms.
- Lying flat down on the ground and raising the body as the rope turns.
- Measuring their full length while lying flat on the ground, rising and letting the rope slip under them.
- Imitating animals such as a kangaroo.
- Walking on all fours.
- Performing various antics.

The rope is kept going the whole time and never varies in pace or pauses for any of the variations. The player who most successfully varies his performance is the winner.

BUROINJIN
Ken Edwards
Appropriate for replication.

Players:

Male and female teens. Played by the Kabi-Kabi people of southern Queensland.

Object of game for players:

The object is for players of one team to run as far as possible with the *buroinjin* (ball) and cross over a line (or a post) at their end of the field. They attempt to do this without being touched by their opponents.

Number of players:

Two teams of up to eight.

Costume, apparel/equipment required:

A size two or three soccer ball as the buroinjin. Use high jump stands or mark lines as the score lines.

Area/arena/field where played—space required:

Use a designated area approximately 50 to 70 meters long and 35 to 50 meters wide. A line is marked (or a post is placed) at each end of the playing area.

Time length of game. How is end of game determined?:

Variable.

Symbolism of game:

The game was played with a ball made of kangaroo skin called a buroinjin. The ball, which was smaller than a football, was sewn with tendons and stuffed with grass. Teams from different groups often played against each other, representing competition between tribes. The game was often played until sunset. Spectators used to mark their applause by calling out "Ei, ei."

Rules of play, including scoring:

This is a running and ball-passing game. The buroinjin is thrown into the air in the middle of the playing area to begin the game. A player from one team then attempts to run as far as possible and cross the line or post at his or her end of the field without being touched by an opponent. There are no positions or offsides and the buroinjin can be thrown in any direction. The buroinjin may be passed from player to player but it cannot be hit or kicked. The game is played by running and passing but does not stop if a player drops the buroinjin. Immediately after a player holding the buroinjin is touched, the ball has to be thrown up and away (at least five meters in the air) by that player for teammates and opposing players to attempt to pick up. The player who was touched may not get the buroinjin on this throw.

If a player is able to run past the score line (or post), one point is scored. The game is then restarted.

Variations of play:
- Use a post at one end of the area only.
- Players may run toward either post when their team gains possession.
- To score, a player would have to run through a marked area ten meters either side of the post.

Safety precaution: Players may not dive on the ball on the ground but must bend over and pick it up.

CHARIOT RACE
Ken Edwards
Not appropriate for replication.

Players:

Males and females of all ages.

Object of game for players:

A team of six players forms a sort of human "chariot," with one jockey standing on the backs of the rear row of players. Teams race each other a distance of 50 meters. Before the start of the race, members of each team join their arms together and remain in that position throughout the race.

Number of players:

Each team consists of six members. The number of teams depends on the space available along the beach.

Costume, apparel/equipment required:

Long-sleeved shirts may be worn or towels may be used to help with holding the chariot together. The jockey holds onto each end of a towel.

Area/arena/field where played—space required:

The beach. Teams race a straight run along the beach (parallel to the water's edge) approximately 50 meters in length.

Time length of game. How is end of game determined?:

The end is determined when one team crosses the finish line.

Symbolism of game:

It represents a chariot race, and the idea of holding the team together and functioning successfully as a homogeneous group.

Rules of play, including scoring:

The formation of the team is three in the front row, two in the rear, in a standing form of a Rugby scrum. A jockey stands with his or her feet on the backs of the rear row members of the team, supported by two towels from the outside front row. The feet of the three front players are on the starting line. The feet of all three front competitors must cross the finishing line and the whole team must be intact for the team to finish the race. Before the commencement of the race the members of each team link their arms together and remain in that position throughout.

Variations:
- Have races without the jockey.
- Hold races where the chariot must go around a marker 20 meters away and return.
- Members of each team run to a line 20 meters away and form their chariot before returning to the start.

CONTINUOUS CRICKET
Ken Hawkins
Appropriate for replication.

Players:

Males and females of all ages.

Object of game for players:

To make the greatest number of runs.

Number of players:

Two teams of six to 12 players. The batting team lines up on the side of the field. The bowling team has one bowler, a wicket-keeper, and fielders spread around the field.

Costume, apparel/equipment required:

A bat (cricket bat), tennis ball, one set of (cricket) wickets (three upright stumps, two inches apart), and a turning marker/base.

Area/arena/field where played—space required:

An area large enough to accommodate a pitch seven to ten meters long and with a turning mark seven meters to the off side of the wicket.

Time length of game. How is end of game determined?:

The game continues until all players of the batting team are "out."

Symbolism of game:

A slightly colorful version of cricket. It represents changing rules to suit all players in differing circumstances.

Rules of play, including scoring:

The bowler bowls the ball underarm close to the ground. The batter guarding the wicket with the bat hits at the ball. If he or she misses, the bowler bowls again. When the ball is hit the batter runs to touch the base and returns to the wicket, which results in one run. The team making the greatest number of runs is the winner. After the ball is hit the fielders return it to the bowler who immediately bowls again whether or not the batter has returned to the wicket.

The batter is out if he or she is:

- bowled (the ball hits the wicket).
- caught.
- hit on the legs while defending the wicket.
- the wicket is hit.
- the ball plays onto the wicket off the bat.
- the batter obstructs a fielder.

Hits behind the wicket are allowed. While the batter is changing the bowler may continue to bowl at the wicket and if he or she hits the wicket then the new batter is out. The game continues until all players of the batting team are out when the teams change over.

Pointers: The batter should place his or her hits between the fielders. Fielders should return the ball quickly to the bowler who should bowl immediately when he or she receives it. The game is accelerated if a rule is made to the effect that if a batter fails to hit the third fair ball bowled, he or she is out and his or her place is immediately taken by the next batter.

Variations:

1. Use a hoop 15 meters out from the middle of the pitch.
2. Change bowlers after every eight to ten deliveries.
3. Vary the distance of the marker.
4. Use different balls or bats.
5. Play with a "leg before wicket" (when the batter prevents the ball hitting the wicket with his or her legs) as a method to dismiss the batter.
6. Play single-inning games.
7. Bowlers can either throw or bowl as in cricket. The ball should hit the ground before it reaches the batter.
8. In indoor play the batter can also be called out if a fielder catches the ball on the full (in the air without bouncing) or if it first bounces off the walls or ceiling.
9. An incoming batter crossing the restraining line, or a player of the batting team leaving the waiting area before the batter is dismissed, is out.
10. After hitting the ball the batter must drop the bat to run around the turning mark.
11. Change the bowler and wicket keeper every eight deliveries.
12. The batter must run when the ball is hit or the ball hits them.

13. When played as a lunch time game the distance the batter must run can be varied. For example, if individual players are difficult to get out then the distance of the run can be lengthened.

14. *Indoor Continuous Cricket:* For this indoor game the bowler bounces the ball for the batter to hit with the palm of his or her hand (or with a short bat held in one hand). Whether the ball is hit or not, the batter has to run to the right, around a marker about five meters away, and back for the next bowl. Every time the bowler bowls the batter must complete a run, even if he or she has missed the ball. Fielders always throw the ball immediately to the bowler, as a bowl that has bounced once and then is caught by the backstop-wicket keeper puts the player out. If a ball is well hit, or misfielded, more than one run can be attempted.

15. *Drop Bat and Run:* If the batter hits the ball, he or she drops the bat and runs round a marker to score a run, pick up the bat, and prepare to face the bowler again. When the first batter is out he or she drops the bat and the next batter runs to pick it up and take his or her place. If the batter hits the wicket when batting or when dropping the bat before running, he or she is out. The bowler may continue to bowl during the changeover and if he or she hits the wicket the batter is out. Batters are also caught out or bowled out.

16. *Small Area Continuous Cricket:* The area is marked with a base placed three to five meters to the right of the wickets and a bowling line is marked five to seven meters in front of the wicket. The batters line up at the side of the playing area while the fielding team selects a bowler and a backstop-wicket keeper. The rest of the team spreads themselves around the field. The bowler must bowl underarm and the batter must run around the base each time the ball is hit. The batter can only be bowled out by the bowler after a ball is fielded. The ball is fielded and thrown to the bowler who immediately bowls again, whether the batter has returned or not. Batters are also out when they are caught or hit their own wickets. When a batter is out the next batter immediately takes his or her place. When a change of batters is being made the bowler may continue to bowl at the wicket. The game continues until all the players of the batting team are out. The teams then change over. The team scoring the most runs after two innings is the winner.

17. The batting team is numbered and stands behind the restraining line. The ball is bowled overarm or underarm to the first batter. If the batter hits it he or she drops the bat and runs around the post to score one run. After this the batter picks up the bat and prepares to face the bowler again. The ball is fielded to the bowler who immediately bowls again whether the batter has returned or not. The batter is out

when: the ball hits the wickets, the batter hits his or her own wicket while batting or when dropping the bat before running, or the batter is caught from a hit. When out, the batter immediately drops the bat and the second batter runs in to pick it up and take his or her place. The bowler may continue to bowl during the changeover, and if the wicket is hit the second batter is out and the third batter runs in to bat. Continue until the whole team is out. The bowler and wicket keeper are changed every eight bowls.

CRICKO (NEE VIGORO)
Ken Hawkins
Appropriate for replication.

Players:

Males and females of all ages.

Object of game for players:

To be the team to score the greatest number of runs.

Number of players:

Ideally, two teams of 12. (No team may take the field with less than six players.)

Costume, apparel/equipment required:

Use a cricket bat, a vigoro ball (red) and a set of vigoro (or cricket) wickets. The wicket keeper may use pads and gloves and batters may use batting gloves.

Area/arena/field where played—space required:

The boundaries of the field are approximately 50 meters from the center of the pitch (40 meters for schools). The pitch is 19 meters long (15 meters long for schools). A popping (batting) crease is marked 1.2 meters from the wicket. A bowling crease and return crease are also marked. A line called the compulsory run mark (crease) is made on the pitch 1 meter in front of the popping crease.

Time length of game. How is end of game determined?:

A good game lasts less than four hours and can have up to 44 wickets fall and well over 400 runs scored.

Symbolism of game:

Cricko is closely related to cricket and vigoro. The game was developed in New South Wales in the 1930s and later spread to Queensland. Cricko is a winter sport and is now played only in Brisbane in a small competition. It represents triumph of people over tricky flying objects.

Rules of play, including scoring:

Each side has two innings taken alternately except in case of a follow on. (A follow on occurs when one side scores so badly that they are forced to bat successively.) The side that bats first and leads by double the number of runs has the option of requiring the other side to follow on their innings. If a second inning is not completed the game can be decided on the first inning.

All batting is done at one end of the pitch. Each batting side has the choice of end for each of its innings. One batter is at each end of the wicket. The batter at the wicket keeper's end is the striker, and the batter at the bowler's end is the nonstriker. One run (or more) must be completed for every ball hit that is fielded in front of the compulsory run mark.

Compulsory run:

- In the case of a compulsory run the striker is out no matter which wicket is knocked down, provided the batters have not crossed in running.
- If the batters have crossed in running then the batter nearest the wicket broken is out.

The striker can be called out if no attempt is made to run from a hit in front of the compulsory run mark.

Noncompulsory run:

- If the batters have crossed each other when attempting a noncompulsory run then the batter running for the wicket that is put down is out.
- If the batters have not crossed then the batter who has left the wicket that is put down is out.

It is optional to run for a bye, leg bye, hit behind the compulsory run mark, or an overthrow. If a no ball is delivered it is not a compulsory run even if it is hit in front of the compulsory run mark.

The ball can be bowled or thrown by an overarm action but must not be delivered from below the shoulder. The penalty for breaking this rule is a no ball. This is an illegal delivery. It counts for nothing and must be repeated with no chance of gaining an out. The bowler must deliver the ball with one foot on the ground behind the bowling crease (at the stumps) and within the return crease. If the bowler fails to do this, he or she receives a no ball. The ball must be bowled in overs of eight balls (six for schools) from one end to the pitch. The bowler is changed at the end of an over. A player can bowl as many overs as required but no bowler may bowl two overs consecutively in one inning. When eight balls have been bowled and the ball is finally back in the bowler's hands the umpire calls "over," which means the end of that bowler's turn and a new bowler takes over. The ball is then dead. Neither a no ball nor a wide ball shall be considered as part of the over.

Variations of play:

1. Use Kanga cricket gear (bats are shaped differently).

2. Play in a smaller area.

3. Play a single inning match.

4. Limit over game. Play a set number of overs to each team. An over is eight balls. Limited over games are usually restricted to 50 overs for each side.

HEAVY BALL
Ken Edwards
Appropriate for replication.

Players:

Male teens and older.

Object of game for players:

To toss a ball into the opposing team's area, while the opposing team tries to catch it or prevent it from landing.

Number of players:

Two teams of five.

Costume, apparel/equipment required:

The game is played with a medicine ball weighing between 1 and 2 kilograms. The weight of the ball can be varied according to the age of the players. Where possible, the medicine ball should be soft, and in a slightly flattened shape.

Area/arena/field where played—space required:

The court is 12 x 7.2 meters. A line divides the court into two areas, each six meters deep. A thin rope (or Badminton net) is stretched across the center of the court at a height of 1.83 meters. Posts are 35 centimeters outside the court. Parallel with the center line, and 1.5 meters from the back line of each area, a dotted line is marked. This line is called the service line.

Time length of game. How is end of game determined?:

Variable.

Symbolism of game:

Heavy ball, called Medicine Ball Tennis, was invented by Australians and first played by Australian soldiers in France during World War I. It was introduced to the Sydney Boys' High School in the early 1920s by Captain O. A. Cropley. In the early years, various rules and court dimensions were used. The rules presented here are based on those outlined by R. A. Anderson in 1984. The game represents cooperation and distress.

Rules of play, including scoring:

Players may move anywhere within their own area but while the ball is being served they must stand in their correct position. The positions are:

- Right forward
- Center forward
- Left forward
- Right back
- Left back

The backs cover the space between the forwards. Each position may be replaced only once during a game.

A medicine ball is thrown over a rope/net to land within the area of the opposing team. The opponents' aim is to catch the ball and prevent it from landing in their area, or, if it is going out of bounds, to avoid touching it.

Basic Rules: The ball is only put into play by a service from one of the backs, standing with both feet behind the service line. The game is commenced by the team losing the toss for choice of ends. After each point is scored the ball is served by the back nearest the ball, regardless of which side won the point.

If the ball lands on the rope/net and falls straight down it is a let. If the ball touches the rope/net without being greatly deflected it is a fair service.

General Play: The ball may be thrown with either or both hands, either under or overarm. When caught the ball must be thrown back over the rope/net by the catcher. If a ball is caught out of bounds or is taken out of bounds, it is returned from just outside the line at the nearest point to where it was caught.

While throwing the ball at least one foot must be kept on the ground. (No player may throw the ball with both feet off the ground.) The ball must be returned quickly. Undue delay (for example to find an opening, or to make a feint) is not allowed. The touching of the ball by one player does not prevent another player on the same team from catching it. However, if the toucher knocks it forward the catcher must go back to the spot where it was touched and throw it from there.

If, in catching a ball, a player, or his foot, passes under the rope into the opponents' area, he must face his own team and throw the ball over their heads in playing it. No player may reach over the rope/net or touch it with any part of his body or with the ball while it is in his hands. (A thrown ball may touch the rope/net while going over it without penalty except when it is being served.)

A ball thrown by one player of a team must not be touched by another player of the same team on its way to the other team's area. The ball may be returned quickly and thrown hard, but must not be thrown by a player (either a forward or a back who has moved from his normal position) directly at an opposing forward. This action constitutes dangerous play, the offender is immediately sent off the court, and no score is made from this throw. A replacement may come on for this player; however, if the player concerned is a replacement, then the position must remain vacant.

Scoring: One point shall be scored by a team each time the ball is thrown fairly over the rope/net and touches the ground within the other teams' area (which includes the side and base lines). Points are also scored when anyone on the opposing team infringes any of the rules relating to:

- A player touching a throw from the opposing team without catching it (even thought the ball would have landed out of bounds).

- The ball being thrown with one or two hands in any manner. (No other method of propelling the ball is allowed.)

- The thrower keeping at least one foot on the ground at the spot where the ball was caught. (If it is caught and taken out of bounds it must be thrown from just inside the area near where it went out.)
- The ball not being returned over the net promptly. (Undue delay is not allowed.)
- Reaching over or touching the rope/net with any part of the body or with the ball while it is in players' hands.
- The ball thrown by one player not being touched by teammates after it is thrown toward the opposing teams' area.

Incorrect service:

Failure to comply with the following rules constitutes a foul (or no ball) and no point can be scored, even though the opposing team may fail to catch the ball.

Incorrect service results in a foul when any of the following occurs:

- The back making the serve does not stand with both feet behind the service line.
- The incorrect team serves to start the game (the team who lost the toss to serve first).
- The nearest back, regardless of the team, does not serve the ball after a point has been won.
- A ball that hit the rope/net and falls to the ground is a let (served again) even if a player attempts to catch the ball.
- The catcher does not return the ball to the correct spot after it has been knocked forward by a teammate. If it is knocked back it is taken from where it was caught.
- A player in catching the ball passes his foot under the net and does not follow the procedure of facing his own team when throwing the ball over their heads to play it.

Match result: The first team to score 21 points in a match or 11 points in a practice game wins the game. The teams change ends when one team has scored 12 points in a match or six in a practice game.

Variation: Use the same rules and a rugby ball to play light ball.

KAI
Ken Edwards
Appropriate for replication.

Players:

Males and females of all ages. This game was played by the people from the Torres Straits.

Object of game for players:

To keep the ball going the best and not allow it to hit the ground as often as the opposition.

Number of players:

Two teams of four to eight.

Costume, apparel/equipment required:

A tennis ball, small beach ball, or small gator skin ball.

Area/arena/field where played—space required:

Indoor or outdoor area.

Time length of game. How is end of game determined?:

Variable.

Symbolism of game:

In this game from the Torres Straits a number of players stood in a circle and sang the *kai wed* (ball song) as they hit a ball up in the air with the palms of their hands. The game was played using the thick, oval, deep red fruit of the kai tree, which is quite light when dry. This fruit, which has a tough rind, varies from about six to seven centimeters in length. This was some time later replaced by a hollow cubicle ball made of *Pandanus* or coconut palm leaves. This ball was introduced by South Sea people. The game teaches patience and hand/eye coordination.

Rules of play, including scoring:

The ball is thrown into a group and each player passes it to another by striking the ball upwards with the palm of the hand. Scoring is determined by how successfully each team keeps the ball going and how successfully they prevent it from hitting the ground. Points are lost every time the ball hits the ground.

Variations:

1. Play as a cooperative game with players all working together to keep the ball in the air as long as possible.

2. The player who makes the most hits without dropping the ball on the ground is the winner.

3. Use a boingo ball, beach ball, or other light ball.

4. Allow players two contacts with the ball instead of one (one to control the ball and one to hit it).

KAILEE

Ken Edwards

Not appropriate for replication.

Players:

Males and females of all ages from Western Australia.

Object of game for players:

To attain the longest possible boomerang flight before catching it.

Number of players:

Any number.

Costume, apparel/equipment required:

A boomerang.

Area/arena/field where played—space required:

An area such as a football field or cricket oval, which is marked with a center circle (10-meter radius) and a 50-meter range circle.

Time length of game. How is end of game determined?:

Variable.

Symbolism of game:

In Western Australia boomerang, or *kailee*, throwing was played. Kailees were thrown almost straight up into the sky. The thrower whose kailee remained longest in the air and flew the highest won the game. The Australians were attempting to connect with the sky.

Rules of play, including scoring:

The competition allows five throws per player. Players throw in a set order so that the competition consists of five rounds of one throw per player. Throws are made from the center circle (10-meter radius), and catches must be made within the 50-meter range circle. To score, the time is recorded from when the boomerang leaves the player's hand until the boomerang contacts the player making a successful catch. The middle result of three timers shall be the official time. If two or more players' best throws are equal, then their second-best times shall determine the winning order.

KALQ
Ken Edwards
Appropriate for replication.

Players:

Males of all ages of the Aboriginal tribes on Cape York Peninsula in North Queensland.

Object of game for players:

To attempt to make the ball circle the ring and return to the thrower.

Number of players:

Six to eight.

Costume, apparel/equipment required:

Each player has a Kanga cricket bat, a small bat, or a tennis racquet, in place of a *woomera* or shield. Use a tennis ball instead of a *kalq*, or a spear.

Area/arena/field where played—space required:

Any designated area.

Time length of game. How is end of game determined?:

Variable.

Symbolism of game:

This was originally a spear game. The men used a throwing stick (woomera) to project a big killing spear (kalq) toward the next player. The spear would travel around the circle of men who were armed only with their woomera, which they used to deflect the spear to the next player. When small boys played they used spears with blunted ends. It symbolizes control of dangerous instruments.

Rules of play, including scoring:

This is a cooperative team game. Players form a circle. One player throws or hits a tennis ball (for the spear) toward the player next to him. This player uses his bat (for the woomera) to deflect the ball to the next player in the circle. If the ball does not complete the circle then the next player has a turn to start it. If a player moves his feet it is regarded as a hit.
Variations:
1. Allow players to move their feet.

2. Players stand on small mats or large carpet tiles.

3. Stand in closer and players use the palms of their hand to hit a tennis ball or soft ball in a circle. A hit is when the bat deflects the ball.

KANGAROO RELAY
Jodie Hawkins
Appropriate for replication.

Players:

Teens.

Object of game for players:

To jump around a marker with ball a between the knees.

Number of players:

Classroom group in teams.

Costume, apparel/equipment required:

One playground or soccer ball per team.

Area/arena/field where played—space required:

Gymnasium, play area, or field.

Time length of game. How is end of game determined?:

When each member has had a turn.

Symbolism of game:

Represents creative use of tools, weapons, or equipment for the daily requirements of community life.

Rules of play, including scoring:

When the teacher says "Go," the first player places the ball between his knees, jumps forward on both feet up and around a marker, and then jumps back to his team. The player gives the ball to the next player and goes to the end of his or her line. If a player loses the ball, he or she must retrieve it and start again where the ball was lost.

KEE'AN
Ken Edwards
Appropriate for replication.

Players:

Males and females of all ages, of the Aboriginal people of North Queensland.

Object of game for players:

To throw a ball or beanbag (originally a bone) over a net and into a bin.

Number of players:

Up to eight. The game is played singly or in teams of two to four players.

Costume, apparel/equipment required:

Use cube beanbags, tennis balls, foxtail, or comet balls (or a ball stuffed into a stocking) for the bone with twine attached. Use a large plastic bin as the pit or hole.

Area/arena/field where played—space required:

For younger players use a badminton court and net. For older players use a volleyball court with the net about 1.8 meters high.

Time length of game. How is end of game determined?:

Variable.

Symbolism of game:

In areas of North Queensland a game of throwing skill was played. A large-sized bone such as a human shin (with twine attached to it) was thrown over a net (used to catch emus) into a pit or hole. Considering the distance to the hole, great skill was required to correctly aim the bone and ensure that it did not touch the net. It represents traditions with a bone, which is very important in aboriginal folklore.

Rules of play, including scoring:

Players attempt to throw the "bone" (ball or beanbag) from the baseline of the court over the net and into the bin. The bin is placed on the inside of the center of the front line of the court (service court line or spiking line, depending on the court used). A bin is set up in each half of the court to allow for two games at the same time. Players take turns throwing the bone into the hole.

Variations of play:
1. Players take turns. The first player to throw the bone into the bin is the winner and the game starts again.

2. Play in teams of four, alternating turns.

3. Use a piece of thick plastic tubing about 30 centimeters in length (to represent the throwing bone) with a piece of cord 20 centimeters long attached.

4. Set up bins on the front line of the court and the opposite baseline. A player has two attempts per turn at each bin. The first player to reach ten points wins.

5. Play in pairs operating from each end of the court. Each player has four turns. The first team to reach 20 is the winner.

6. Use badminton shuttles.

7. Put a handkerchief or similar cloth over a tennis ball, rubber ball, or styrofoam ball with a rubber band around it to hold it in place.

8. Play a miniversion using rolled up balls of paper thrown into a small rubbish bin half a meter beyond the end of a table tennis table. Players throw from behind the other end of the table.

9. Throw fleece or sponge balls into a small bin or bucket about three to five meters away.

10. Play the game outdoors in the traditional manner using a shin bone and a net.

KEENTAN
Ken Edwards
Appropriate for replication.

Players:

Males and females of all ages of the northwest central districts of Queensland.

Object of game for players:

A running, passing, and catching game in which the object is to keep the ball away from the other team.

Number of players:

The game can be played either singly or in teams of four to ten.

Costume, apparel/equipment required:

Use a ball such as a size three soccer ball or gator ball.

Area/arena/field where played—space required:

Any designated area.

Time length of game. How is end of game determined?:

Variable.

Symbolism of game:

A keep-away game of catch played everywhere by both genders in the northwest central districts of Queensland. Because the action of the players jumping up to catch the ball resembled the movements of a kangaroo the Kalkadoon people sometimes described this game as the "kangaroo play." The ball itself was made of a piece of opossum, wallaby, or kangaroo hide tied up with twine. The players tried to imitate animal mobility.

Rules of play, including scoring:

When played in teams the ball is thrown from one player to another player of the same team. The players of the opposing team attempt to intercept the ball while they are off the ground; the ball can only be intercepted if it is caught while the player is literally in the air. If the ball is dropped or knocked to the ground by a player the other team gains possession. This is also the case if a thrown ball is not caught by a player of the same team and falls to the ground. No physical contact is allowed. Players cannot stop opposing players from moving around the area; no interference is allowed. A player cannot be guarded or obstructed while he or she is attempting to pass the ball.

Variations:
1. When played in pairs the ball is thrown from one player to another player and is caught when the player is in the air.
2. Passes must be from a minimum of three meters.
3. The ball must be in the air to be caught but players do not have to be to catch it.

KOMBE BURRONG
Ken Edwards
Appropriate for replication.

Players:

Male and female teens of the Ngungar people of the southwest part of Western Australia.

Object of game for players:

To elude the defender and take emu feathers off the stick they are tied onto.

Number of players:

Four to six.

Costume, apparel/equipment required:

A piece of a soft rubber hose about 30 centimeters in length can be used to represent a bundle of feathers attached to a stick.

Area/arena/field where played—space required:

Any designated area.

Time length of game. How is end of game determined?:

The game is played until the piece of hose is taken away from the defender, five minutes have elapsed, or the attacking players become tired and give up.

Symbolism of game:

Defense against odds.

Rules of play, including scoring:

One player holds the piece of hose (bundle of feathers). The other players attempt to take the piece of hose away, but they are not allowed to interfere with the defender in any other way. The defender protects the piece of hose by pushing the other players away. No kicking is allowed.

Variation: One player kneels on a large gym mat and is given a football or small medicine ball. The other players attempt to take it from him. Set a time limit for this version.

MEETCHE KAMBONG
Ken Edwards
Appropriate for replication.

Players:

Male and female teens of the Ngungar people of the southwest part of Western Australia.

Object of game for players:

To retrieve a ball that has been buried in the ground while the opposing team tries to prevent capture.

Number of players:

Two teams of four or five.

Costume, apparel/equipment required:

A rounded stone or tennis ball used as the meetche nut.

Area/arena/field where played—space required:

Any designated area.

Time length of game. How is end of game determined?:

When fatigue sets in.

Symbolism of game:

A wrestling game of the Ngungar people of the southwest part of Western Australia was called *meetche kambong* (nut game) or *boojur kombang* (ground game). In the Swan district it was called *boojoor-el-eeja*. A team beaten at this game might resume the contest in a month or so. The game represents team competition.

Rules of play, including scoring:

The meetche (tennis ball) is buried about 20 centimeters into the ground. Four or five players guard it while an equal number of attacking players attempt to break through and "capture" the meetche. All players' actions are restricted to pushing and pulling; no kicking is allowed. The game continues until one team becomes tired (at least five minutes) or until the meetche is secured. This would be a good game to play on the sand at the beach. The winners shout: *Kaia, kaia, yaang, yaang, yaang doojara. Ngai jinnong, jinnong. (Beat them. See, see, I've got it.)*

MILLIM BAEYEETCH
Ken Edwards
Appropriate for replication.

Players:

Male and female teens. In this game boys and girls play separately. It is from the Aboriginal people from parts of Victoria.

Object of game for players:

To keep the ball away from the other team by kicking it among your own players.

Number of players:

Two teams of up to 20 or more.

Costume, apparel/equipment required:

An Australian football, soccer ball, or gator skin ball.

Area/arena/field where played—space required:

A designated area such as a cricket oval.

Time length of game. How is end of game determined?:

Variable.

Symbolism of game:

One of the favorite games of the Aboriginal people in parts of Victoria was a game of football. There were a few variations of the game and the one outlined below was observed in the 1840s. Among some people of the western district of Victoria, ball players were referred to as *beiin*. Another Aboriginal group in a nearby area named them *millim baeyeetch*. The game was an imitation of animals, birds, and reptiles fighting.

Rules of play, including scoring:

To start the game the ball is kicked in any direction by the leader of one team. Players may run around the area and, after gaining the ball, they run and kick it as soon as they can, and usually as far as they can. A player may be allowed up to five meters to run and kick the ball. If the ball is kicked farther the opposing team gains possession.For safety reasons and to allow for the involvement of all players no intentional physical contact or obstruction is allowed. Players are allowed to kick the ball only if they catch it or otherwise gain possession. If the ball is dropped or knocked along the ground the player closest to it is allowed to pick up the ball and run with it and/or kick it. A player may not dive on the ground to gain the ball. The ball may be kicked off the ground. If the ball goes out of the playing area the nonoffending team gains possession. If any rules are violated, it is considered a foul and an opposition player will be allowed to pick up the ball and continue play. The team that kicks the ball the most or retains possession the longest wins the game.

Variations:
1. Players can only run with the ball for five meters before they kick it.
2. Players can pass the ball with the hands or hand the ball to each other as in Australian football.
3. Kicks have to be ten meters or more or they result in a change of possession.
4. Possession changes if a kick is dropped.
5. The first player in position calls "mark" for the ball and is allowed to try to catch the ball without any other player attempting to do so.
6. A team scores one point if they are able to make ten consecutive passes to players on the same team. The team scoring the most points in the game is the winner.
7. Allow physical contact in attempting to gain the ball.
8. Use two balls.
9. Play marks (a catch on the full) as in Australian football. Any time a player catches the ball on the full (ball doesn't hit the ground), it is called a mark.

In the traditional game the player (beiin) who kicks the ball the highest during the game is considered the best player and has the honor of burying it in the ground in preparation for a game the next day. The game ends with a shout of applause and the best player is complimented on his or her skill.

PILLOW FIGHT
Ken Edwards
Not appropriate for replication.

Players:

Males and females of all ages.

Object of game for players:

To knock everyone else off the pole. Players begin the game by sitting on a pole. Each player holds a pillow in one hand and with their other hand they hold their costume (or shorts) behind their back. Players are not permitted to cross their legs under the pole. Blows are then to be delivered by the pillow in a round arm or swinging action to the person next to them or across from them on another pole. The first player to fall is the loser.

Number of players:

As many starters as desired, to be reduced to eight for the final rounds and eventually down to four final players. Player #1 plays player #4 and player #2 plays player #3. The winners of these matches meet in the grand final with the losers taking third and fourth place.

Costume, apparel/equipment required:

The pillow to be used should be made from a durable semihard material with a handle-like grip to prevent the competitors from wrapping the pillow around their fists like a boxing glove. It must be made of noninjurious material. The pole on which the competitors sit is 12.5 centimeters in diameter and marked off clearly with lines 60 and 80 centimeters apart. The pole is supported by a structure so that it is about 1.8 meters from the ground.

Area/arena/field where played—space required:

A sandy area with soft sand underneath the pole.

Time length of game. How is end of game determined?:

Each round lasts no longer than one minute. The end of the game is determined by the elimination of players each round until the final round held between the last two players.

Symbolism of game:

Previously this was a competition conducted at lifesaving championships. It essentially is a game of motor skills and balance.

Rules of play, including scoring:

As mentioned earlier, each player holds a pillow in one hand and their costume in the other behind his or her back. All blows must be made only by the pillow and in a round, swinging motion. The first one to fall loses. Players will be disqualified if they release the grip on their costume, use their feet against their opponent, or hold the pole. Willful punching, butting, or jostling with the elbows, head, knees, or legs results in disqualification after two clear warnings.

Variations:

1. Competitors are allowed to cross their legs under the pole.

2. Use a pole over a large mat or swimming pool.

3. Use large sponge balls or beach balls in a sack. No contacts on the head.

4. Players compete while standing on a low balance beam or plank.

5. Players use low raised blocks about one meter apart.

6. Players sit on circular sponge mats (gym mat) about half a meter high. These are placed one meter apart on a large soft gym mat.

ROGAINING
Ken Edwards
Appropriate for replication.

Players:

Male and female teens and older.

Object of game for players:

A rogaining competition is a race between teams traveling on foot and limited by time. The aim of this cross-country navigation exercise is to visit as many checkpoints as possible in a specified time.

Number of players:

Teams may have two and five members, although two is the most common at the competitive level.

Costume, apparel/equipment required:

Standard topographical maps, compasses, and natural aids. One of the challenges of rogaining is to be able to determine which features are reliable and to use these to navigate when there is doubt as to the accuracy of other features. (Features help to find the checkpoints.)

Area/arena/field where played—space required:

Any designated area.

Time length of game. How is end of game determined?:

When a team reaches the final destination within the limited time.

Symbolism of game:

Rogaining is a team sport based on cross-country navigation. The sport originated as the Melbourne University 24 Hour Walk, held annually since 1947, and developed with enthusiastic university and scouting groups into rogaines, as they are held today. The concept of rogaines existing as a sport in its own right originated in Australia in 1976. It has since spread to Canada, the United States, New Zealand, Great Britain, and Ireland.

Rules of play, including scoring:

A rogaining course consists of a number of controls (or checkpoints) that are assigned point values depending on their location—their distance from the start, elevation, terrain, and the difficulty of navigation to reach them. The aim of the game is to visit as many checkpoints as possible in a specified time: six, eight, 12, or 25 hours. All players begin together. Maps with checkpoints shown are given out before the event and the players plot the checkpoints and plan their routes. Route choice refers to the sequence in which checkpoints are visited, as there are choices of routes between checkpoints. Most of the longer rogaines involve night navigation. Whenever possible these are held at the time of a full moon. Teams must remain together at all times. The length of the rogaines means that most teams walk with only the top teams running for part of the course. The team with the highest number of points gained from visiting the various checkpoints wins.

ROPE QUOITS
Ken Edwards
Not appropriate for replication.

Players:

Male and female teens and older.

Object of game for players:

The object of the game is to throw rope quoits (a quoit is a rung made up of rope wrapped around wire) from a toeblock onto a peg without missing. (Rope quoits are like rings in a ring toss.)

Number of players:

Played by singles or in team competitions, a team usually consists of six players or a minimum of four.

Costume, apparel/equipment required:

A set of six standard rope quoits and a peg. School-quality sets are available from sports stores. Use a small gym mat .8 meters behind the peg as the backdrop.

Area/arena/field where played—space required:

The throwing distance must be 2.74 meters from the center of the peg to the toeblock (toeline). Use a toeblock or mark a line with floor markers or tape.

Time length of game. How is end of game determined?:

School matches are played to 51 or 101 up (meaning number of tosses). When playing singles, open championship matches are played to 1001 up with no limit break. Junior and ladies championships are played to 351 up, and intermediate is played to 701 up with no limit break.

When playing in teams, open teams championships are eight rounds with no time limit. An extra round or rounds will be played to break a tie. Ladies teams championships play a minimum of seven rounds, with one-and-a-half hours of play and a maximum of ten rounds. Extra rounds will be played to break a tie.

The maximum number of throws in team championship are:

- Open Teams = 60 limit (played over eight rounds)
- B Grade Team = 30 limit (played over ten rounds)
- Ladies Team = 24 limit (minimum seven rounds, maximum ten rounds = 1.5 hours)

Symbolism of game:

Rope quoits was played extensively throughout Britain as early as the fifteenth century and was introduced by early settlers to Australia at many mining centers. The Australian Rope Quoits Council was formed in 1947, and the sport has developed its own Australian identity.

Rules of play, including scoring:

The number of quoits to be thrown is six. All quoits must be thrown directly at the peg one at a time with the feet behind a toeblock (toeline). If a player lands all six quoits on their first throw they continue on the break until they miss the peg or reach the required total (go out). A break is a turn that continues successfully. After the conclusion of a break (when a player has reached the total or passed the other player's final score) players should not throw additional quoits. The player winning the toss can toss first or send their opponent to the peg. If a quoit is dropped by a player in the act of placing or taking a quoit into the throwing hand, it is considered not thrown, no matter where the quoit finishes. Dropping the quoit in this case is accidental and is not penalized. A quoit thrown or partly thrown is recorded against the player. If a player has been interfered with in any way he or she will have the quoit back to throw again.

A game is played to a set number of points or can be played to the most points (successful throws) after a set number of rounds (six to ten). Only quoits on the peg at the completion of a throw count. For instance, if a quoit goes on the peg and then comes off it does not count. A quoit that lands on top of the peg can be thrown again or not (at the choice of the thrower). Once players take their stance at the toeblock they may not walk toward the peg until the completion of all six quoits. The exception to this is if there is a spinning quoit that can be knocked down with the hand or foot. In the event of a tie in any game the players have an extra throw (or throws) until a decision is reached. It is possible for a player to win the toss, go first, and go out (reach the total) in one throw. If this occurs the opponent will still have his or her turn. Play extra throw(s) for the tie.

Handicapping is a useful feature of the game. With handicaps, the higher the handicap, the better the thrower. There are difficulties involved with establishing these in the school situation, especially if quoits is played only occasionally.

Suggestions:

1. Randomly assign handicaps and readjust where necessary. A player is given a handicap that is added to the total points scored and this is the score that must be made. For a game to 51 up the handicap ranges from zero to 20. A player given a 20 handicap needs to score 71 to go out while a player on a handicap of two needs to score 53.

2. Play a number of rounds and assign a handicap. Before a handicap is assigned the players play a number of games. For example, let each player play ten rounds and record the scores in each game. If they make a total of 60 their handicap is six (60 divided by ten). If the total is 120 the handicap is 12. Repeat the procedure at least twice and average the two scores. Most players will be given a handicap of two to five.

3. Assign a bonus based on the number of quoits thrown to reach a set total. Let each player throw to 51 up and count the number of quoits thrown to reach this score. Repeat this a couple of times to find an average. If a player takes 70 throws then their bonus is 19 and they need to throw 32 quoits to go out. The maximum bonus allowed is 25. Readjust the bonus based on results in the contests.

4. Limit play with handicaps. If handicaps are to be used for players 15 and over they can vary from one to a maximum of eight (based on 101 up). Players handicapped six or under will be permitted to throw in any one shot more than double their handicap. All players handicapped seven or eight are restricted to a limit of 15. Players play (to 101 up) in two games before being rehandicapped.

Competitions:

1. No handicap: Play singles matches to 51 up with no limit break.

2. Handicap events: Either play with players of different abilities or a handicap total (and limit break) which is the same for all teams.

Terms:

- *Handicap:* a number designated by the handicapper.
- *Limit:* double the player's handicap.
- *Break:* number of rope quoits throw without missing.
- *Possible:* maximum quoits thrown in a game without missing.

- *Unfinished throw:* the throw by the last player in the competition who stops throwing after passing opponent's score.

Variations:

1. Players do not finish throws until they miss, even when reaching total (no break limit).

2. Place the pegs four meters apart. Play to one peg and throw back.

3. Play blindfolded.

4. Play an elimination contest for beginners. Players drop out of the competition if they cannot put four out of six throws on the peg at every turn.

5. Give a bonus of three for new players for every six quoits they throw. Play from six to ten rounds for each player.

6. Old quoits: Move the peg out to ten to 15 meters. Each player has three quoits. Play to 21 up.

7. Handicap players by the number of quoits to throw each turn. One player throws all six and then his or her opponent throws a set number. Play ten rounds.

8. Team competition: Play round-robin competition.

9. For younger players or less skilled place the peg at 1.8 meters.

10. Hoop quoits: Use plastic hoops that must be thrown over large markers. Markers can be placed at different distances.

11. Wall quoits: Place a peg or several pegs at a slight angle against a wall.

12. Pegboard Quoits: Use two pieces of board at right angles to one another. A peg is placed in the middle of the two pieces of wood and at the end of each "arm." Use rope or rubber quoits. Count two points for the middle peg and one for each of the other pegs or take turns throwing a quoit on each peg.

13. Novelty contests: Players alternate throwing with one hand and then the other, throwing two or more quoits at a time, or sitting in a chair while throwing.

14. Play a team competition of four rounds, the team having the highest total winning; handicaps may be used. The limit for any player is eight. Extra round or rounds to be played if teams tie.

15. Play a championship competition to 351.

Skills:

Stance: Keep both feet firmly on the ground and hard against the toe-block. Make sure to maintain good balance.

Grip: Rest the quoit on the thumb, and with the fingers gripping lightly on the quoit, throw with an even and consistent action.

Aim: Beginning players usually sight the peg through the quoit. For better players this is not necessary as they develop an arm action that tells them where the peg is.

Arm action: After the arm action is perfected do not watch the top of the peg at all.

Achievement: A world record throw of 4002 unfinished was made by Bill Irby, Sr. of Melbourne in the 1967 Australian Championships.

SPHAIREE

Ken Edwards

Appropriate for replication.

Players:

Male and female pre-teens.

Object of game for players:

To master skills similar to those employed in Tennis, Paddle Tennis, and to a lesser extent, Table Tennis.

Number of players:

Two in singles and four in doubles.

Costume, apparel/equipment required:

The bats are of plywood, plastic, or other material. A pimpled rubber, sandpaper, or other surface can be used. The bats should be about eight millimeters thick and 35 centimeters in length. The width should be 18 centimeters. The ball shall be a perforated plastic playball (a Unihoc or Cosom ball) about six centimeters in diameter. A net and stands are needed. Temporary lines may be marked on board surfaces with colored plastic self-adhesive tape or special floor markers.

Area/arena/field where played—space required:

Court dimensions are 6.2 x 2.8 meters with a center line running the full length of court. The court surface can be of any suitable material (such as concrete or board.) The net is 55.8 centimeters high at the posts with a maximum sag of 23 millimeters at the center.

Time length of game. How is end of game determined?:

Play for a set may be long or short. Long sets are played to advantage (to six or more games with a lead of two games.) In short sets, a tie-breaker is played if the score reaches five-all. A rubber match consists of the best of three sets.

Symbolism of game:

Pronounced *Sf-i-ree* (with an *i* as in *dine*), the game of sphairee employs skills similar to those used in tennis or its other forms. The name of the game comes from the Greek work *sphaira*, meaning ball. The game was invented by Fred Beck of Sydney in 1961.

Rules of play, including scoring:

Start of Play: To begin, players toss a coin to decide who will serve first. The winner of the toss has the choice of serving or receiving the serve.

Service: In singles play, service alternates between the two players. Ends are changed after the first game and again whenever the games total of both players in a particular set is an uneven number. If the players neglect to change ends and continue play then the match will continue until the games count again results in a change of ends (uneven number of games). To serve, the player must stand behind the baseline and within the area defined by an imaginary continuation of the center- and sidelines. No part of the server's feet may touch the baseline, and the service is underhand. It is delivered from a level not higher than the waistline. The server must hit the ball in the air. It is not allowed to bounce the ball on the ground and then hit it.

Service Court: The first serve in each game is delivered from the right hand side of the center line. After each point, the server changes to the other side of the center line. All serves are made into the diagonally opposite service box, and only one serve is allowed from each side. The score determines the correct court for the current point. If the game has been allowed to continue on the basis of an incorrect score then the server must still serve to the court determined by the corrected score and without a replay of points previously played.

Let: Under the following conditions a let is called and the serve is replayed: a) if the ball touches the top of the net and then lands in the correct service box, b) if the player serves to the wrong court (if, however, the next point has been commenced before the error has been noticed then the point will stand and service changes courts), c) if there is any disturbance that interferes with a rally, d) if an umpire is used and there are doubts about a decision, and e) if the ball is defective and affects the rally.

Rally: A point is scored when one player fails to fairly return the ball within the confines of the court as defined by the outside edges of the lines. A ball landing on the lines is considered in. Any type of stroke may be played in a rally. A rally is not over until the ball becomes dead (the point is awarded to the nonoffending player). A point is scored when:

- a player is unable to return the ball fairly (for example, missing or not returning a hit, a hit after the ball bounces twice, or a hit into the net that does not go over it).
- the ball lands out of court.
- the ball drops back into the striker's court after failing to clear the net.
- the ball, before bouncing, touches the body or clothes of a player.
- a player catches a ball before it has bounced.
- the ball in play hits walls or fixtures other than the net fixture or net posts.
- a player contacts the ball more than once in any stroke.
- a player catches the ball on his or her bat and throws it over the net.
- a player reaches over the net to hit the ball before it has reached the net.
- a player after allowing the ball to cross the net touches the net with his or her bat or body before the ball is dead.

If a player hits the ball around and outside the net posts the stroke is legal. If a player volleys a ball that would have landed out then the ball is still regarded as being in play and the ball must be returned fairly.

Receiving Serve: The receiver must allow the serve to bounce before playing it. Players may receive the service by standing anywhere in their court area. In singles matches only the server must observe the one bounce rule and allow the return of service to bounce before it is played. After this both players may play volleys or allow the ball to bounce.

General Play: Basically the same as for tennis, play is continuous but a player may choose to have a short break between games on the change of ends (up to 45 seconds) and after the second set a five-minute break is allowed.

Doubles Play: At the service both the server's and the receiver's partners must be behind the baseline at the moment when the server strikes the ball in the act of delivery. After the service both players of a team move anywhere in the court to play their strokes. They are allowed to be at the net at the same time, one up and one back, or to both be in the back of the court area. The players serve in rotation and the players in each pair decide from which service box they will receive service and continue to receive from the same service box until the end of the set. The system of scoring in sphairee is the same as that used in Tennis: 15, 30, 40, game. At 40-all the score is called deuce. When deuce is called the next point won is advantage to the player winning it. If the player holding advantage wins the next point he or she wins the game; but if the player loses it the score returns to deuce, and so on, until the player holding advantage wins the next point. A set normally ends when one player reaches a score of six games.

THA'AN
Ken Edwards
Not appropriate for replication.

Players:

Males of all ages of the Aboriginal people of the upper reaches of the Batavia River and McDonnell Ranges in North Queensland.

Object of game for players:

To push the other players with padded poles until they fall over, or step over a boundary.

Number of players:

Two to four.

Costume, apparel/equipment required:

Use a strong pole about four to five meters in length and padded at both ends.

Area/arena/field where played—space required:

Any designated area.

Time length of game. How is end of game determined?:

When a specific push is over.

Symbolism of game:

The pushing game of tha'an, similar in nature to tug-of-war, is played by young and old men on the upper reaches of the Batavia River and at

McDonnell in North Queensland. It demonstrates ruggedness and willpower.

Rules of play, including scoring:

Instead of pulling, players push against each other. One player plays against another, or two players play against two others.

Comment:

The fun of the activity consists mainly in balancing the pole side against side for a few minutes and then letting it fall with a deep grunt of relief.

THONG THROWING
Ken Edwards
Appropriate for replication.

Players:

Male and female pre-teens and teens.

Object of game for players:

The thong was christened in the mid 1950s. This casual form of footwear is sometimes called the flat sandal, flip flop, or jandal. The World Thong Throwing Championship is held every year in Pomona, 20 kilometers inland from Noosa. People come from as far as the United States, Japan, New Zealand, and Malaysia to compete for the coveted Bronzed Thong. The Pomona event began in 1985 and is part of the famous King of the Mountain contest, also held at Pomona.

Number of players:

Unlimited.

Costume, apparel/equipment required:

A rubber thong, size 10, which must measure 29 centimeters long and weigh 145 to 150 grams.

Area/arena/field where played—space required:

Any designated open area.

Time length of game. How is end of game determined?:

Three rounds.

Symbolism of game:

Heaving light instruments for distance.

Rules of play, including scoring:

The thong is thrown from a 2.135 diameter circle to land in a 30-degree arc. Contestants have to throw the thong as far as they can in the best of three attempts. A thrower cannot leave the throwing circle until the thong has landed.

The world record for the thong throwing event is held by a Queenslander at 42.8 meters.

Thongs have a down-side: They can be dangerous for the feet if used too often.

TOUCH IN SEVEN
Ken Edwards
Appropriate for replication.

Players:

Suitable for males and females of all ages and body sizes.

Object of game for players:

The object of the game is to score more touchdowns than the opposing team.

Number of players:

Seven-per-side with up to seven replacement players. A minimum of five players is needed for the game to continue.

Costume, apparel/equipment required:

A touchball (like a football) and appropriate clothing and footwear (which might be bare feet).

Area/arena/field where played—space required:

An area 70 meters long by 50 meters wide.

Time length of game. How is end of game determined?:

Fifty minutes.

Symbolism of game:

The game has its origins in the training routines employed by the rugby union and the rugby league in the 1960s. The first competition was held by the South Sydney Touch Football Club in 1968. The game was adopted in other states with wide variations in the rules. The NSW rules were largely adopted with the formation of the Australian Touch Association in 1978. The game is also similar to other versions such as Gridiron in the United States.

Rules of play, including scoring:

General Points:

1. The object of the game is to score touchdowns in order to gain points and also to prevent the opposition from scoring. The team with the most points at the end of the game is the winner.
2. Players may make substitutions at any time.
3. The game is divided into two halves of 25 minutes each. There is a five-minute break at half-time and the teams change direction in the second half.
4. Unless infringing the rules the team with the ball is entitled to six touches prior to changing possession with the opposing team.
5. All players wear approved clothing with an identifying number on the shirt and wear suitable footwear.
6. An approved touchball is used.
7. The normal team of seven is made up of two wingers, two links, and three middle players. These positions are not critical to success and players should be capable of playing in any position.
8. The ball must not be hidden under the attire of a player.

Commencement of Play:

1. A coin is tossed to decide the direction of play and possession of ball for the start of the game.

2. Play is commenced with a tap at the center of the halfway line after indication from the referee. The defending team is ten meters back from the tap and cannot move forward until the ball is tapped.

3. A tap is also used to recommence play after a touchdown, after half-time, and for some infringements. There must be minimum delay between the scoring of touchdowns and the recommencement of play.

General Play:

1. A player in possession of the ball may pass, flick, knock, throw, or otherwise deliver the ball to any other outside player in the attacking team. The ball cannot be propelled forward (tap penalty).

2. The ball may be passed to a teammate who is positioned behind the ball carrier (onside). The ball cannot be passed forward (tap penalty).

3. The ball carrier may run with the ball until touched by an opponent.

4. If the ball is dropped to the ground possession changes (rollball).

5. An advantage rule is used in the game to determine play-on situations, or to determine the positions of play.

6. The ball becomes dead when it, or a player in possession, touches or crosses the sideline and a change of possession results. However, if a player in possession is touched prior to crossing the sideline, the touch counts (rollball where touched).

7. When a defender effects a touch on the ball carrier within five meters of the attacking scoreline, the player in possession must move directly behind the mark and out a distance of five meters. An attacking team is not required to rollball within five meters of their own (defending) scoreline.

Offside:

1. A player on the attacking team is offside when that player is forward of the player who has possession or who last had possession.

2. The defending team must stand not less than ten meters from the ball at a tap to start/restart play or at a tap penalty.

3. All defending players must stand 5 meters back from the rollball and cannot move until the halfback touches the ball (tap penalty). If no half-back is in place, the defending team can move when the roll ball is performed.

4. An attacking player may not receive the ball if he is standing in front of the last player of his team to touch the ball (offside). Forward passes to previously onside players are penalized.

5. Offside infringements are usually penalized (tap penalty).

6. Players from attacking and defending teams should return to an onside position as soon as possible.

Effecting a Touch:

1. All touches must be made with minimum physical force and may be made by a defending player or by the player in possession. Defending players should call all touches.

2. For a touch to be effected, a contact is made on any part of the body of a player in possession or a defending player. A touch includes contact on the ball, hair, or clothing of a player.

3. The player touched must bring the ball back into play with a rollball at the place (mark) where a touch was effected. There should be little delay.

4. A player cannot pass the ball after a touch has been effected (tap penalty).

5. A penalty touchdown may be awarded for any action by a player or spectator that prevents an attacking team from scoring.

Rollball:

1. A player must perform a rollball when a touch is effected, after the sixth touch, the ball is to ground, there is infringement at the tap, or when directed by the referee.

2. The rollball is usually made by placing the ball on the ground and rolling it back between the legs with the hand(s). Other variations are permissible as the rules allow.

3. All players on the defending team must move back five meters from the player performing the rollball.

4. The halfback is an attacking player receiving the ball from the player performing the rollball. The halfback may run with the ball, but if touched possession is lost.

5. The halfback usually passes to a teammate standing behind who may run or pass the ball to another teammate in support. (Players use deception, overlay, and ball-handling skills to score.)

6. If the ball is not returned to the mark for a penalty or rollball but is thrown away to cause delay, a penalty of ten meters is awarded down-field from the original mark.

7. Attacking players cannot delay the rollball while awaiting a halfback.

8. The halfback is permitted to use the foot to control the ball.

Scoring:

A touchdown is worth one point. The team with the highest score at the end of the game is the winner. Scoring is achieved by out-maneuvering the opposition through passing, running, deception, and overlap to cross the scoreline and ground the ball without being touched by an opponent.

1. A touchdown is awarded when a player places the ball on the ground on or over the team's attacking scoreline without being touched.

2. For the recommencement of play following the scoring of a touchdown, the team against which the score was made is to recommence play at halfway.

3. The halfback cannot score a touchdown but can cross the scoreline before passing to another player.

4. A penalty touchdown may be awarded for any action by a player or spectator that prevents an attacking team from scoring.

Discipline and Player Misconduct:

1. Players who infringe the rules of touch are liable to penalties or other appropriate action according to the seriousness of the infringement.

2. Any player may be dismissed for a period of time or for the remainder of the game.

Referees:

1. The referees are the sole judges on matters of fact in the game. Line judges may be appointed to assist referees.

Penalty Tap:

1. A penalty tap is to be awarded for certain infringements by players in accordance with the rules.

2. After a penalty is awarded, the defending team must move back at least ten meters from the mark.

3. A penalty tap is awarded in such cases as:

   • Obstruction: a deliberate attempt by an attacking player to gain an unfair advantage by preventing a defending player from effecting a touch.

   • Offside infringements by the defending team.

   • Forward passes.

   • Player misconduct.

Change of Possession:

1. The nonoffending team performs a rollball in cases such as after the sixth touch, a dropped ball, or an incorrect rollball.

Rule Changes Being Considered for the Game Include:

• Teams to consist of six players on each team (now implemented at some representative levels of play).

• A defensive player cannot shadow a halfback once he or she has effected a touch on a ball carrier, but must retreat along a similar line from which he or she came.

- Players are to be seven meters back in defense.
- The attacking team may choose to rollball within five meters of the attacking scoreline.

The Federation of International Touch (F.I.T.) Playing Rules: The current F.I.T. rules (as of June 1994) have seen changes that bring the international game closer in line to that being played in Australia. The forward pass has been removed, as have the ability of the halfback to score and the method of scoring, which only required a player to run over the scoreline.

The Main Rule Changes in Place Now Involve:

1. Interchange Area: An area 20 meters long and five meters wide is marked on both sides of the field, extending ten meters either side of halfway and one meter back from the sideline.

2. Mode of Scoring: A touchdown is scored by placing the ball on the ground over the attacking scoreline and within the touchdown zone. The touchdown zone extends from the scoreline to five to ten meters behind this line.

3. Actions within five meters of the defending scoreline: When defenders are required to defend on or within five meters of their defending scoreline, they must move forward beyond the five-meter line in an attempt to effect a touch on the player in possession (no holding the line allowed). A penalty will result. Two consecutive infringements may result in a player being removed from the field until possession is regained by their team.

TRUGO

Colin Riley

Appropriate for replication (if equipment is adapted).

Players:

Males or females over 55 years of age.

Object of game for players:

The object is to strike as many rubber rings (or balls) as possible with a mallet (or bat) between the goal posts at the other end of the court.

Number of players:

Singles or two teams of up to six.

Costume, apparel/equipment required:

The goal posts are 1.5 meters apart. To set up positions for the goal posts use flat vinyl floor markers or floor marking tape for inside courts and marking paint for outside courts. Use wooden skittles or a kanga cricket stump placed in a stump base for the goal posts. Two *trugo* mats (or carpet squares with rubber backing) are required for each court. For outside courts, mats may be pegged to the ground. The mats should be marked with at least two lines at right angles to each other. One line is lined up with the goal posts and the other faces down the court and is used to assist in placing the ring (or ball) to be hit. For outside play, pieces of carpet or carpet squares can be placed on each side of the mats for players to stand on. For inside play, do not use mats or flat vinyl floor mats. Use rubber trugo rings or balls (kanga, tennis, croquet, or cricket balls). Mallets can be made to suit, or use school-quality croquet mallets available from sports stores. Catchers are used to catch the rings after they have passed between or outside the goal posts. These can be canvas bags on a broomstick, broom, softcross stick, or something similar. Two catchers are required for each single court. Score cards/boards may be used.

Area/arena/field where played—space required:

An outdoor or indoor area. Use a court area 15 to 25 meters long depending on the age and skill level of players. Each court should be five meters apart. Four goal posts are required for a single court—two at each end.

Time length of game. How is end of game determined?:

The end of the game is determined after 12 rings have been tossed by each player on each side.

Symbolism of game:

Trugo is a uniquely Australian sport that evolved from a lunchtime game played by workers at Melbourne's Newport Railway Yards in the 1920s. It is still played in Melbourne by men and women where players must be over 55 years of age; elsewhere players are typically much younger. The game appears to be a hybrid of Lawn Bowls and Croquet. It symbolizes skills common to all ages.

Rules of play, including scoring:

After a coin toss for choice of ends the players from each team take their places at opposite ends of the court. A player places the ring (or ball) on the mat in the center of the goal posts. A player can hit the ring (or ball) sideways or between the legs, as preferred. Each player must hit a total of 24 rings (or balls), 12 from each end. No player shall leave his or her end of the court or hit a ring (or ball) as part of his or her turn until all rings (or balls) have been returned from the opponents' end. Players are not allowed to interfere with the striker. If time is available, each player is allowed four practice rings (or balls) before a game commences. If the rings (or balls) hit any obstacle and bounce back onto the court and go through the goal posts no score is recorded. If playing with two on a team, the two players from each side hit four rings each and their opponents then hit four rings back from their end. This continues until each player has hit a total of 12 rings. The players then change ends and proceed in a similar manner as before until a further 12 rings each have been hit. If playing with teams of four, when the first two players on a team have finished their 24 hits this completes the first half of the game. The second half of the game is played by the other two players of each team.

One point is scored for each ring or ball that passes between the goal posts at the opposite end of the court without touching the posts. The ring or ball must pass over the goal line to score a point. Should the ring or ball go over the goal line and fall or roll back into the court it is still deemed a goal. A player acting as a catcher stands at the end of the court one meter behind the goal posts and catches the ring or balls that have been hit from the other end. The catchers indicate a goal by raising their arm straight over their head, and a miss by waving their arm across the body. The catcher calls the scores (such as "1, 2, 3, 4") at the end of each four hits, and his or her decision is final. After each hit the catcher places the rings or balls on the ground behind the goals.

TWO UP
Ken Hawkins
Appropriate for replication.

Players:

Adult men.

Object of game for players:

To bet against the House (the host institution, usually a pub) in a coin toss by calling heads, tails, or five consecutive odds.

Number of players:

As many as desired.

Costume, apparel/equipment required:

Two pennies slotted in a flat board used for the spin.

Area/arena/field where played—space required:

A ring in any designated area.

Time length of game. How is end of game determined?:

Depends on how many spinners participate in the game. A spinner is a person who throws the pennies in the air from the flat board.

Symbolism of game:

Two up is a game made famous by World War I diggers. "Come in spinner!" they called, and tossed two coins high, in the trenches of France, on the slopes of Gallipoli, and in the shadows of the Pyramids.

Rules of play, including scoring:

The game is played with two penny coins spun in the air by a volunteer spinner from among the players around the ring. The spinner spins for pairs of heads or tails in sets of three consecutive results. When the coins show odds (a mixed head-tail pair) all bets stay until the next result. Both the spinner and the players bet against the house. They may bet on the coins coming down and showing heads, tails, or on five consecutive odds. All bets on heads and tails lose when five consecutive odds are thrown. When a pair of heads or tails come up the bets on five consecutive odds lose. If the spinner spins the opposite of what he or she has elected to spin for, or spins five consecutive odds, he or she must leave the ring and make way for the next volunteer.

Comments:

The Winning Odds on Two Up Are:

Heads	Even money
Tails	Even money
Five Consecutive Odds	27/1
Spinners bet on Heads or Tails	7.5/1

Two Up Terms:

Kip	Implement used to spin coins
Heads	Both coins showing Heads
Tails	Both coins showing Tails
Odds	One coin showing Heads, the other Tails
Boxer	The dealer controlling the game
Floater	One or both coins not spinning
"Come in Spinner"	Term used by the Boxer calling for the coins to be thrown

WALLA RUGBY

Ken Edwards
Appropriate for replication.

Players:

Male and female teens.

Object of game for players:

To develop in children the basic skills of running, ball handling, kicking, and tackling evident in adult rugby.

Number of players:

Twenty.

Costume, apparel/equipment required:

A ball and proper uniforms.

Area/arena/field where played—space required:

Like the number of players on a team, the size of the field is flexible, but it is usually 50 x 70 meters. If the number of players on the team exceeds nine, the extra players play in the backline and a full rugby field is used.

Time length of game. How is end of game determined?:

Two 15-minute halves.

Symbolism of game:

Walla rugby is a modified version of rugby union played by school-children using half of a full-sized rugby field. The game is played ten on a side on a noncompetition ladder basis. No tackling is permitted and players use the Walla tag, a two-handed tag below the waist. The game represents a battle of brains over brawn.

Rules of play, including scoring:

There are nine players, five forwards who take part in the scrum and lineout and four backs. Up to six substitutions can be made during the game. In the kicking game, an extra backline player (fullback) is included. If fewer than nine players are used in a team, a three-player scrum and lineout are used.

The attacking team carries the ball downfield by running, passing, or handing back, in order to score a try (touchdown) by placing the ball over the goal line. The ball can only be transferred to a player behind the ball carrier. No forward handling or passing is allowed. The defending team attempts to halt the running progress of the attacking team by tagging (touching) the ball carrier.

Basic Rules:

1. Play begins at the center of the halfway line. The team winning a coin toss chooses an end and stands within that half of the field, at least ten meters away from the half-way line, facing the opponents' goal line. The team losing the toss stands in the other half of the field and places the ball in the middle of the halfway line. A player place kicks the ball forward at least ten meters toward the opposition. If the ball travels less than ten meters, another kick is taken from the center. After a team scores a try, the nonscoring team recommences play from the center with a dropkick. From the kickoff, if the ball crosses the opposing team's goal line without being touched by the defending team, that team may have a scrimmage at the center of the halfway line.

2. Offside: There is no offside when running, tagging, or passing, but offside lines apply for set plays (scrum and lineout) and the ball take. These are imaginary lines drawn across the field parallel to the goal lines. In general play, offside players may not advance toward a player waiting to play the ball until they have been put onside.

3. Tagging and Ball Take: To tag (touch), a player must contact the ball carrier with two hands (simultaneously) below the waist.

When tagged, the ball carrier must either immediately pass the ball backwards, as any attempt to gain territory without trying to pass will result in loss of possession, or stop, turn, and wait for a support player to ball take, and the support player must then pass the ball without running. For a ball take, the tagged player is joined by a support player who takes the ball and then passes it. The defending team provides two defenders, a tagger who remains in contact with the ball carrier, and a second defender who must be in contact with either the tagger or the ball carrier. Neither may interfere with the transfer of the ball. The ball carrier may continue moving forward providing the support player has a grip on the ball and the tagger is the only defender. Defenders not taking part in the ball take must be at least five meters away in the direction of their goal line. The number of ball takes permitted during a period of play where one team has continuous possession is two. This prevents teams from gaining ground by having a number of successive ball takes. If a team has used two ball takes, and a player is tagged and has no support to make an immediate pass, play restarts with a scrum. The other team puts in the ball.

4. Gaining Possession:
Intercepting the Ball: An opposition pass may be intercepted.

Gathering a Dropped Ball: If the attacking team drops, knocks, or throws the ball to the ground, the defending team picks up the ball and plays on. If the attacking team picks up the ball, the scrum is formed with the defending team putting the ball into the scrum.

Forward Pass: A forward pass is an infringement, and when this occurs a scrum takes place with the noninfringing side putting the ball into it.

Ball Out: A ball out is when one team carries or puts the ball out over the touchline (sideline). A lineout is formed with a player from the non-infringing team throwing the ball into the lineout.

Goal Line Tags: When a ball carrier is tagged over any goal line, a scrum is formed five meters in from the goal line with the tagger's team putting the ball into the scrum.

5. Kicking: If a kick other than a penalty-line kick goes over the touch line on the full (in the air), a lineout takes place level with the point from where the ball was kicked. When a penalty kick is kicked directly into touch the same team will have the throw in. If a kick bounces out, the lineout takes place where the ball crosses the line. If a free kick is kicked into touch on the full, the team will not gain ground. A player kicking for touch from a free kick may only punt or dropkick the ball. When a player receives the ball outside the 15-meter area and runs behind this line before kicking for touch, that player may not gain ground from the kick. A quick kick may be taken by a team either at a penalty kick or

free kick without waiting for players of that team to retire behind the ball providing those players do not become involved in play. At a quick throw-in, the ball may be thrown in from any point along the touch line near to the defending teams' goal line, providing the player uses the same ball and retrieves it. The touchlines extend approximately ten meters behind the goal line defining the area in which a try can be scored. If the ball is kicked over the goal line and out of this area, play is restarted with a kick by the noninfringing team 15 meters in from the goal line. This kick must travel at least five meters and all players from the kicking team must remain behind the kicker. The defending players stand set distances away:

- Kick offs (ten meters).
- Tap kicks (five meters).
- Penalty kicks (ten meters).

6. Infringements: A free kick is awarded for the following infringements:

- The ball carrier fails either to pass immediately or return to the mark for a ball take.
- The ball is not thrown down the line of touch after two attempts.
- The ball is not kicked off ten meters downfield within two attempts.
- Players leave the lineout before the halfback has the ball or the referee calls break.
- Players not in the lineout move closer than ten meters to the lineout before the halfback has the ball or the referee calls break.
- An incorrect scrum formation or incorrect put in is made.
- The defending halfback moves beyond the scrum midline before the opposition halfback has the ball.
- An incorrect ball take occurs or defenders move closer than five meters from a ball take.
- An intentional knock-on is played.
- Using another player in a line-out for support in jumping.
- Moving beyond the end of the line-out.
- Handling or picking up the ball in a scrum or ruck.
- Delaying or wasting time.

The opposition must be at least five meters away from the place where the tap kick is taken. A line kick may be taken as an alternative to a tap kick from a penalty kick. Following a line kick, play is restarted with a lineout formed where the ball crossed the touchline (throw-in to the team taking the penalty kick). When an infringement occurs, the referee may apply the advantage law by allowing play to proceed if the noninfringing team gains an advantage.

7. Walla Rugby Options: The competitive elements of the scrum and line-out may be omitted until teams become confident rugby players. The number of players in the lineout may vary from two to four, increasing the number of running players, and providing greater flexibility for attacking moves and lineout tactics. The team throwing in the ball determines the maximum number of jumpers in the lineout. Failure to comply results in a tap kick.

8. Lineout: A lineout restarts play after the ball goes out over the touch-line (sideline). A maximum of six players form the lineout (five for-wards and a halfback). The four forwards from each team stand in two lines, one meter apart and no longer than five meters in length. The first player in each line must stand at least three meters from the touch-line. There is no requirement of a set distance between players of the same team. The fifth forward of the noninfringing team stands outside the touchline and throws the ball down the middle of the lineout (line of touch). The fifth forward from the other team stands near the thrower. The halfbacks wait beside their line, ready to receive the ball. If the ball is not thrown down the line of touch at the first attempt, another throw-in is allowed. A tap kick is given to the other team if the second throw is not thrown straight. After the ball is thrown in, play-ers in both lines compete for the ball by jumping and trying to control the ball to their halfback. When jumping for the ball a player must use both hands or the insides of the arms to catch the ball. The act of jump-ing for the ball does not allow a player to step across the line of touch. Players in the line cannot make a tag and are not permitted to leave the line until the halfback has the ball or the referee calls break. Failure to comply results in a tap kick. All other players must stand at least ten meters away (behind the offside line), until the halfback has the ball or the referee calls break. Failure to stand ten meters away results in a tap kick ten meters in from the touchline along the line of touch.

9. Scrum: A scrum occurs when

- a player drops the ball and a player from the same side picks it up.
- a forward pass is made.
- the player accidentally becomes involved in play while offside.
- the player with the ball is tagged behind the goal line.
- more than two consecutive ball takes occur.

Five players from each team, three front row forwards and two second row forwards, join to form a scrum. The three forwards stand side by side and correctly bind on each other. The second row also binds with the front row with their heads in between, just below the level of the hips of the front row forwards. The opposing scrum crouches, binds, and engages on each other with the front row players of each team coming to rest shoulder to shoulder with the opposition. In forming a scrummage, the front rows must be within one arm's length of their opponents and they may not form the scrummage until the referee has marked the place of engagement. The halfback in possession puts the ball into the scrum from the lefthand side. The opposition halfback remains behind the scrum midline until the ball has been picked up by the halfback feeding the ball. The halfback may not take any action while the ball is still in the scrummage to convey to opponents that the ball is out. The hooker may raise the foot when the ball leaves the hands of the player putting the ball in. All other players must remain behind their offside line which is the imaginary line behind the feet of the second row players in the scrum. Players can only move beyond their offside line, when the halfback has picked up the ball. The middle player of the front row (hooker) is the only player permitted to hook the ball. No pushing or lifting is permitted. For this and other infringements, a tap kick is awarded. When a five-meter scrum is awarded it will take place opposite the place where the ball became dead and not where it crossed the goal line.

10. Safety in Walla Rugby: The modified laws (no tackling or pushing in scrums) enable children to play in a variety of positions, and learn the running and passing skills of a backline player, as well as the positioning, tactics, and skill of a forward player.

11. Scrum Safety: In a scrum, children with long, thin necks are not suitable for the front row or second row and must not be selected to play in these positions. Even though the laws of Walla Rugby have been modified to exclude pushing, the principle of selecting appropriate body types starts at this level. Players in the scrum should always keep their head up and above the height of their hips. When an injured player leaves the field, particular attention must be given to the physique of the replacement player. It may be necessary to reallocate playing positions.

Variations:

1. If full Rugby scoring is used the following will apply:
   Try: Five points
   Penalty goal and a dropped goal: Three points
   Conversion of a try by place kick or drop kick: Two points
   The team awarded a free kick may not score a dropped goal until after the ball next becomes dead.

2. Use one-handed tagging, which requires the defender (tackler) to touch the ball carrier with only one hand on any part of the body.

3. Use eight players, three forwards and five backs. If kicking is used then an extra player (fullback) is included. Allow up to six substitutes.

WALLE NGAN WERRUP
Ken Edwards
Appropriate for replication.

Players:

Young males of the Gooniyandi in the West Kimberly area of Western Australia.

Object of game for players:

To hunt and capture the kangaroo.

Number of players:

A group of four or more.

Costume, apparel/equipment required:

None.

Area/arena/field where played—space required:

Any suitable outdoor area.

Time length of game. How is end of game determined?:

When chase is over.

Symbolism of game:

Food hunting simulation.

Rules of play, including scoring:

In the West Kimberley area of Western Australia the young men were very fond of playing a version of hide and seek called the hunting or bush game (*wallee ngnan weerup*). The game is based on Kangaroo and emu hunting. One player represents the kangaroo (*jamarra*) or emu and the other players are the hunters. The kangaroo is given a short time to disappear into the bush. The other players pretend to hunt the kangaroo. When the hunters find the kangaroo, they imagine they have captured it and return with this player back to the camp. The game is then restarted.

Suggestion: This could be used as an acting game for younger children.

Language: A few Gooniyandi sentences are used by the players:

Pindan yangarrama: We will play the bush game.
Joon wanjoolboo: You drive him.
Nowloo goon weerup: Hit with club.
Joona joodoo joodoo wongoola: You throw him down there.
Booroo ngan dammajinna: I missed him.
Kai! kala! ngan barrin: Hurrah! I've got him.

WEME

Ken Edwards
Not appropriate for replication.

Players:

Male and female teens of the Waljibiri people of Central Australia.

Object of game for players:

Similar to bowling, players roll balls or rounded stones in an effort to hit the stones of the other player.

Number of players:

Between one and four. The game can be played alone, one player against another player, or by pairs of players against each other.

Costume, apparel/equipment required:

Two sets of kanga cricket wickets or two lines (each five-meters long) marked five to ten meters apart—the distance depends on the age and ability level of the players. Use rounded stones or balls/bowls.

Area/arena/field where played—space required:

Any designated area.

Time length of game. How is end of game determined?:

When one player or pair of players has reached 20 points.

Symbolism of game:

The Waljibiri people of Central Australia play a stone-bowling game. One player throws a stone, which is used as a target by the second player. Players alternate turns with each aiming at the other's stone. This is the Aboriginal version of kanga cricket. It represents cooperation in games.

Rules of play, including scoring:

The game is a bowling game where balls or rounded stones are rolled underarm along the ground. Players may toss a coin to choose who starts. Turns are taken from behind designated lines. One player starts the game by rolling his or her ball or stone toward the wickets (or line marked on the ground). If the ball passes beyond the mark then the stone is rolled again. If this happens a second time the other player scores one point. After a fair roll that stops between the lines (or before the wickets), the second player attempts to roll the stone to hit the first. If the stone is hit by the second player that player scores one point. Both players alternate turns. The second player now has the first turn. If the game is played in pairs the players stay at one end and their partners are at the other end. Play continues until the game is decided. One point is scored for each hit. The first player or team to reach 20 points is the winner.

Variations of play:

1. No scoring in the game. Play for fun.

2. No restriction on how far the stones can be thrown/rolled.

3. One point is scored by a player when they hit the stone of the other player. If a player misses, the other player gains the point.

4. Play a set number of ends (the number of bowls from one direction).

5. If the second player misses with their attempt then the first player has the next turn. The winner is the player who delivers his or her stone first for most of the game.

6. For younger children, set up kanga wickets three to five meters apart.

7. Use indoor bias bowls or bocce balls on a carpet area about seven meters long and two or three meters wide.

Comment: The unpredictable nature of rounded stones makes for a more interesting game.

WITTCHIM
Ken Edwards
Appropriate for replication.

Appropriate age of players:

Male and female teens from Victoria, Australia.

Object of game for players:

This game consists of stalking a feather in imitation of hunting an emu. It is recognized that individuals will hunt in different ways.

Number of players:

Five.

Costume, apparel/equipment required:

Feather and stick.

Area/arena/field where played—space required:

An open area.

Time length of game. How is end of game determined?:

Approximately five minutes for each chase.

Symbolism of game:

Chasing and silence.

Rules of play, including scoring:

In Victoria a corroboree game was played by different groups. Depending on the area it was played in it was called tarratt or wittchim. A feather is tied to the end of a long stick, which is held by a player in the center of a large circle of players. The performer, who is dressed in a corroboree costume, enters the circle with a shield and boomerang, and moves around the circle for about five minutes with his or her eye on the feather. The player crouches and runs in imitation of stalking the emu and finishes by stooping and touching the feather. After the performance another player has his or her turn. This continues until four or five players have gone through the same movement. The contest is conducted in silence.

A number of judges decide on the best performance and present that player with the feather. The winner is expected to repeat his or her performance and present the feather to the other players as a compliment and a way of removing any feelings of jealousy.

Variation: Have a competition with each player allowed two to three minutes to complete his or her performance.

ZICH BALL

Chris Aichy Woinarsky
Appropriate for replication.

Players:

Male and female teens.

Object of game for players:

To move balls from hoop to hoop by running and tagging, develop decision making, which can be applied to tennis, and develop rapid movement across the court, which is required for tennis. Also, to have fun and warm up in an active way, to develop the cardiovascular system, and to develop rapid-change-of-direction skills.

Number of players:

Classroom group.

Costume, apparel/equipment required:

Fifteen tennis balls or beanbags and five hoops.

Area/arena/field where played—space required:

Gymnasium, play area, or field.

Time length of game. How is end of game determined?:

When one team has six balls in their hoop.

Symbolism of game:

Represents the skills required for food hunting and survival and the ability to work as a community.

Rules of play, including scoring:

Teams are placed behind their respective hoop and in a line. In the center is a hoop containing 15 tennis balls. To win a team must have at least six balls in their hoop (a big basket). A team cannot stop a member of another team from taking balls out of their hoop. Only one member from each team may run at a time. Only one tennis ball can be carried at a time. Balls have to be placed in the hoop, not thrown, and a tag must be made to the next person for him or her to run. Balls can be taken from any hoop around the gym.

New Zealand

LUMMI STICKS

Tom Sharpe
Not appropriate for replication.

Players:

Male and female pre-teens and young teens. This game is played by the Maoris of New Zealand.

Object of game for players:

Cooperation and sharing.

Number of players:

Unlimited, with a minimum of two.

Costume, apparel/equipment required:

Native New Zealand Maori costumes, and a pair of lummi sticks for each player. Lummi sticks can be made from wooden dowels, one inch in diameter, and decorated. Sticks should be between 12 and 48 inches in length. Players can choose any length stick, but be sure all sticks are the same length.

Area/arena/field where played—space required:

Outdoor area with hard surface or indoor gymnasium.

Time length of game. How is end of game determined?:

Lummi stick activities usually follow the length of the chant or music. As players become more skilled, the games last longer.

Symbolism of game:

Lummi sticks represent fair play, cooperation, and sharing. The rhythm of the chant adds to the significance of cooperation between friend and foe alike.

Rules of play, including scoring:

The key element of the game is rhythm and the game is traditionally set against the background of a chant or rhythmic song. Players try to maintain the rhythm and tempo of the chant or song and speed up or slow down as the spirit moves them. Players click their lummi sticks on the ground, together, or with other members in the group. Complex patterns of lummi sticks can include clicking and tossing sticks between players.

The following are some basic lummi sticks patterns:

1. On each beat, hit bottom end of sticks on ground; then hit your two sticks together; then hit partner's right stick with your right stick. Repeat, but hit your left stick to partner's left stick.

2. Same sequence, except hit both partners' sticks on the third beat.

3. Same sequence, except toss (pass one stick from right to right) on the third beat. Repeat tossing on each subsequent third beat. Keep sticks in a vertical position and toss with a slight lift to give partners time to catch them.

No scoring.

Variations:

This game can be started in a circle as a clapping game during which motions and rhythm can be learned before lummi sticks are introduced. Follow the Leader, Mirroring Motions, and Add-On games are excellent lead-up activities for this game.

MAORI
Colin Spanhake
Not appropriate for replication.

Players:

Males from the age they are strong enough to hold their own body weight when suspended from a vine.

Object of game for players:

To leap farther than anyone else.

Number of players:

No limit.

Costume, apparel/equipment required:

None.

Area/arena/field where played—space required:

A deep pool with overhanging trees.

Time length of game. How is end of game determined?:

No limit.

Symbolism of game:

Evidence of strength, skill, and courage.

Rules of play, including scoring:

Look for one or more trees with a rata vine (a common vine in New Zealand forests). Where a pool exists but has no trees, sometimes a kauri (*agathis australis*) sapling embedded in the earth and leaning over the pool is supported by shorter, crossed manuka (*Leptospermun scoparium*) poles lashed with flax (*Phormiun tenax*) at about one third the way up the sapling from the ground. Each participant takes turns grasping the vine at full stretch, running to the bank, lifting knees, and swinging as far as possible out into the pool. The participant who lands farthest out has the honor of being best for the day.

MAORI HAND GAMES
Colin Spanhake
Appropriate for replication.

Players:

Males and females of all ages.

Object of game for players:

To trap the opponent into making the same hand signal as the caller.

Number of players:

No limit.

Costume, apparel/equipment required:

None.

Area/arena/field where played—space required:

Any casual gathering place.

Time length of game. How is end of game determined?:

The game ends when one player reaches nine points.

Symbolism of game:

Develops alertness and quick movement, outthinking the opponent. Valued for developing alert warriors.

Rules of play, including scoring:

Two players face each other and perform an action simultaneously with the call from the hand signaller. One player, the defender, gives the first call while the first action is performed by both players. Then the challenger answers with the same call while the second action is performed. The players continue to call alternately until one player wins the round—a round is won by the player who is calling when both players do the same action at the same time. When the challenger wins a round, he or she wins the right to become the defender. When the defender wins a round, he or she scores a point and restarts with another call. A point is scored only by the player who starts the round. The actions are performed in any order. The calls are standardized according to the type of hand game played. More than two players can participate, the additional players becoming the challengers, in turn, of the winner of the preceding round. The first to reach nine points is the winner.

Variations:

1. *Toro and Piko*: Only one hand is used. Clench fist palm facing the opponent. On the call "Toro," the forefinger is raised fully extended. On the call "Piko," the clenched fist remains.

2. *Hipitoitoi*: Played with the thumbs only. Four different positions are used while the fists are clenched and the hands are held close together in front of the body. The positions are (a) both thumbs down, (b) both thumbs upright, (c) right thumb upright and left down, and (d) left thumb upright and right down.

3. *Hei Tama Tu Tama*: Played with arms. The four positions used are (a) both hands on hips, (b) both arms raised, fists clenched, and elbows out sideways, (c) right forearm raised with clenched fist, left hand on hip, and (d) left forearm raised with fist clenched, right hand on hip.

4. *Whakaropiropi*: Played with hands. There are five positions (a) both fists clenched, (b) both hands open, parallel and pointing away from the body, (c) both hands open with fingertips touching in a V shape, (d) both hands open with heels of the hands touching and fingers pointing away in a V shape, and (e) fingers of both hands extended, pointing diagonally across the body and the right hand (or left) on top with the left (or right) thumb in the right (or left) palm.

MAORI STICK DANCE
Colin Spanhake
Appropriate for replication.

Players:

Young Maoris of both sexes.

Object of game for players:

To manipulate the sticks to the prescribed rhythm and movement without making a mistake.

Number of players:

No limit.

Costume, apparel/equipment required:

Sticks like relay batons.

Area/arena/field where played—space required:

Usually a public place where elders can admire and/or criticize.

Time length of game. How is end of game determined?:

Until prescribed movements have been completed.

Symbolism of game:

Hand, eye, and foot coordination, and rhythm development.

Rules of play, including scoring:

An even number of players stand in line. Players stand with feet together, hands on hips, with backs of hands facing forward, grasping sticks by the center. At the commencement of the music players perform various foot movements while simultaneously twirling the sticks. The players proceed to do a variety of exchange movements with players on each side, the end players performing individual variations. Foot movements and exchange movements are developed and modeled by the leader. The players making the least number of mistakes while following the prescribed rhythms wins.

MAORI STICK GAMES
Colin Spanhake
Appropriate for replication.

Players:

Originally played by young warriors of the Maori people, but now played for recreation by all. Male and female teens can play.

Object of game for players:

Originally, to be the last remaining player fault free, but now the game is played as a drill for fun.

Number of players:

No limit.

Costume, apparel/equipment required:

No special costume is needed unless the game is part of a demonstration of Maori arts. In this case both males and females wore a *piupiu*, a skirt-like garment made of hard fern stalks, bleached and dyed with patterns. Females also wear a pleated bodice. Also, a pair of matched sticks 14 to 16 inches long are needed.

Area/arena/field where played—space required:

Any public space.

Time length of game. How is end of game determined?:

No special time. Players continue until prescribed sequence is completed. Originally, game continued until only one player remain fault free.

Symbolism of game:

Developing quickness of hand and eye, anticipation, and agility.

Rules of play, including scoring:

Each player has a pair of matched sticks (*rakau*) 14 inches to 16 inches long. The game was originally played in a circle but is now played in two lines. The players kneel, sitting back on their heels, with knees slightly apart and backs straight, leaning slightly forward at the hips. The game is played to the rhythm of a song accompaniment, originally chants (since lost), but since late the 1980s a European melody to which Maori words are added has become the standard. The game finishes when only one person remains fault free.

In time with the rhythm of the song, holding the sticks by the center and keeping them vertical, the players tap the ends of the sticks simultaneously on the ground, one on each side of the body, bring them together in front of the body to click against each other, then throw one or both across to the partner who has simultaneously performed the identical movement. Various sequences are prescribed. Right to right and left to left, right to left and left to right, both simultaneously, without throwing, tap right to right and left to left. Added to these are more difficult sequences such as holding the sticks near one end and tapping the ground to one side of the player, swinging the sticks to the front and twirling them, initially half a rotation, the later with one full rotation. Repeat to the other side. Add various exchanges with partner, as for the opening moves.

OMANAIA ROUNDERS
Colin Spanhake
Appropriate for replication.

Players:

Male and female pre-teens.

Object of game for players:

To score more runs than opponents.

Number of players:

Classroom group in two teams of 10 to 20.

Costume, apparel/equipment required:

Normal school clothes; bats and balls.

Area/arena/field where played—space required:

Outside area with a designated home base 20 x 20 feet. Circuit lengths vary according to the natural features of the area.

Time length of game. How is end of game determined?:

Any agreed number of innings.

Symbolism of game:

A fun game that symbolizes a coeducational activity without violence.

Rules of play, including scoring:

There are two courses, one short and one long. The courses may be around buildings, trees, or natural features. Before the ball is pitched, the batter shouts "short" or "long." Batters strike the ball with their hand, stick, or bat forward of the base and runs the chosen course. Fielders attempt to catch on the full (in the air), in which case the batter is out. If the ball is not caught, the fielder who retrieves it must run the chosen course in the opposite direction to the batter. When the fielder is in sight of the home base he or she may attempt to throw the ball to land in home base before the runner arrives. The batter is out when caught on the full or by being beaten by the ball landing in home base when thrown by a fielder. The batter scores three points for the long course, one point for the short course. When three batters are out, the side is out.

SHARKS
(Also played in Australia and throughout the South Pacific)
Colin Spanhake
Appropriate for replication.

Players:

Male and female pre-teens and teens.

Object of game for players:

To safely reach a designated island in an ocean. Raise awareness of earth sciences through games.

Number of players:

Groups of three to six.

Costume, apparel/equipment required:

Hula hoops for each group.

Area/arena/field where played—space required:

Gymnasium.

Time length of game. How is end of game determined?:

When everyone has crossed the ocean.

Symbolism of game:

Safety in the oceans.

Rules of play, including scoring:

Students try to cross a body of water filled with sharks. In groups of three to six, each group uses their hula-hoop as a ship. Everyone holds onto the hoop or ship to move across the ocean but they jump into the hoop when the teacher calls out, "SHARKS!" The players are safe from the sharks in their ship as they move across the ocean or from one end of the gym to the other. Play continues until everyone has safely reached a designated island in an ocean.

TAPAUAE
Colin Spanhake
Appropriate for replication.

Players:

Male and female pre-teens and young teens of the Maoris in New Zealand.

Object of game for players:

To score points by knocking down opponents' skittle.

Number of players:

Mixed teams with no definite number.

Costume, apparel/equipment required:

Two large identifiable balls, such as a basketball or rugby ball, and two skittles. Ropes, hoops, and lines can be used to designate the various areas.

Area/arena/field where played—space required:

Two circles with one skittle in each.

Time length of game. How is end of game determined?:

No limit.

Symbolism of game:

The game was first played at Tapauae School in the lower half of the North Island of New Zealand. Some translators suggest that the name is derived from the Maori words *tapu*, sacred, forbidden, and *waewaw*, steps.

Rules of play, including scoring:

Each team is in its own circle. Each has a ball. The game begins with each team moving to knock down the opponents' skittle. The game requires skill in catching, passing, and teamwork. Sometimes played with no referees or umpires, the players are honor bound to relinquish the ball to the nearest opponent if a rule is breached. There is a stepping rule as in basketball. Players must not cross any lines and the ball must not be held longer than five seconds. The ball must be touched by a center when passing to opposite circle. One point is given for knocking down a skittle with the player's own ball, two points for knocking down a skittle with the opponent's ball, and three points are given to opponents of the defender who knocks down his or her own skittle.

On signal, each team tries to pass to their own shooters, who try to knock down the skittle. Defenders and rovers try to intercept or retrieve the balls and pass to their own shooters via the centers, so that two balls may be used to attack one skittle. When a skittle is knocked down play is restarted at the center. In small country schools children under eight years sometimes play as additional rovers with special dispensation to run with the retrieved ball and pass it to an older rover who passes it to their own shooters.

Papua New Guinea

BIM (MAT)
Philip J. Doecke
Appropriate for replication.

Players:

Male and female pre-teens and older. This game is from the Lemusmus Village.

Object of game for players:

To correctly guess the identity of the person coming toward your team.

Number of players:

Any number, in two equal groups.

Costume, apparel/equipment required:

Woven coconut leaf mat (*bim*) or blanket.

Area/arena/field where played—space required:

Any designated area.

Time length of game. How is end of game determined?:

No limit.

Symbolism of game:

This game is played by children and adults in Lemusmus Village, located on the western end of New Ireland. It is a long narrow island about 500 kilometers northeast of mainland Papua New Guinea. The game symbolizes alertness under pressure.

Rules of play, including scoring:

It is a game played by young people, but sometimes joined in by older people, to make the guessing more difficult. The two groups stand some distance apart across a level space. One of the first group members wraps himself in the bim. Identity concealed by the bim, he or she slowly walks toward the other team. This team tries to guess the identity of the player walking toward them. He or she will then slowly return to his or her team. The team has a prescribed number of guesses allowed. If they are not able to guess who it is, the first team wins a point. If the second team correctly guesses the identity of the individual, then he or she must hand over the bim. The game continues until everyone is tired or the correct names are regularly being called out.

BLIND MAN
Philip J. Doecke
Appropriate for replication.

Players:

Male and female pre-teens and young teens.

Object of game for players:

For a blindfolded person to guess the identities of the other players he or she touches.

Number of players:

Classroom group.

Costume, apparel/equipment required:

Clean handkerchief or cloth.

Area/arena/field where played—space required:

Any designated circle area during moonlight.

Time length of game. How is end of game determined?:

No limit.

Symbolism of game:

Fun and perceptual activity.

Rules of play, including scoring:

All the players form a circle with the blind man in the middle. The blind man looks around the circle trying to remember the position where each player is standing. The cloth is then tied over his or her eyes. The teacher gives a signal to the players to move two or three steps clockwise or counterclockwise so that they are no longer standing in their original positions. They must remain silent during the game. The blind man must then move to find the players. When he or she touches a player he or she tries to guess who the player is. If the player is guessed correctly, then the two exchange places. Each time a new blind man is selected the players change their positions in the circle.

DOLANDOL

Philip J. Doecke
Appropriate for replication.

Players:

Male and female pre-teens and young teens from Baluan, in the Manus Province.

Object of game for players:

For one person to figure out who in a group has the ball.

Number of players:

Any number.

Costume, apparel/equipment required:

A small ball or other soft hand-held object.

Area/arena/field where played—space required:

A designated circle area.

Time length of game. How is end of game determined?:

No limit.

Symbolism of game:

Alertness in competition.

Rules of play, including scoring:

Players sit in circle formation with crossed legs and knees touching their neighbors' knees. Their hands should be opened, the palms placed down on each knee. Someone is chosen to be it and is given the small ball, which is held in the hand. The one who is it stands in the center of the circle with eyes closed, turning around while the song, "Dolando," is being sung. When the players start singing, the one who is it begins turning around. With eyes still closed, he or she throws the ball to anyone sitting in the circle, who then passes the ball to the right. When the song comes to the last word, "there," all hands must be together in the circle and the one who is it opens his or her eyes, trying to guess who has the ball. If the guess is correct, that person becomes the next one to be it. If the guess is wrong, the song begins again and the same player who was it continues the same routine until a correct guess is made.

Song:
Dolandol how you wonder
From the one hand to the other
Is it fair? Is it fair?
To keep poor (name of person) standing there?

MUMU (SMOKE)
Philip J. Doecke
Appropriate for replication.

Players:

Male and female pre-teens and young teens.

Object of game for players:

Not to get caught by the person with closed eyes in the center of the circle.

Number of players:

Any number.

Costume, apparel/equipment required:

None.

Area/arena/field where played—space required:

Any designated circle.

Time length of game. How is end of game determined?:

No limit.

Symbolism of game:

This game is played in the Southern Highlands Province, which is a mountainous region located in the geographical center of the island of New Guinea. The name smoke relates to the mountains. The game represents alertness in competition.

Rules of play, including scoring:

One player is in the center of a circle of players. He or she has closed eyes while the others come into the center and touch his or her head saying "mumu." When the center child feels that a player is close enough, he or she reaches out and tries to grasp the person while his or her eyes are still closed. Whoever is caught becomes the next player in the center. This activity can be repeated using two players in the center.

STALKING THE WILD BOAR
John Cheffers
Appropriate for replication.

Players:

Male and female teens. This game is from the Baining Tribe who live near Rabaul.

Object of game for players:

To trap (but not kill) the wild boar.

Number of players:

Ten to 15.

Costume, apparel/equipment required:

Headbands made from coconut twine.

Area/arena/field where played—space required:

Gymnasium, play area, or field (usually about 30 x 50 yards).

Time length of game. How is end of game determined?:

Until boar is trapped or pursuers give up.

Symbolism of game:

Represents food gathering experience, fitness, and courage.

Rules of play, including scoring:

An "invisible" make-believe spear is used, no physical contact is allowed, and the game finishes when the boar is surrounded. The village center is the arena. The game is for very energetic players and requires lots of running. The pursuit is always accomplished with vocal cries and is often watched by the entire village.

One player is chosen as the boar. He can run anywhere in the area. Others run to surround and trap him, so that he cannot run through any spaces between, over, or under the circle of bodies. The game finishes when the boar's head is tapped by the leader of the pursuers. The boar wins if the pursuers become exhausted and give up.

TARGET SHOOTING
Philip J. Doecke
Not appropriate for replication.

Players:

Male pre-teens and older.

Object of game for players:

To hit the target with your own arrows more times than the other team.

Number of players:

Any number, in two equal groups.

Costume, apparel/equipment required:

Two banana stem centers erected in the ground on a slight angle, leaning away from the thrower, and placed in the center of lines marked on the ground at a chosen distance, which are the targets. Many sage palm stalks about one meter long with sharpened points for arrows or darts, which are the arrows. An equal number of arrows is needed for each group.

Area/arena/field where played—space required:

Any designated area.

Time length of game. How is end of game determined?:

No limit.

Symbolism of game:

Accuracy in target shooting.

Rules of play, including scoring:

From behind the line marked on the ground (with the opposite team's banana stem target stuck in it alongside the thrower) each player takes a turn throwing his arrow at the target. Being soft, it will stick in if thrown accurately. Every miss will be an extra throw for the other team. The game continues until one team runs out of arrows. Because the arrows are quite sharp, the other team stands back from the target as they are being thrown.

TUTUBIM
(HIDE AND SEEK ON THE MAT)
Philip J. Doecke
Appropriate for replication (if clarified).

Players:

Male and females of any age. Usually pre-teens and young teens of mixed gender. This game is from the Lesmusmus people of New Ireland Province.

Object of game for players:

To find the person hiding.

Number of players:

Any number.

Costume, apparel/equipment required:

Woven coconut leaf mat.

Area/arena/field where played—space required:

Any designated area.

Time length of game. How is end of game determined?:

No limit.

Symbolism of game:

This common game is played in Lesmusmus of New Ireland Province and symbolizes patience when searching.

Rules of play, including scoring:

One player lies face down on the mat. Another player comes to the face-down player, taps him or her on the back, and recites some village rhymes. When finished, the reciter runs away and hides. The player lying down has to go and search for the other player. The other players watch; they may hide the reciter.

VEKAMO VEKAMO (KNOW EACH OTHER)

Philip J. Doecke
Appropriate for replication.

Players:

Male and female pre-teens and young teens. This game is commonly played in Central Province, located on the south coast of Papua New Guinea.

Object of game for players:

For a group of young people to get to know each other. This game is a deliberate attempt to get young boys and girls together to exchange friendship.

Number of players:

Any number.

Costume, apparel/equipment required:

None.

Area/arena/field where played—space required:

Any designated area.

Time length of game. How is end of game determined?:

No limit.

Symbolism of game:

It enables children to learn about each other and symbolizes deliberate gender inquiry.

Rules of play, including scoring:

This game starts with a group of male players sitting at the end of the playing area and a group of female players sitting at the other end. A male walks up to the group of females and picks one out. The female then walks back with the male to his group, and on the way they talk to each other and get to know one another, mainly by asking questions. In some villages the players walk holding each other's hands. When the first couple returns to the group of males the male remains in the group and the female then picks another male and they walk back to the group of females where the same procedure is followed. The game goes on until everyone gets to know each other or until everyone is tired of walking. When males or females join the group, they should begin talking to one another.

Appendix A

THE PLACE OF GAMES IN THE ACADEMY
by John Cheffers

To those of esoteric persuasion the mention of the word games brings to mind peripheral activity for human beings. Something merely recreational, important perhaps for young children, certainly useful during vacations, and a break from important activities—in schoolyards, gymnasiums, and on playing fields. The tendency to relegate games to second rung status in the academy is strong. But perhaps this is a mistaken viewpoint. In Book Seven of *The Republic*, Plato begins the discussion, "Therefore, you best of men . . . don't use force in training the children in studies, but rather play. In that way you can also better discern what each is naturally directed towards." Many a thinker from Huizinga to Callois to Wittgenstein has borrowed the concept of games to explain matters as divergent as simple play and as complex as language communication. Perhaps the nature of games is such that adults indulge equally as much as children and their forms encompass the spectrum of human activity. George Sage, amongst others, has examined the concept of play, games, and sport. To him, play is an unshackled, creative, human activity that can take many forms and that takes place regardless of external human organization and management. Play is creative and is very much the province of the individual concerned. It is fanciful or serious, it is imitative or creative. Play can represent stories or feelings. It can involve materials, toys, or throwing objects. It can be competitive or comparative. Play's forms can be as disparate as a child sitting in a sandlot pushing a car or a mischievous office clerk playing tricks on his or her coworkers. Play is, in and of itself, an entity.

When this *play* takes the form of competition, with goals and teams, we tend to call it a *game*. Games have no set lengths of time, can be changed radically midstream, and have the objective of immediate resolution as their rationale. Two pick-up teams playing three-on-three basketball at lunch hour is a typical example of playing a game. And play fits into the concept of games in the sense that it brings vitality and resolution to the purpose of that game. The participants play by the agreed-upon rules and regulations of that contest.

When games generate more serious elements such as schedules, fixtures, regular teams with referees, and strict management regulations, then games become institutionalized, and the enterprise is called a *sport*. Obviously, all the professional sports are examples of this. So, too, are amateur sports, such as Little League and any human endeavor that settles on merit ladders (rankings), and adherence to agreed upon formulae; where lines are drawn, permanent teams assume strict rules, numbers of participants, and regular schedules, and where control is centered not in the players but in legitimized and centralized organizations, games are sports. It is hoped, of course, that the beneficial and enjoyable aspects of play are absorbed into the games and that the spirit of well-played games is absorbed into sports. Sport theorists and those who study these things have found the overall situation in society today to be less than ideal as far as games and sports are concerned. Enormous sums of money tied up in professional sports have placed an emphasis on winning, which has reduced much sport today to combative enterprises needing heavy policing and strict systems of retribution. It is not true that every competitor fits into this mold but there is ample evidence of this perversity to justify the need for a critical study of modern sport. The intervention of politics, commercial enterprise, nationalities, and secondary rewards have further complicated the situation. This book includes descriptions of popular games that have become sports. The emphasis, however, is centered on the description of games, leaving the essence of play and sport for discussion elsewhere.

Jan Huizinga presents a refreshing view of play, the kind of definition that appeals to the human spirit. He insists it is inventive, not simply normal functioning, and that it does not need to be practiced or explained. Taking these attributes into a game, Callois offers four categories: The algon, which is competition; the alea, which is chance; mimicry, which is simulation; and ilinx, which is vertigo. Callois' four categories certainly explain the popularity of games and begin the discussion of the diversity and importance of playing them. Suits disputes the linkage of play and games, certainly a tenable position, because games mean the containing of individual wants and needs and the surrendering of much independence, in order to allow the combatants to wage contest. He does not, however, explain the presence of playfulness, which is obvious in games that are constructed impromptu and that bring so much joy to the participants.

The tendency for games to become institutionalized has produced a phenomenon called New Games. New Games are not fixed in number or nature and are subject to agreed-upon changes by the participants at any time. The motto of New Games is "play hard, play fair, everybody included, and nobody is hurt." So the concept of traditional games with fixed rules and the existence of new games with flexible rules give great variety to the use of games as part of the spectrum of human physical activity. We have included rare games in this discussion because we feel it is of interest to teachers and youth leaders for purposes of enjoyment, pursuit of cultural realities to cross-cultural studies, and the general education of both young people and adults.

Games require human activities that go beyond physical expression. Cognition, along with control of emotions, are two such activities. Cafias (Cheffers' Adaptation of the Flanders Interaction Analysis System) is a descriptive instrument used to describe teacher or coach behavior, student or player behavior and the interaction between the two. It has been used in over 100 publications on teaching and coaching. Where the originator Flanders explained two student behaviors, Cheffers felt it necessary to add a third category in order to explain more fully the types of activities students engage in. Flanders (8) describes predictable human behavior, such as the following of orders, the direct answering of questions and the close maintenance of regulations. Flanders (9) describes student's unpredictable, self-initiated, and creative behaviors that are not bound by rules or regulations. Cheffers' third category, called eine (8\), describes human behaviors, predictable and anticipated, yet allows broad individual interpretation leading to much wider cognitive activity, with individual creativity still remaining within the scope of prediction.

As an example, when basketball players are performing drills (lay-ups, two on ones, passing drills, dribbling, setting-up of plays, etc.) the recorded behavior according to Cheffers' system would be an eight (8). When players are playing the game (predictable activities, yet accompanied by considerable initiative and guile) the rating would be eine (8\). When players are ad-libbing, as do the Harlem globetrotters, the coding would be nine (9). This template occurs with all drills, all games, and all impromptu behavior. From a cultural perspective, Lawrence Olivier, rehearsing his lines in Hamlet would constitute an eight (8). The performance of Hamlet would be an eine (8\), and post-performance playfulness with words and sayings would be a nine (9). When Issac Stern is practicing the notes and cadenzas of a violin concerto, he would register an eight (8), when performing the concerto in front of the audience, his behavior would be an eine (8\), and when "jamming" at the post-performance dinner, he would register a nine (9).

Cheffers added the third student behavior because he wanted to register the considerable importance of student activity when playing a game. From a cognitive viewpoint this behavior represents the knowledge learned within the constraints of the enterprise and under the conditions of limiting discipline. This activity, especially in a game, is also accompanied by the need to maintain personal discipline even under extreme emotional pressure, and the eine (8\) behavior is one of being always on task (which, most of the time, is a good thing). As most creativity represents humans building on the work of others who came before them, especially in the applied areas, the presence of the eine (8\) is essential if distribution is needed in describing human endeavor. The game then, according to Cheffers, represents applied and usually very skillful examples of human cognition, especially under the influence of strong feelings.

Many philosophers have attempted to place games in philosophical perspective. Some have felt that meaning must be ascribed to games, and they represent a spectrum of opinion. Aristotle linked "the well ordered state with leisure," implying that activities such as games were essential to human functioning. Sartre saw play, unlike work, as an outlet for mass subjectivity, especially in game form. Merleau-Ponty saw the body as needing something other then skills, treadmills, and expressive development in order to flourish. Schiller stressed that play and games are totally absorbing and comprise a creative enterprise that harmonizes the two important facets of human existence, the rational and the sensual. Some lesser known philosophers, like Margaret Cheffers, make much sense in ruefully lamenting the disappearance in the modern-day United States of Saturday and Sunday as times for play and recreation for the masses. She predicts the inordinate emphasis on commercial endeavors and spectator activities will eventually lead to the disappearance of play altogether.

One of the most interesting uses of the word games is found in the writings of Ludwig Wittgenstein. After his period of important involvement with Bertrand Russell and Gottloib Frege at Cambridge University at the turn of the century, he presented his interpretation of Logical Atomism, which reduces human expression and communication to very simple sentences ready for logical interpretation. With reflection, however, he rejected this position and went on to a metaphysical position that centered around the meaning of the words we use. He came to the conclusion that primitive language took the form of "language games." In his classic, unfinished, text called *Philosophical Investigations*, he included a full list of games. "It includes obeying and giving orders, describing the appearance of objects, giving measurements, constructing an object from a description, reporting an event, speculating about an event, forming and testing a hypothesis, presenting the results of experiments in tables and diagrams, making up stories, acting plays, singing catches, guessing riddles, telling jokes, translating from one language into another, asking, thanking, cursing, greeting and praying." He saw great difficulty in our craving for generalities in communication and came to the conclusion that when we see simple language games, we see activities and reactions, which are clear cut and transparent, and on which we can build more complicated forms of expression. He did not see language merely as a means of communicating but through games, as evidenced in language games, our expression became part of the logic of description and meaning. Further, he maintained that words could only be determined as having meaning when their *use* was understood. The intricacies of language had meaning when examined in the context of how it was used.

Perhaps the same thing can be said about games in general. Games are developed for a purpose and the language that describes them also has a purpose. Some games have cultural imperatives, which make them serious portrayers of national philosophy. They tend to be played with vigor and pride. Unfortunately for Germany, for example, games developed by Jahn at the turn of the twentieth century embodied militarism and a "Boot Camp" mentality leading to preparation for war—in spite of their other worthy goal of providing fitness, good health, and human hardiness.

It is wrong to read too much into the facets of children's games however, especially when they are in full flight of fancy. Children often drew swastika's at the height of World War II, for example, not because they were supportive of Hitler's Nazism and brutality but because it was a fascinating emblem to draw. Those who studied German and Danish literature knew Teutonic history emphasized the Swastika for vastly different reasons long before the advent of Adolf Hitler. So we must be careful in presuming on the meaning of games of the innocent. Certainly, games are some of the first tools of indoctrination used in education and shaping the minds of our young. We cannot ignore but must scrutinize games, and not reject their implications. Play, or lack of it, is often an indication of unhealthy development in young children. Game playing can signify the same thing. To those of esoteric persuasion who deprecate the position of games in society we direct a simple question: *Because both children and adults play games with whimsical and serious intent, predictive meaning, and for emotional release, can we afford to ignore such behaviors and dare we underestimate their importance?*

Appendix B

A GUIDE FOR EDUCATORS:
THE ROLE OF COOPERATIVE GAMES
IN MOVEMENT EDUCATION
by Eileen Crowley Sullivan

How Does an Educator Select an Appropriate and "Fun" Game?

A common denominator of all children is that they enjoy playing and participating in games. A visit to playgrounds, backyards, the schoolyard, and most anywhere there are children, moving, playing, active boys and girls probably playing games. Tag games, running games, ball games, jump rope chants, sport-related movements, and blacktop activities are all examples of games children play. Early elementary school children might be playing freeze tag, pick-up basketball, double-Dutch jumping, or four-square on the pavement. These games provide children with opportunities to practice their physical skills, interact with their peers, function as part of a team or group, and apply moral judgment by adhering to the established rules of play.

Games should be studied and critiqued before implementation with children in a school and educational setting. A developmental perspective is recommended where the age/grade of the children is considered. A multi-dimensional approach, in contrast to just examining the physical domain, should be used in the planning and teaching of games. Games should be selected for specific purposes and reasons. The attributes of the games chosen must compliment the children who play the game. Games should be played not only because they are fun but because they meet the objectives of a lesson for a specific student population.

The preschool years require an abundance of opportunities for exploration and practice of fundamental motor skills through simple, game-like experiences. The fundamental movements preschoolers practice through their physical games provide the foundation for lead-up skills to specific sports. Toddlers and preschoolers should be involved with physical games that stimulate their curiosity, involve their imagination, and allow them varied opportunities to apply their basic motor skills. Controlled running, chasing, dramatization, and games with simple rules should be played. Cooperative games that do not exclude participants are particularly essential for child development during these years from age two to five.

The early elementary school years, from Kindergarten through grade four, require a continuation of the physical and motor skills established in the preschool years. While the preschool years of fundamental motor skills through games is the foundation for the early elementary years, these early elementary years form the building blocks for sport specific motor skills that come into play later on. Children ages five through nine or ten should be playing physical games that refine their locomotor, non-locomotor, and manipulative motor skills. The games should contain the use of rules to establish a base for games that then evolve into designated sports. There has been a dilemma in physical education in the past ten years about whether children are taught sports too soon and should instead be playing lead-up games or presport activities in the early elementary years. As in the preschool years, the five- to nine-year-old needs to practice physical, intellectual, social, and moral attributes through game playing, which allows maximum participation with the element of "fun" competition.

The purpose of playing a game should be to apply the movement skills that have already been learned. Games usually are not played to teach a new motor skill, but often skill drills help students focus on a designated motor skill. In order to be able to play a game, a child should have some mastery of the motor skill needed for play. A one-year-old is not taught tag games that require proficient running, dodging, and fleeing because he or she has not yet mastered these skills. Educators also need to select developmentally appropriate games. Children need the right opportunities to practice and master motor skills prior to applying them in game situations. Teachers should be informed of the physical characteristics of their students before selecting or modifying a game for educational purposes.

This chapter defines the characteristics of *cooperative games* so that a knowledge base is acquired to select, create, modify, implement, and change games for educational objectives in the classroom or the gymnasium. The safety, physical, intellectual, social/emotional, and moral attributes are described and then applied to the chart, The Cooperative Games Attributes work sheet. The chart assists educators in the selection of games that should be used in the elementary curriculum for prekindergarten through grade four.

Guidelines for Analysis of Cooperative Games

Agreed on the assumption that games serve an educational purpose in the elementary school curriculum, teachers must become comfortable with the elements of an appropriate game experience. This section reviews the content of the chart, The Cooperative Games Attributes, found on the following page. Educationally sound cooperative games for the early elementary school years should meet the attributes defined in this section. Safety, physical, intellectual, social/emotional, moral, and play elements are outlined and discussed with examples supporting and disagreeing with the established guidelines of cooperative games.

Safety

Safety should be foremost in an educator's mind when selecting a game to play with the class. Is the game active or is it one that requires only limited movement and space needs? The playing area of the game should be checked prior to play. Running games should not be played in the classroom because of space limitations but nonlocomotor, circle games are encouraged. The physical skills needed to play the game must be in agreement with the designated playing area. If the class is planning on playing on the field outside, take precautions to check the area for protruding objects, holes, and other unsafe items. Students could walk the field in paths to check for unsafe items. Place cones over holes in the grass where students could trip or sprain an ankle. If the playing area is too large for a certain game, use markers, boundaries, or cones so that students can visualize the field of play. The size of the playing field is a factor because if the field is too large or too small, students will become frustrated and the game will lose its focus. Running games and active activities should not be played on asphalt or hard surfaces. Consider the movement, skills, playing surface, and the size of the playing area for safety.

Physical

Developmentally appropriate physical skills should be used for games with children. One of the purposes of game playing is to reinforce motor

The Cooperative Games Attributes (Crowley Sullivan, 1999)

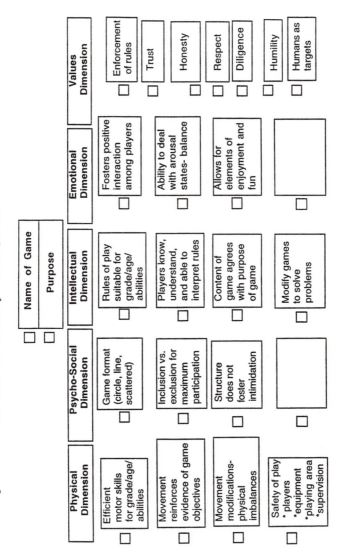

| Name of Game |
| ☐ |
| Purpose |
| ☐ |

Physical Dimension	Psycho-Social Dimension	Intellectual Dimension	Emotional Dimension	Values Dimension
☐ Efficient motor skills for grade/age/ abilities	☐ Game format (circle, line, scattered)	☐ Rules of play suitable for grade/age/ abilities	☐ Fosters positive interaction among players	☐ Enforcement of rules
				☐ Trust
☐ Movement reinforces evidence of game objectives	☐ Inclusion vs. exclusion for maximum participation	☐ Players know, understand, and able to interpret rules	☐ Ability to deal with arousal states- balance	☐ Honesty
				☐ Respect
☐ Movement modifications- physical imbalances	☐ Structure does not foster intimidation	☐ Content of game agrees with purpose of game	☐ Allows for elements of enjoyment and fun	☐ Diligence
				☐ Humility
☐ Safety of play *players *equipment *playing area *supervision		☐ Modify games to solve problems		☐ Humans as targets

abilities, not to "teach" the motor skills through play. Participants of a game must be proficient in the motor skills needed to play the game. The motor skills should not be too simplistic or elaborate. The age, grade, population of the school, and other variables must be considered when selecting an appropriate game to play with a class. Locomotor, nonlocomotor, and manipulative motor skills are enhanced through games. These movement actions become the focus of the game so that players are practicing their motor abilities through a fun, interactive, game-playing approach. A first-grade class plays Red Lion, Red Lion, which is a line tag game. The six-year-olds tiptoe up to a row of students who are pretending to be red lions asleep in their den. As the line of students calls out, "Red Lion, Red Lion, Come Out of Your Den," the lions wake up and chase the callers. While the first graders enjoy the drama, creativity, and excitement of being a lion or runner, they are actually practicing running, dodging, and fleeing skills. Efficient motor skills can be reinforced through games but games should use safe skills. Most tag games or locomotor games should not use running backwards, timed hopping, or prolonged jumping for game playing. These and other skills do not constitute efficient skills for elementary games. Young children should not be using animal behaviors as apart of a tagging event as the use of animal behavior does not promote quality, efficient, and appropriate motor skills. Instead, use animal movements for the creative drama portion of the game but use running skills for the tagging games.

Intellectual

The players of a game should know and be able to apply the rules of play. Children playing the designated game must have the mental capability to grasp the objectives and strategies of play of the game. The content should not be too simple or complex for the selected age of the players or they will become frustrated and there could be cause for safety concerns as well. Knowing the intellectual capabilities and academic skills of students, and combining these factors with physical skills, creates developmentally appropriate games. There should be opportunities to increase the level of play both through the intellectual domain and the physical. If a number- or shape-circle game is played with kindergarten children then perhaps the same format of the game could be used for third and fourth graders with multiplication facts or skip-counting skills. If players are uncomfortable with the rules of play, modify the rules to meet specific needs. Often a class or group establishes its own rules for a traditional game.

Social/Emotional

Players of a game should be comfortable with the social interaction of the game and the rules of play. Often a game is first played in pairs or small groups and then tried in a large group setting. The children playing the game must have the ability to function as individuals and as part of a small group or team. The participants must accept others into the play and have a sense of give-and-take when it comes to taking responsibility, if a team strategy game is played. Respect for others' opinions and skill abilities as well as an understanding of the needs of the team are essential components of teamwork. There should be both planned and unplanned brief discussions of team play in the more advanced game situations. Emotional release of positive tension and anxiety over play should be allowed and funneled through physical play, but negative outbursts and behavior that do not agree with the concept of "team" should not be fostered or tolerated.

Values

The name of the game and the behaviors used for the game should enforce and reflect positive values of learning and play. The name of the game, Steal the Bacon, for example, does not inform children of positive behaviors, as the name reflects a dishonest behavior, stealing. Players participating in selected games should agree on a proper and improper code of behavior and play. Players should not be intimated if they are less proficient in the skills required for the game. There should be opportunities for all players to use their physical and mental skills for the benefit of themselves and/or the team so that each player experiences success at his or her own level of play. Rules of a game as well as the infringement of rules should be settled on mutually agreeable terms by the players and teachers.

Play Elements

Fun and excitement should be included in a game. Players should play the game at their own level, but there should be maximum participation of play during most or all of the game time. True cooperative games allow players to switch roles in the course of the game. It is acceptable to play a tag-type game where players are tagged or penalized, but they should not then be excluded from the game. Perhaps their role in the game changes to a different level, but the tagged players should remain an essential part of the game playing.

As an example, in the game Octopus, a tagged player becomes a tentacle and becomes a stationary tagger until everyone is tagged. The tagged players do not sit on the sidelines, but are given a different role in the game. Inclusion, not exclusion, is a requirement for cooperative play, and elimination of players is not recommended for the early childhood years. Since the tagged players are often given a new role in the game, the less-skilled children are not intimated because they remain a significant aspect of the game playing. The primary focus of a game should not have children or people used as targets in the game. The traditional games of Dodgeball or Bombardment, for example, use people as targets. This devalues the individual and these traditional games should be modified. Games should be modified to meet the needs of different populations. The boundaries, equipment, type of movement, physical skills, and content of a game can be revised to meet various specific class needs and classroom/gymnasium requirements.

References

Albert, Rabil, Jr. *Merleau Ponty: Existentialist of the Social World.* New York: Columbia University Press, 1967.

Aristotle. *Introduction to Aristotle.* (ed. Richard McKeon). New York: Modern Library, 1992.

Ashlock, R. B. and Humphrey, J. H. *Teaching Elementary School Mathematics Through Motor Learning.* Springfield, IL: Charles C. Thomas, 1976.

Barbarash, Lorraine. *Multicultural Games.* Champaign, IL: Human Kinetics, 1997.

Barlin, A. and Barlin, P. *The Art of Learning Through Movement.* Los Angeles: Ward Publications, 1971.

Barrett, K. *Exploration: A Method for Teaching Movement.* Madison, WI: College Printing and Typing, 1971.

Bryant, B. and Oliver, E. *Complete Elementary Physical Education Guide.* New York: Parker Publishing, 1974.

Cheffers, J. and Crowley Sullivan, E. *The Instruments of Involvement: Individual Reaction Gestalts (IRG), Version I–IV, 1990 Revision.* Available from the authors, Boston University. Revision.

Cheffers, J. "Tuesdays and Thursdays with Boston's Inner City Youth," *Quest,* 1997, 49, pp. 50–56.

Cheffers, J., Mancini, V., and Martinek, T. *Interaction Analysis,* (2nd Ed.). St. Paul: P.S. Amidon, 1980.

Cratty, B.J. *Active Learning.* Englewood Cliffs, NJ: Prentice Hall, 1976.

Doray, M. *J Is for Jumping: Moving into Language Arts.* Belmont, CA: Pitman Learning, 1982.

Eitzen, S. and Sage, G.. *Sociology of North American Sport.* (6th Ed.). Dubuque, IA: W.C. Brown, 1996.

Fluegelman, A. *More New Games.* Garden City, NY: Doubleday and Co., 1981.

Gilbert, A. G. *Teaching the Three R's Through Movement Experiences.* Minneapolis: Burgess Publishing, 1977.

Hemery, D. *Another Hurdle.* New York: Taplinger Publishing Co., 1976.

Hoffman, H., Young, J., and Klesius, S. *Meaningful Movement For Children.* Boston: Allyn and Bacon, 1981.

Kirchner, G. *Physical Education for Elementary School Children.* Dubuque, IA: William C. Brown, 1992.

Melograno, V. *Designing the Physical Education Curriculum: A Self Directed Approach.* Champaign, IL: Human Kinetics, 1995.

Morgan, W. J., and Meier K. *Philosophic Inquiry in Sport.* Champaign, IL: Human Kinetics, Inc., 1988.

Morris, G. S. D. and Stiel, J. *Physical Education: From Intent to Action.* Columbus, OH: Merrill, 1985.

Mosston, M. *Teaching Physical Education.* Columbus, OH: Merrill, 1981.

Orlick, T. *The Cooperative Sports and Games Book.* New York: Pantheon, 1978.

Pangrazi, R. B. and Dauer, V. P. *Dynamic Physical Education for Elementary School Children.* Boston: Allyn and Bacon, 1995.

Plato. *The Republic,* Book VII (trans. Allan Bloom). New York: Basic Books Harper Collins Publisher, 1991.

Rohnke, K. *Silver Bullets: A Guide to Initiative Problems, Adventure Games, Stunts and Trust Activities.* Hamilton, MA: Project Adventure, Inc., 1984.

Russell, B. *The Problems of Philosophy.* New York: Oxford University Press, 1967.

Sartre, J. P. *Existentialism and Human Emotion.* New York: Citadel Press, 1990.

Schiller, F. W. *On the Aesthetic Education of Man.* New York: Frederick Ungar Publishing Co., 1988.

Schurr, E. L. *Movement Experiences for Children: A Humanistic Approach to Elementary School Physical Education.* Englewood Cliffs, NJ: Prentice-Hall, 1980.

Seagraves, M. *Bridge to Learning: Motor Skill Development.* Winston-Salem, NC: Hunter Textbooks, 1986.

Werner, P. H. and Burton, E. C. *Learning Through Movement: Teaching Cognitive Content Through Physical Activities.* St. Louis: C.V. Mosby, 1979.

Whitehead, A. N. *Adventures of Ideas.* New York: Macmillan Company, 1933.

Wickstrom, R. L. *Fundamental Motor Pattern.* Philadelphia: Lea and Febiger, 1970.

Wittgenstein, L. *Philosophical Investigations.* (Trans. G. E. M. Anscombe). New York: Macmillan, 1968.

Index of Games by Continent, Country, and Contributor

General Index

About the Editors and Contributors

DORIS CORBETT is a Sport Sociologist and Professor at Howard University. She is the author of *Outstanding Athletes of Congress*.

JOHN CHEFFERS is Professor of Education and Coordinator of the Human Movement Program at Boston University.

EILEEN CROWLEY SULLIVAN is Assistant Professor in the Human Movement Program at Boston University.

MARGALITH AKAVYA, The Educational Center For Games, Israel.

A. K. BANERJEE, University of Kalyani, India.

BETTY SUE BENISON, Texas Christian University, USA.

VERA REGINA TOLEDO CAMARGO, consultant, Campinas, Brasil.

JEPKORIR ROSE CHEPYATOR-THOMSON, The University of Georgia, USA.

SUSANNA CHOW, Hong Kong Polytechnic University, Hong Kong.

CHRISTINE M. CONBOY, consultant, Colorado Springs, USA.

HOWARD DARBON, Bedford University, England.

S. DHABE, Indigenous Sports Association of India, India.

MIKE DAVEY, Western Illinois University, USA.

BRIAN DEVANEY, International Student at Boston University, USA.

PHILIP J. DOECKE, National Sports Institute of Papua New Guinea.

DONNA DUFFY, Student at University of North Carolina at Greensborough, USA.

KEN EDWARDS, Brisbane Grammar School, Australia.

HERBERT HAAG, University of Kiel, Germany.

JODIE HAWKINS, Central Queensland University, Australia.

KEN HAWKINS, Central Queensland University, Australia.

JASON HOLDER, Boston University, USA.

TOM JACOBY, Educational Consultant, Pennsylvania, USA.

ADNAN D. JALLON, King Abdul Aziz University, Saudi Arabia.

JONG-HOON YU, International Student at Boston University, Korea.

ROSABEL S. KOSS, consultant, New Jersey, USA.

MARCH KROTEE, University of Minnesota, Minnesota, USA.

FRANCIS D. MAGNO, Miriam College Foundation, Inc., Philippines.

KEVIN MCALLISTER, Student at Boston University, USA.

AMINU MOMODU, Edo State University, Nigeria.

GREG NARLESKI, Student at Boston University, USA.

REGINALD OCANSEY, SUNY College at Brockport, USA.

MAURICE PIERON, University of Liege, Belgium.

WILLY PIETER, University of North London, England.

ABDEL NASER QADOMI, AN-Najah National University, Palestine.

EDNA B. REYES, consultant, Philippines.

COLIN RILEY, Royal Melbourne Institute of Technology, Australia.

JEAN ROBERTS, Australian Institute of Sport, Australia.

MYRNA SCHILD, Missouri, USA.

ARLENE SEQUINE, consultant, New York, USA.

TOM SHARPE, Purdue University, USA.

JIMOH SHEHU, Kenyatta University, Kenya.

BERNARD SMITH, Warwick University, England.

DELL SMITH, Arkansas, USA.

CHARLIE SONG, Xavier University, USA.

OK SOO CHA, Chinju National University of Education, Korea.

COLIN SPANHAKE, Massey University, New Zealand.

SHELLY AGNEW SWEENEY, Salem State College, USA.

DAVID CHANG SZN-MIN, University of Tai Pei, Taiwan.

RISTO TELAMA, University of Jyvaskyla, Finland.

ELENIE TSARHOPOULOS, International Student at Boston University, USA.

HAMBDI URKUNDT, International Student at Boston University, USA.

CARLOS LOPEZ VON VRIESSEN, Universidad Catolica de Valparaiso,

ERIK DE VROEDE, Sportmuseum Vlaanderen, Belgium.

CHRIS AICHY WOINARSKY, University of Ballarat, Australia.

GREG WOOD, Memorial University of Newfoundland, Canada.

SHEN XUN-ZHANG, Chang-ning District Adolescent Sport School, China.